Contents

◀◀ Xidan shopping ◀ Ghost Street at night, northeast Beijing

Introduction to Beijing

Beijing is China at its most dynamic: a vivid metropolis spiked with high-rises, changing and growing at a furious, unfettered pace. Yet this forward-looking capital of the world's newest superpower is also where, for a thousand years, the drama of China's imperial history was played out, with the emperor sitting enthroned at the centre of the Chinese universe. Though Beijing is a very different city today, it still remains spiritually and politically the heart of the nation. Shanghai and Hong Kong may be where the money is, but it's Beijing that pulls the strings, and its lure is irresistible to many Chinese, who come here to fulfil dreams of success in business, politics or the arts.

The Chinese character *chai* (demolish), painted in white on old buildings – and the cranes that skewer the skyline – attest to the speed of **change**, affecting not just the city's architecture: as China embraces capitalism, social structures are also being revolutionized. The government is as determined as ever to repress dissent, but outside the political arena, just about anything goes these days. Students in the latest fashions while away their time in internet cafés, dropouts mosh in punk clubs, bohemians dream up boutiques over frappuccinos. New prosperity is evident everywhere – witness all the Mercedes-driving businessmen – but not everyone has benefited: migrant day-labourers wait for work outside the stations, and homeless beggars, not long ago a rare sight, are now as common as in Western cities.

Beijing's facelift

Beijing has always been **image-conscious** – anxious to portray a particular face to the world. When Mao took over, he wanted the feudal city of the emperors transformed into a "forest of chimneys"; he got his wish, and the capital became an ugly industrial powerhouse of socialism. In the 1980s, when the Party embraced capitalism "with Chinese characteristics", bland international-style office blocks were erected with a pagoda-shaped "silly hat" on the roof as a concession to local taste.

Modern Beijing, eager to be viewed as a cool and **stylish** world city, and to express China's new global dominance, has undergone the kind of urban transformation usually only seen after a war. In recent years, factories were banished to the suburbs, six new subway lines opened, a new terminal (designed by Norman Foster) was added to the airport, and some $10 billion has been spent on greening projects including a tree belt around the city to control the dust storms that whip in from the Gobi Desert. Now, **statement architecture** – the kind of massive, prestige project that not long ago would have been derided as bourgeois and decadent – is all the rage, designed by the world's hottest (and most expensive) architects.

As well as the fantastic venues built for the 2008 **Olympics** (the most famous of which, the "Bird's Nest", is shown below), there's Paul Andreu's **National Opera House** (the "Egg"), and perhaps most striking of all, the new **state television station** (the "Twisted Doughnut") by Dutch architect Rem Koolhaas, which appears to defy gravity with its intersecting Z-shaped towers.

All this has been made possible by light planning laws, deregulation and the willingness of the government to allow developers to sweep homes away without much compensation to residents. Regrettably, little of **old Beijing** has been preserved, with *hutong* neighbourhoods such as those around Qianmen levelled en masse. The city has been left with a disjointed feel; there's something arbitrary about the skyscrapers and single-use zones around them. Beijing today looks modern, indisputedly, but it has some way to go before you could call it beautiful.

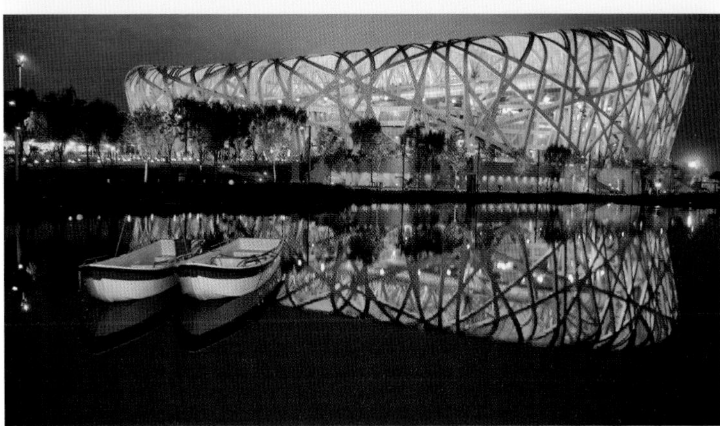

Chinese script

Chinese characters are simplified images of what they represent, and their origins as pictograms can often still be seen, even though they have become highly abstract today. The earliest known examples of Chinese writing are predictions, which were cut into "oracle bones" more than three thousand years ago during the Shang dynasty, though the characters must have been in use long before, for these inscriptions already amount to a highly complex writing system. As the characters represent concepts, not sounds, written Chinese cuts through the problem of communication in a country with many different dialects. However, learning the writing system is ponderous, taking children an estimated two years longer than with an alphabet. Foreigners learning Mandarin use the modern *pinyin* transliteration system of accented Roman letters – used in this book – to help memorize the sounds. For more, see p.185.

The **first impression** of Beijing, for both foreigners and visiting Chinese, is often of a bewildering vastness, not least in the sprawl of uniform apartment buildings in which most of the city's 22 million-strong population are housed, and the eight-lane freeways that slice it up. It's a perception reinforced on closer acquaintance by the concrete desert of **Tian'anmen Square**, and the gargantuan buildings of the modern executive around it. The main **tourist sights** – the Forbidden City, the Summer Palace and the Great Wall – also impress with their scale, while more manageable grandeur is on offer at the city's attractive **temples**, including the Tibetan-style Yonghe Gong, the Taoist Baiyun Guan, and the astonishing Temple of Heaven, once a centre for imperial rites.

With its sights, history and, by no means least, delicious **food** (all of China's diverse cuisines can be enjoyed cheaply at the city's numerous restaurants and street stalls), Beijing is a place almost everyone enjoys. But it's essentially a private city, one whose surface, though attractive, is difficult to penetrate. The city's history and unique character are in the **details**: to find and experience these, check out the little antique markets; the local shopping districts; the smaller, quirkier sights; the *hutongs*, the city's twisted grey stone alleyways that are – as one Chinese guidebook puts it – "fine and numerous as the hairs of a cow"; and the parks, where you'll see

▲ Chaoyang Theatre

Beijingers performing *tai ji* and old men sitting with their caged songbirds. Take advantage, too, of the city's burgeoning nightlife and see just how far the Chinese have gone down the road of what used to be deemed "spiritual pollution". Keep your eyes open, and you'll soon notice that **Westernization** and the rise of a brash consumer society is not the only trend here; just as marked is the revival of **older Chinese culture**, much of it outlawed during the more austere years of communist rule. Witness, for example, the sudden re-emergence of the **teahouse** as a genteel meeting place, and the renewed interest in traditional music and opera and **imperial cuisine** – dishes once enjoyed by the emperors.

What to see

In the absolute centre of Beijing, **Tian'anmen Square** is the physical and spiritual heart of the city. Some of the most significant sights are very close by, including the **Forbidden City**, two colossal museums, and the formidable buildings of the modern executive, as well as the corpse of Chairman Mao, lying pickled in his sombre mausoleum.

The road leading south from here, **Qianmen Dajie**, once the pivot of the ancient city, is now a busy market area that leads to the magnificent **Temple of Heaven**. These days the main axis of the city has shifted to the east–west road, a showcase of grandiose architecture that divides Tian'anmen Square and the Forbidden City. Changing its name every few kilometres along its length, the thoroughfare is generally referred to as **Chang'an Jie**. Westward, this street takes you past the shopping district of **Xidan** to the **Military Museum**, monument to a fast-disappearing overtly communist ethos. To the east, the road zooms past more giant buildings and glamorous shopping districts – notably **Wangfujing**, **Jianguomen** and the **Silk Market** – to the little oasis of calm that is the **Ancient Observatory**, where Jesuit priests used to teach the charting of the heavens.

Once, dark, twisting little alleys – or **hutongs** – formed a web between the grid lines of the major streets; now, almost all have been bulldozed. The charming heritage district centred around the **Houhai lakes**, north of the Forbidden City, is one of the few areas to retain this traditional street plan. Many sights here are remnants of the imperial past, when the area was home to princes, dukes and eunuchs. They might be tricky to navigate, but this is one of the few parts of the city where aimless rambling is rewarded. Easier to track down is **Beihai Park**, the imperial pleasure grounds, just north of the Forbidden City, and the fine **Yonghe Gong**, a popular Lamaist temple in the northern outskirts.

▲ Panjiayuan antique market

▶ Temple ornament

Beijing's sprawling outskirts are a messy jumble of farmland, housing and industry, but it's here you'll find the most pleasant places to retreat from the city's hectic pace, including the two **summer palaces**, the giant parks of **Badachu** and **Xiangshan**, and the **Tanzhe**, **Fahai** and **Jietai temples**. Well outside the city – but within the scope of a day-trip – is the **Great Wall**, which winds over lonely ridges only a few hours' drive north of the capital.

A week is long enough to explore the city and its main sights, and get out to the Great Wall. With more time, try to venture further afield: the imperial pleasure complex of **Chengde** is easily accessible from the capital by train and bus.

Chinese traditional medicine

Chinese traditional medicine has been used for 2200 years – ever since the semi-mythical Xia king compiled his classic work on medicinal herbs. Around eight thousand "herbs" derived from roots, leaves, twigs, fruit and animal parts are used – usually dried or roasted, but sometimes stir-fried. They are generally taken as a bitter and earthy tasting tea.

Diagnosis involves feeling the pulse, examining the tongue and face, and listening to the tone of voice. Infections are believed to be caused by internal imbalances, so the whole body is treated, rather than just the symptom. In the treatment of flu, for example, a "cold action" herb would be used to reduce fever, another to induce sweating and so flush out the system, and another as a replenishing tonic.

Just as aspirin is derived from willow bark, many Western drugs come from traditional herbal remedies: artemisin, an effective anti-malarial treatment, for example.

With their presentation boxes of ginseng roots and deer antlers, traditional Chinese pharmacies are colourful places; a good one to check out in Beijing is Tongrentang on Dazhalan, which also offers on-the-spot diagnosis.

▲ Beihai Park

When to go

The best time to visit Beijing is in the **autumn** (Sept & Oct), when it's dry and clement. Next best is the short **spring**, in April and May – it's dry and comfortably warm, though a little windy. Fortunately, the spring dust storms that once plagued the city have lessened of late. In **winter** (Nov–Feb) it gets very cold, down to -20°C (-4°F), and the mean winds that whip off the Mongolian plains feel like they're freezing your ears off. **Summer** (June–Aug) is muggy and hot, with temperatures up to 30°C (86°F) and sometimes beyond.

The run-up to **Chinese New Year** (falling in late Jan or early to mid-Feb) is a great time to be in the country: everyone is in festive mood and the city is bedecked with decorations. This isn't a good time to travel around, however, as much of the population is on the move, and transport systems become hopelessly overstretched. It's best to avoid Beijing during the first three days of the festival itself, as everyone is at home with family, and a lot of businesses and sights are closed.

Average daily temperatures and rainfall

	Jan	Feb	Mar	Apr	May	Jun	Jul	Aug	Sep	Oct	Nov	Dec
Temperature												
Max/min (ºC)	1/-10	4/-8	11/-1	21/7	27/13	31/18	31/21	30/20	26/14	20/6	9/-2	3/-8
Max/min (ºF)	34/14	39/18	52/30	70/45	81/55	88/64	88/70	86/68	79/57	68/43	48/28	37/18
Rainfall												
Rainfall (mm)	4	5	8	17	35	78	243	141	58	16	11	3

things not to miss

It's not possible to see everything Beijing has to offer in one short trip – and we don't suggest you try. What follows is a selective taste of the city's highlights: stunning temples, delicious food, fantastic markets and fascinating excursions beyond the city – all arranged in colour-coded categories to help you find the very best things to see and experience. All entries have a page reference to take you straight into the Guide, where you can find out more.

01 **Beijing opera** Page **149** • Largely incomprehensible to foreigners, and many Chinese, but still a great spectacle.

02 Nightlife Page **146** • Experience Beijing's cultural explosion by catching one of the new bands in a smoky bar, or just bop with the beautiful people.

03 Temple of Heaven Page **63** • A gorgeous temple in an elegant park.

04 Houhai Lake Page **87** • Beautiful and serene in the early morning, Houhai Lake is the perfect setting for a lazy cappuccino – and has a wonderfully laidback bar scene after dark.

05 Forbidden City Page **52** • For five centuries centre of the Chinese universe and private pleasure ground of the emperor, this sumptuous palace complex ranks as the city's main attraction.

06 Hutongs Page **87** • The tangle of alleys behind Houhai Lake reveals the city's real, private face.

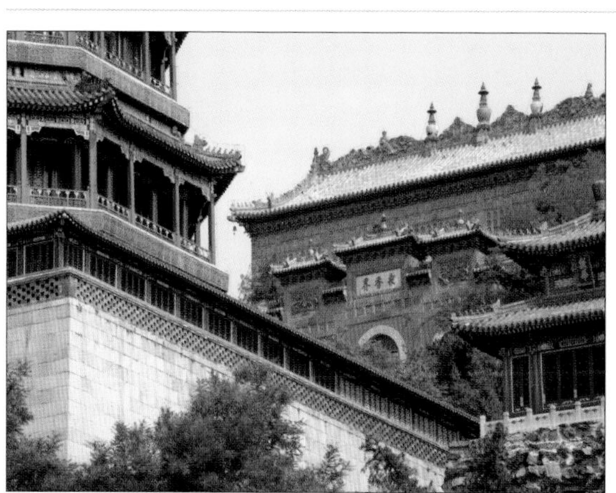

07 Summer Palace Page **99** • Once the exclusive retreat of the emperors, this beautiful landscaped park, dotted with imperial buildings, is now open to all.

08 Mao's mausoleum Page **50** • Join the queue of awed peasants shuffling past the pickled corpse of the founder of modern China in his giant tomb.

09 Great Wall at Simatai Page **106** • A dramatic stretch of crumbly, vertiginous fortifications three hours from Beijing.

10 Yonghe Gong Page **90** • A lively Tibetan temple, flamboyantly decorated and busy with devotees and monks.

11 Nanluogu Xiang Page **90** • This trendy *hutong* of restaurants and boutiques has a Left Bank feel to it – the perfect spot for a quick cappuccino and a read of the paper.

12 Markets Page **160** • The city's jumbled cornucopias of bric-a-brac, souvenirs, curios and fake antiques are great for a browse and a haggle.

13 798 Art District Page **82** • This huge complex of art galleries has become Ground Zero for the city's bohemians and fashionistas.

14 Teahouses Page **149** • Experience the ancient and relaxing tea ceremony in one of Beijing's elegant teahouses.

15 Acrobatics Page **152** • The style may be vaudeville, but the stunts, performed by some of the world's greatest acrobats, are breathtaking.

16 Beijing duck See ***Capital cuisine* colour section** • Though heavy on calories and very rich, Beijing's culinary speciality is supremely tasty.

17 Dazhalan Page **60** • An earthy, hectic shopping street with some grand facades and plenty of opportunities for bargain hunting.

18 Baiyun Guan Page **62** • See China at prayer in this attractive and popular Taoist temple, where devotees play games such as throwing coins at the temple bell.

19 Tian'anmen Square Page **47** • The grandiose heart of Communist China, a concrete plain laden with historical resonance.

Basics

Basics

Getting there

Beijing is China's main international transport hub, with plenty of direct flights from European capitals and from American, Australian and Asian cities. Though most travellers arrive by plane, you can also get here by rail from elsewhere in China or, more romantically, from Moscow (on the Trans-Siberian Express; see p.20).

Airfares vary with season, with the highest fares charged from Easter to October and around Christmas, New Year, and just before the Chinese New Year (which falls between late Jan and mid-Feb). Note also that flying at weekends is slightly more expensive; price ranges quoted below assume midweek travel.

Flights from the UK and Ireland

The only **nonstop flights** to Beijing **from the UK** are Air China and British Airways flights from London Heathrow (10hr). It's not a problem to fly from other UK airports or **from the Republic of Ireland**, though you'll end up either catching a connecting flight to London or flying via your airline's hub city.

There are plenty of **indirect flights** to Beijing from London with airlines such as Emirates, Qatar Airways, Lufthansa and Aeroflot, stopping off in the airline's hub city. These are a little cheaper than direct flights, with prices starting from around £400 in low season, rising to £700 in high season. If you're flying from the Republic of Ireland, reckon on €1000 in low season, €1500 in high season.

Flights from the US and Canada

There's no shortage of **direct flights** to Beijing **from North America**; carriers include Air China, Air Canada and United. It takes around thirteen hours' flying time to reach Beijing **from the West Coast**; add seven hours or more to this if you start **from the East Coast** (including a stopover on the West Coast en route). Air Canada's flight from Toronto and Continental's from Newark cross the North Pole, shaving a couple of hours off the flight time.

In low season, expect to pay US$650–900/CDN$1100–1250 from the West Coast (Los Angeles, San Francisco, Vancouver), or US$850–1100/CDN$1350–1800 from the East Coast (New York, Montreal, Toronto). To get a good fare during high season it's important to buy your ticket as early as possible, in which case you probably won't pay more than US$200/CDN$320 above low-season tariffs.

In addition to the usual **online booking agents**, North American travellers can check ⓦwww.flychina.com.

Flights from Australia, New Zealand and South Africa

You can fly **direct** to Beijing **from Melbourne and Sydney** with, among others, Singapore Airlines, JAL, Malaysia Airlines and China Eastern. Otherwise, you will need to **stop over**, probably in Hong Kong. Alternatively, once in Hong Kong, you have the option of continuing your journey on the Kowloon–Beijing train (see p.24); consider taking a short hop on the train to Guangzhou and flying on to Beijing from there, as it's cheaper than flying direct from Hong Kong.

Good deals include the Air China flights from Melbourne or Sydney direct to Beijing (Aus$1500); and Cathay Pacific to Hong Kong (Aus$1500 in low season; far steeper at other times). Some of the cheapest fares are with Royal Brunei Airlines, though they only serve Brisbane and Darwin. Their return fares to Hong Kong, via a stopover in Brunei, are around Aus$1100. Qantas or British Airways are the only two operators to fly direct from Perth to Hong Kong (Aus$1800).

The only direct flight to Beijing **from New Zealand** is with Air New Zealand (around NZ$2000). About the best deal is on

Air New Zealand or Singapore from Auckland to Hong Kong (NZ$1750). Air New Zealand, Malaysia Airlines and other carriers also fly via other Southeast Asian cities to Hong Kong and Beijing.

There are no direct flights from **South Africa** to Beijing. You can fly from Johannesburg for around SA$1000 off season; the trip will take around 19 hours.

Organized tours

Tour operators generally include Beijing as one of a number of destinations in a tour of China. There are very cheap off-season **flight-and-hotel packages** to Beijing, which, at prices that sometimes go as low as £600/US$1000/€700, provide six or seven nights in a four-star hotel effectively for free, considering the cost of the flight alone. Don't forget, though, that quoted prices in brochures usually refer to the low-season minimum, based on two people sharing – the cost for a single traveller in high season will always work out far more expensive.

From Moscow: the Trans-Siberian Express

The classic **overland route to Beijing** is through Russia on the **Trans-Siberian Express**, a very memorable way to begin or end your stay in China. The fabulous views of stately birch forests, velvety prairies, misty lakes and arid plateaus help time pass, and there are frequent stops during which you can wander the station platform, buying food and knick-knacks.

There are two rail lines from Moscow to Beijing: the first, the **Trans-Manchurian line**, runs almost as far as the Sea of Japan before turning south through Dongbei to Beijing, and takes six days. The second **Trans-Mongolian** line is more popular with tourists as it rumbles past Lake Baikal in Siberia, the grasslands of Mongolia, and the

Six steps to a better kind of travel

At Rough Guides we are passionately committed to travel. We feel strongly that only through travelling do we truly come to understand the world we live in and the people we share it with – plus tourism has brought a great deal of **benefit** to developing economies around the world over the last few decades. But the extraordinary growth in tourism has also damaged some places irreparably, and of course **climate change** is exacerbated by most forms of transport, especially flying. This means that now more than ever it's important to **travel thoughtfully** and **responsibly**, with respect for the cultures you're visiting – not only to derive the most benefit from your trip but also to preserve the best bits of the planet for everyone to enjoy. At Rough Guides we feel there are six main areas in which you can make a difference:

- Consider what you're contributing to the **local economy**, and how much the services you use do the same, whether it's through employing local workers and guides or sourcing locally grown produce and local services.
- Consider the **environment** on holiday as well as at home. Water is scarce in many developing destinations, and the biodiversity of local flora and fauna can be adversely affected by tourism. Try to patronize businesses that take account of this.
- Travel with a purpose, not just to tick off experiences. Consider **spending longer** in a place, and getting to know it and its people.
- Give thought to how often you **fly**. Try to avoid short hops by air and more harmful night flights.
- Consider **alternatives to flying**, travelling instead by bus, train, boat and even by bike or on foot where possible.
- Make your trips **"climate neutral"** via a reputable carbon offset scheme. All Rough Guide flights are offset, and every year we donate money to a variety of charities devoted to combating the effects of climate change.

desert of northwest China. It takes around five days. The trains are comfortable and clean: second-class compartments contain four berths, while first-class have two, and even boast a private shower. There are two direct trains a week, but it's also possible to break up the journey with stops in, for example, Irkutsk or Mongolia.

Meals are included while the train is in China. In Mongolia, the dining car accepts payment in both Chinese and Mongolian currency; while in Russia, US dollars or Russian roubles can be used. It's worth having small denominations of US dollars as you can change these on the train throughout the journey, or use them to buy food from station vendors along the way. Note that trains via Dongbei arrive in Beijing at 5.20am, so remember to change money at the border stop if you're using this route.

You'll need tourist **visas** for Russia, and if you use the Trans-Mongolian train you may have to apply for visas for Mongolia as well (US citizens don't need these). For detailed, up-to-date **information** on all ways to get tickets, check Ⓦwww.seat61.com/trans-siberian.htm.

You'll need to **reserve** at least a couple of weeks ahead to ensure a seat, with tickets for winter travel easier to get hold of than for the peak summer season. Sorting out your travel arrangements on your own from abroad is a complex business and almost certainly more trouble than it's worth, and simply turning up in Russia and buying a ticket from a train station is unlikely to succeed as tickets sell out quickly. British travellers can cut the complications by using the **online booking system** offered by **Real Russia** (Ⓦwww.realrussia.co.uk); they mark up prices about 20 percent but do save you a lot of hassle. A second-class Moscow to Beijing ticket booked with them costs around £870 – and of course they will then help you sort out your visas for a small fee (as will all other agencies). They also offer **tours**, as do a number of Russia-based agencies. For details of these and companies at home that can sort out Trans-Siberian travel, see p.22.

If you're planning to take the train home, you could buy your train ticket in Beijing, at the CITS office on the ground floor of the *International Hotel* on Jianguomennei Dajie, just north of the train station (daily 8.30am–5pm; Ⓣ010/65120507; see p.78). You can check fares at Ⓦwww.cits.net. BTG Travel, on Fuxingmenwai Dajie (see p.25) have a desk for Trans-Siberian tickets that charges about the same. These are the inexpensive options (tickets for Moscow start at about US$600), but involve a certain amount of hassle as you'll have to get your visas yourself.

Airlines, agents and operators

Airlines

Aeroflot Ⓦwww.aeroflot.com
Air Canada Ⓦwww.aircanada.com
Air China Ⓦwww.airchina.com.cn
Air France Ⓦwww.airfrance.com
Air New Zealand Ⓦwww.airnewzealand.com
Alitalia Ⓦwww.alitalia.com
All Nippon Airways (ANA) Ⓦwww.anaskyweb.com
American Airlines Ⓦwww.aa.com
Asiana Airlines Ⓦwww.flyasiana.com
Austrian Ⓦwww.aua.com
British Airways Ⓦwww.ba.com
Cathay Pacific Ⓦwww.cathaypacific.com
China Airlines Ⓦwww.china-airlines.com
China Eastern Airlines Ⓦwww.chinaeastern.co.uk
China Southern Airlines Ⓦwww.cs-air.com
Continental Airlines Ⓦwww.continental.com
Emirates Ⓦwww.emirates.com
Finnair Ⓦwww.finnair.com
Garuda Indonesia Ⓦwww.garuda-indonesia.com
Gulf Air Ⓦwww.gulfairco.com
JAL (Japan Air Lines) Ⓦwww.jal.com
KLM (Royal Dutch Airlines) Ⓦwww.klm.com
Korean Air Ⓦwww.koreanair.com
Lufthansa Ⓦwww.lufthansa.com
Malaysia Airlines Ⓦwww.malaysia-airlines.com
PIA (Pakistan International Airlines) Ⓦwww.piac.com.pk
Qantas Airways Ⓦwww.qantas.com
Qatar Airways Ⓦwww.qatarairways.com
Royal Brunei Ⓦwww.bruneiair.com
Royal Jordanian Ⓦwww.rja.com.jo
SAS (Scandinavian Airlines) Ⓦwww.flysas.com
Singapore Airlines Ⓦwww.singaporeair.com
Swiss Ⓦwww.swiss.com
Thai Airways Ⓦwww.thaiair.com
United Airlines Ⓦwww.united.com
US Airways Ⓦwww.usair.com
Vietnam Airlines Ⓦwww.vietnamairlines.com

Agents

North South Travel UK ⓣ01245/608291, ⓦwww.northsouthtravel.co.uk. Discounted fares worldwide. Profits are used to support projects in the developing world, especially the promotion of sustainable tourism.
STA Travel UK ⓣ0870/160 0599, US & Canada ⓣ1-800/781-4040, Australia ⓣ1300/733 035, New Zealand ⓣ0508/782 872; ⓦwww.sta-travel.com. Worldwide specialists in low-cost flights and tours for students and under-26s, though other customers are welcome too.
Trailfinders UK ⓣ0207/628-7628, Republic of Ireland ⓣ01/677 7888, Australia ⓣ02/9247 7666; ⓦwww.trailfinders.com. One of the best-informed and most efficient agents for independent travellers.

Specialist tour operators

Abercrombie & Kent US ⓣ1-800/323-7308 or 630/954-2944, ⓦwww.abercrombiekent.com. Luxury tours; US$4000 buys you a twelve-day "Highlights of China" trip covering Shanghai, Guilin, Xi'an and Beijing.
China Highlights China ⓣ+86/773 2831999, ⓦwww.chinahighlights.com. China-based company that offers a set of tours of Beijing and the surrounding area.
China Odyssey China ⓣ+86/773 5854000, ⓦwww.chinaodysseytours.com. Short city tours and longer trips that take in other destinations in China.
Destinations Worldwide Holidays Republic of Ireland ⓣ01/855 6641, ⓦwww.destinations.ie. Two-week tours that include Hong Kong and Beijing.
Hayes and Jarvis UK ⓣ0870/898-9890, ⓦwww.hayesandjarvis.co.uk. Among the most inexpensive Beijing flight-and-hotel-only packages available to British travellers.
Intrepid Adventure Travel UK ⓣ0207/354-6169, ⓦwww.intrepidtravel.co.uk; Australia ⓣ1300/360 667 or 03/9473 2626, ⓦwww.intrepidtravel.com.au; New Zealand ⓣ0800/174 043. Small-group tours, with the emphasis on cross-cultural contact and low-impact tourism. Covers the staples, including hikes along the Great Wall near Beijing.
The Russia Experience UK ⓣ0208/566-8846, ⓦwww.trans-siberian.co.uk. Besides detailing their Trans-Siberian packages, the website is a veritable mine of information about the railway. More expensive than similar tours offered by Russian agencies, but probably the most hassle-free option.
Travel China Guide US & Canada ⓣ1-800/892-6988, all other countries ⓣ+800/6668 8666; ⓦwww.travelchinaguide.com. A Chinese company with a wide range of three- and four-day group tours of Beijing and around.
World Expeditions UK ⓣ0208/870-2600, Australia ⓣ1300/720 000, US ⓣ1-888/464-8735, Canada ⓣ1-800/567-2212; ⓦwww.worldexpeditions.com. Offers a 21-day Great Wall trek, starting in Beijing and heading well off the beaten track, for US$2500, excluding flights.

Russian agencies and Trans-Siberian Express tours

All Russia Travel Service ⓦwww.rusrailtravel.ru. A reliable agency for Trans-Siberian train journeys and tours, cheaper than its Western competitors.
Monkey Business ⓦwww.monkeyshrine.com. A wide range of inexpensive tours: a Moscow to Beijing trip, including a couple of nights in a youth hostel, costs around US$950 in standard-class.
Ost West ⓦwww.ostwest.com. A Russian operator offering competitively priced Trans-Siberian train journeys.
Real Russia ⓦwww.realrussia.co.uk. An efficient booking service for journeys on the Trans-Siberian Express plus tours – a nine-day option, including a couple of nights in Moscow, costs £1400 per person, a little less if you book as a group.

Arrival

Those who arrive by train are lucky to find themselves already at the heart of the city; all others will find themselves outside the Second Ring Road with a long onward journey. It's best not to tussle with the buses with luggage, so head for the metro or a cab rank. There aren't many shady cabbies in Beijing, but the few there are hang around arrival points – ignore offers from freelance operators and head straight to the officially monitored taxi ranks.

Orientation

Beijing's **ring roads** – freeways arranged in nested rectangles centring on Tian'anmen Square – are rapid-access corridors around the city. The Second and Third ring roads, **Erhuan** and **Sanhuan Lu**, are the two most useful, as they cut down on journey times but extend the distance travelled; they are much favoured by taxi drivers. Within the Second Ring Road lie most of the **historical sights**, while many of the most modern buildings – including the smartest hotels, restaurants, shopping centres and office blocks – are along or close to the third. You'll soon become familiar with the experience of barrelling along a freeway in a bus or taxi, not knowing which direction you're travelling in, let alone where you are, as identical blocks flicker past.

By air

Beijing Capital Airport (Ⓦwww.bcia.com.cn) is 29km northeast of the centre. **Banks** and an **ATM** are on the right as you exit Customs (and there are more ATMs upstairs). There's an accommodation-booking service opposite Customs, but you may get lower prices if you call the hotels yourself and bargain for a discount.

You'll be pestered in the Arrivals Hall itself by charlatan taxi drivers; ignore them. Use the **taxi rank** to the left of the main exit from Arrivals (just outside Gate 9). A trip to the city centre will cost around ¥150, including the ¥10 toll. The most convenient way to get into town on public transport is with the new light-rail **Airport Express**, which starts from terminal 3, and calls at terminal 2 and Sanyuanqiao before terminating at Dongzhimen, where you can transfer to the subway network. Note that cabbies at the Dongzhimen exit commonly gouge new arrivals, so if you're getting a cab walk a little way and hail one from the street. Trains run every fifteen minutes from 6.30am to 10.30pm; the ride takes about twenty minutes and tickets cost ¥25.

Beijing transport terminals

Beijing	北京	*běijīng*
Beijing Capital Airport	北京首都机场	*běijīng shǒudū jīchǎng*
Bus stations		
Deshengmen bus station	德胜门公共汽车站	*déshèngmén gōnggòng qìchēzhàn*
Dongzhimen bus station	东直门公共汽车站	*dōngzhímén gōnggòng qìchēzhàn*
Haihutun bus station	海户屯公共汽车站	*hǎihùtún gōnggòng qìchēzhàn*
Zhaogongkou bus station	赵公口公共汽车站	*zhàogōngkǒu gōnggòng qìchēzhàn*
Train stations		
Beijing Zhan	北京站	*běijīng zhàn*
Xi Zhan	西站	*xī zhàn*
Xizhimen Zhan	西直门站	*xīzhímén zhàn*
Yongdingmen Zhan	永定门站	*yǒngdìngmén zhàn*

Street names

Beijing street names appear bewildering at first, as a road can have several names along its length, but they are easy to figure out once you know the system. Each name varies by the addition of the word for "inside" or "outside" (**nèi** or **wài** respectively), which indicates the street's position in relation to the former city walls, then a direction – **běi**, **nán**, **xī**, **dōng** and **zhōng** (north, south, west, east and middle respectively). Central streets often also contain the word **men** (gate), which indicates that they once passed through a walled gate along their route. **Jiē** and **lù** mean "street" and "road" respectively; the word **dà**, which sometimes precedes them, simply means "big". Thus Jianguomenwai Dajie literally refers to the outer section of Jianguomen Big Street. More confusingly, in the northwest section of the Third Ring Road you'll come across both Beisanhuan Xi Lu (for the bit east of the northwest corner) and Xisanhuan Bei Lu (the stretch running south of that corner). Some of these compound street names are just too much of a mouthful and are usually shortened; Gongrentiyuchang Bei Lu, for example, is usually referred to as Gongti Bei Lu.

Comfortable, if cramped, **airport buses**, can be found outside Gate 11. Buy tickets (¥16) from the desk directly in front of the exit. They leave regularly on nine routes: most useful are **Line 1, which** stops at Dongzhimen (for the subway), Dongsishitiao and Yabao Lu, and finishes at the Airline Office in Xidan); **line 2, which** goes to the far north and west of the city; **line 3** to Guomao and Beijing Zhan; and **line 4** to Zhongguancun.

If the airport bus doesn't pass close to your destination, it's best to do the remainder of your journey by taxi rather than grapple with more buses, as the public transport system is confusing at first and the city layout alienating. Be wary, however, of the taxi drivers waiting at the bus stop – hail a cab from the street instead.

By train

Beijing has two main train stations. **Beijing Zhan**, the central station, just south of Jianguomennei Dajie, is where trains from destinations north and east of Beijing arrive. At the northeastern edge of the concourse is the subway stop, on the network's loop line. The taxi rank is over the road and 50m east of the station; another 50m on is a major bus terminal, from where buses serve most of the city.

Approaching from the south or west of the capital, you'll arrive at the west station, **Xi Zhan**, Asia's largest train terminal and the start of the Beijing–Kowloon line. There are plenty of **buses** from here – bus #122 heads to Beijing Zhan, bus #21 to Fuchengmen subway stop – as well as taxis, from the rank 50m in front of the main entrance.

You're unlikely to use Beijing's new south station (**Yongdingmen Zhan**) just inside the Third Ring Road, unless you have come on the new fast train link from Tianjin.

Leaving Beijing

Booking **onward transport** is a simple matter. But at the peak seasons – the two-week long holidays and just before Chinese New Year (see p.30) – it's best to organize your onward transport long in advance.

By air

You can buy **airline tickets** from hotels and all travel agencies, which sometimes charge a small commission (¥30 or so); the Aviation Office at 15 Xichang'an Jie in Xidan (Ⓣ010/66013336 for domestic flights, Ⓣ010/66016667 international; 24hr); from CAAC offices in the *Beijing Hotel* on Dongchang'an Jie and in the China World Trade Centre (Ⓣ010/65053775); or from CITS offices at 103 Fuxingmenwai Dajie (Ⓣ010/66039321), and in the *International Hotel* (Ⓣ010/65126688), just north of Beijing Zhan. Alternatively, buy your ticket **online** with Ⓦwww.elong.com.cn or www.ctrip.com.cn. Your ticket will be delivered the same day at no extra charge, provided you're within the Third Ring Road. You need a phone number to confirm your purchase.

Airport buses (call ⓣ010/64594375 for enquiries) leave from the Aviation Office at 15 Xi Chang'an Jie (every 15min 5.40am–9pm), and from outside Dongzhimen subway station (the stop is 50m east of the big intersection). Another bus also leaves from the east side of the Beijing Zhan station concourse (every 30min 6am–7pm), but this one is a little confusing to find as there are so many buses in the area. Trips take an hour (90min in rush hour), and cost ¥16.

By train

At **Beijing main station**, the ticketing office for foreigners (5.30–7.30am, 8am–6.30pm & 7–11pm) is on the northwest corner of the first floor, at the back of the soft-seat waiting room. You don't have to buy your tickets here, but the queues are much shorter than at the main ticket booking office on the west side of the station; you may be asked to show your passport. At **Beijing West** station, the foreigners' ticketing office is on the second floor (24hr). You can also book train tickets **online** at ⓦwww.51piao.com/train or call the reservation centre on ⓣ010/95105105 – your ticket will be delivered for a ¥10 fee, or you can pick it up at an agent near you. For train **timetables**, check ⓦwww.chinahighlights.com/china-trains/index.htm.

By bus

You're unlikely to encounter Beijing's fearsomely busy bus stations, unless you're going to **Tianjin** or **Chendge**, or as part of an independent trip to the **Great Wall**. There are many **terminals** for long-distance buses, each one serving only a few destinations. Stations are located on the city outskirts, matching the destination's direction from the city.

Dongzhimen, on the northeast corner of the Second Ring Road, is the largest bus station, connected by subway to the rest of the city; it handles services to and from Shenyang and the rest of the northeast. **Deshengmen** (Beijiao), the north station serving Chengde and Datong, is just north of the Second Ring Road (Erhuan Bei Lu); it's on the route of bus #328, which terminates at Andingmen, from where you can catch the subway's loop line. **Zhaogongkou**, on the south side of the Third Ring Road (Nansanhuan Lu), serves southern and eastern destinations including

Travel agents

There are plenty of **travel agents** in Beijing. The biggest (though certainly not the best) is the state-run **CITS**. They offer tours of the city and surroundings, and advance ticket booking within China for trains, planes and ferries, with a commission of around ¥20 added to ticket prices. You'll find CITS next to the *Gloria Plaza Hotel* at 28 Jianguomenwai Dajie (daily 8.30–11.30am & 1.30–4.30pm; ⓣ010/65050231); next to the Parkson Building at 103 Fuxingmen Dajie (daily 9am–5pm; ⓣ010/66011122); in the *Beijing Hotel*, 33 Dongchang'an Jie (ⓣ010/65120507); and at the *New Century Hotel* (ⓣ010/68491426), opposite the zoo. The government-run **CYTS** (China Youth Travel Service), at 3C Dongjiaominxiang (ⓣ010/65243388) is another large agent that runs tours and sells tickets but, again, don't expect too much from them.

Good, privately run alternatives include **China Swan International Tours** on the 4th floor of the Longhui Building, 1 Nanguang Nanli, Dongsanhuan Lu (ⓣ010/87372266, ⓦwww.china-swan.com) and **BTG International** at 206 Beijing Tourism Building (ⓣ010/96906798, ⓦwww.btgtravel.com.cn); both are well geared up for corporate groups.

For adventure travel within China, contact **Wild China**, Room 801, Oriental Place, 9 Dongfang Dong Lu, Dongsanhuan Bei Lu (ⓣ010/64656602, US Office ⓣ1-888/902-8808; ⓦwww.wildchina.com). Beijing's most unusual tour agency is **Koryo Tours**, at 27 Beisanlitun Nan (East Courtyard), Chaoyang District (ⓣ010/64167544, ⓦwww.koryogroup.com), who arrange visits (heavily controlled, of course) to the paranoid hermit kingdom of North Korea. Expect to pay at least US$2000 for the privilege.

Tianjin; it's on the route of bus #17 from Qianmen. Close by, to the west, **Haihutun**, at the intersection of the Third Ring Road and Yongdingmenwai Dajie, is for buses for Tianjin (see below) and cities in southern Hebei; it's connected with the centre by bus #2 to Qianmen.

By boat

International **ferries** to Japan and Korea leave from Tanggu port in Tianjin, an hour from Beijing. Boats (run by a Japanese company) are clean and comfortable, (there's ping pong and karaoke) and third-class – a *tatami* mat on the floor of a communal dorm – is certainly the cheapest way to do the trip. The trip to Kobe in Japan leaves every Monday and takes two full days. Tickets start at around ¥1600 and can be bought at CITS (see p.21). The twice-weekly ferries to Inchon in Korea take 24 hours, and cost around ¥850.

Getting around

Getting around Beijing isn't quite the challenge it once was, thanks to the new subway lines. Still, the public transport system often feels overstretched. Buses can be a hassle and taxis get stuck in gridlock, so sometimes the best way to get around is to hire a bike.

Anyone staying more than a couple of weeks and intending to use a lot of public transport should consider buying a **swipe card**, available from subway stations and valid for bus and subway tickets. The deposit is ¥20, which you receive back when you return it, and you can put as much money on the card as you like.

Beijing is divided into **districts** that, unfortunately, aren't marked on standard city maps. Broadly, Dongcheng is the eastern half of the centre, Xicheng the western half. Xuanwu is the southwest, Chongwen the southeast, Haidian the north and west outside the Second Ring Road, and Chaoyang north and east outside the Third Ring Road. It's helpful to know these districts when trying to locate addresses.

By subway

Clean, efficient and very fast, the **subway** (daily 5am–11pm), is preferable to the bus – though be prepared for enforced intimacies during rush hour. Station entrances are marked by a logo of a rectangle inside a "G" shape. All **stops** are marked in *pinyin* (the anglicized spelling out of Chinese characters) and announced in English and Chinese over the intercom when the train pulls in.

Line 1 runs across the city from the western suburbs, through Tian'anmen, Wangfujing and the China World Trade Centre, and terminates out beyond the eastern section of the Third Ring Road. **Line 2** is a loop line running around the city, making useful stops at Beijing Zhan, Jianguomen (under the flyover, close to the Ancient Observatory and the Friendship Store), Yonghe Gong (50m north of the temple of the same name), Gulou (near the Drum Tower) and Qianmen, at the northern end of Qianmen Dajie. There are **interchanges** between this and line 1 at Fuxingmen and Jianguomen stations. Handy **line 4** runs north–south on the west side of the city, with useful stops at both summer palaces, the zoo, Xidan and Xisi. **Line 5** runs north–south on the east side, and connects with the loop line at Yonghe Gong. There is no **line 3**.

Line 10 is suburban, and of little interest to visitors. **Line 13** serves the far north of the city: built for the Olympic Village, it's in fact an overground light-rail system, though the stations use the same logo as the subway. You can get onto it from the loop line at

Xizhimen or Dongzhimen, though you have to leave the station, walk a short distance and buy new tickets (same price) to do so. The only useful stations for tourists are Dazhongsi – for the Dazhong Si – and Wudaokou – for Beijing Daxue and the summer palaces. There's also a line that connects the two main train stations, a dedicated line for the Olympic Green, and a line that shoots up to the aiport from Dongzhimen.

Tickets on the ordinary subway cost ¥2 per journey and can be bought from the ticket offices at the top of the stairs leading down to the platforms.

By bus

Even though every one of the city's 140 **bus and trolleybus services** (¥1) runs about once a minute, you'll find it hard work getting on or off at rush hour. **Double-deckers** (¥2), operated on five services, are comfortable – you're more likely to get a seat on these – and run along main roads. **Luxury buses** (¥3–10), which run around certain tourist sights, are modern, air-conditioned, and quite pleasant. **Tourist buses** (¥10–60) – which look like ordinary buses but have route numbers written in green – make regular trips (mid-April to mid-Oct) between the city centre and certain out-of-town attractions, including sections of the Great Wall; we've listed useful routes in the text of the Guide.

Bus routes are efficiently organized and easy to understand – a handy feature, since stops tend to be a good kilometre apart. The routes are indicated by red or blue lines on all good maps; a dot on the line indicates a stop. Next to the stop on the map you'll see tiny Chinese characters giving the stop's name (the Beijing Tourist Map has stops marked in *pinyin*).

Useful bus routes

All buses display their route numbers prominently. Routes numbered #1–25 run around the city centre; buses numbered in the #200s run only at night; numbers in the #300s navigate the periphery of the city centre; and numbers in the #800s are the luxury buses.

Bus #1 and double-decker bus #1 From Xi Zhan east along the main thoroughfare, Chang'an Jie.

Double-decker bus #2 From the north end of Qianmen Dajie, north to Dongdan, the Yonghe Gong and the Asian Games Village.

Double-decker #4 From Beijing Zoo to Qianmen via Fuxingmen.

Bus #5 From Deshengmen, on the Second Ring Road in the northwest of the city, south down the west side of the Forbidden City and Tian'anmen to Qianmen Dajie.

Bus #15 From the zoo down Xidan Dajie, past Liulichang, ending at the Tianqiao area just west of Yongdingmennei Dajie, close to Tiantan Park.

Bus #20 From Beijing Zhan to Yongdingmen Zhan, south of Taoranting Park.

Bus #52 From Xi Zhan east to Lianhuachi Qiao, Xidan Dajie, Tian'anmen Square, then east along Chang'an Jie.

Bus #103 From Beijing Zhan, north up the east side of the Forbidden City, west along Fuchengmennei Dajie, then north up Sanlihe Lu to the zoo.

Bus #104 From Beijing Zhan to Hepingli Zhan in the north of the city, via Wangfujing.

Bus #105 From the northwest corner of Tiantan Park to Xidan Dajie, then west to the zoo.

Bus #106 From Yongdingmen Zhan to Tiantan Park and Chongwenmen, then up to Dongzhimennei Dajie.

Bus #300 Circles the Third Ring Road.

Bus #332 From Beijing Zoo to Beijing University and Yihe Yuan (Summer Palace).

Luxury bus #808 From just northwest of Qianmen to the Yiheyuan.

Luxury bus #802 Xi Zhan to Panjiayuan Market in the southeast.

Taxis

Taxis cost ¥2 per kilometre, with a **minimum charge** of ¥10; after 11pm, there's a surcharge of twenty percent. Drivers are good about using their meters; if they don't put them on, insist by saying "dǎ biǎo" ("put on the meter"). **Tips** are never expected.

Don't let yourself get hustled into a taxi, as unscrupulous drivers look out for newly arrived foreigners with luggage; walk a short distance and hail one, or find a rank (there's one outside each train station). Having a map open on your lap deters some drivers from taking unnecessary detours. If you feel aggrieved at a driver's behaviour, take his number (displayed on the dashboard) and report it to the taxi **complaint office** (Ⓣ010/68351150). Indeed, just the action of writing his number down can produce a remarkable change in demeanour.

Bicycle rental

Renting or buying a **bike** gives you much more independence and flexibility – and they're often faster than taxis. There are **bike lanes** on all main roads and you'll be in the company of plenty of other cyclists. If you feel nervous at busy junctions, just dismount and walk the bike across – plenty of Chinese do.

Almost all hotels – certainly all the hostels – **rent** out bikes for around ¥30 a day plus a ¥200–400 deposit. Upmarket hotels charge ¥50 a day for the same bikes. You can also rent from many places in the **hutongs** around Houhai (see p.88).

You can **buy** cheap city bikes for about ¥250; try Carrefour (see p.144) or the strip of bike shops on the south side of Jiaodaokou, just west of the Ghost Street (Gui Jie) restaurants (see p.142).

Always test the brakes on a rented bike before riding off, and get the tyres pumped up. Should you have a problem, you can turn to one of the bike repair stalls – there are plenty of these on the pavement next to main roads.

You'll need a good **lock**, as **theft** is very common. The best place to leave a bike is at one of the numerous **bike parks**, where you pay ¥0.3 to the attendant.

Car rental

Given the state of Beijing's traffic, you'd have to be pretty intrepid to want to **drive** yourself around the city, and it's not possible for anyone with an "L" or tourist visa. You'll need a Chinese driver's licence, a Beijing Residence Permit and a credit card to cover the deposit. **Avis** is at 16 Dongzhimennei Dajie (Ⓣ010/84063343, Ⓦwww.avischina.com).

City tours

Organized tours of the city and its outskirts offer a painless, if expensive, way of seeing the main sights quickly. All big hotels offer them, and **CITS** has a variety of one- and two-day tour packages, on "Dragon Buses" which you can book from their offices (see p.25), or from the information desk in the Friendship Store. These tours aren't cheap, though the price includes lunch and pays for a tour guide: a trip to the Summer Palace, Yonghe Gong and a pedicab jaunt around the *hutongs* is ¥260. Similar tours are run by two other official agencies, **CTS** and **CYTS** (see p.25). **City Bus Tour** scores for convenience, as you can book online (Ⓦwww.citybustour.com; freephone Ⓣ4006500760). Coaches are modern and you'll have an English-speaking guide. A day trip with them costs ¥380.

The one-day tours offered by the **cheaper hotels** offer better value than similar jaunts run by classier places, and you don't have to be staying with them to go along. All the **youth hostels** offer good-value evening trips to the acrobatics shows and the opera a few times a week, and day (and occasionally overnight) trips to the Great Wall (April–Oct daily; Nov–March weekly; ¥60–80). You must book these at least a day in advance.

One good, inexpensive tour that's more imaginative than most is the **hutong tour** (see p.86), which offers the opportunity to see a more private side of the city. **China Culture Club** (Ⓣ010/64329341, Ⓦwww.chinaculturecenter.org) also has plenty of imaginative city **walking tours** (3–4hr; around ¥200) and hiking trips into the countryside, including jaunts to little-known sections of the Great Wall (see p.103).

The media

Hopes that a newly wealthy, post-Olympics China would relax its hardline on dissent have been dashed; if anything, the heavy hand of the state censor has tightened in the last few years. All Chinese media is so heavily controlled that it shouldn't be relied on. That said, the official English-language newspaper, the *China Daily*, has improved of late. Imported news publications (sometimes censored) such as *Time*, *Newsweek* and the *Far Eastern Economic Review*, and Hong Kong's *South China Morning Post*, can be bought at the Friendship Store or at the bookstands in four- and five-star hotels.

Listings magazines

The English-language **Beijing This Month** has listings and light features aimed at tourists; you can pick it for free in the lobbies of the upmarket hotels, from any tourist office or the counter inside the front door at the Friendship Store on Jianguomenwai Dajie.

Much more useful, though, are the free magazines aimed at the **expat** community, which contain up-to-date entertainment and restaurant listings and are available at expat bars and restaurants. Look for *City Weekend* (Ⓦwww.cityweekend.com.cn/beijing) and *Time Out* (Ⓦwww.timeout.com/cn/en/beijing). Both have listings sections that include club nights, art happenings and gigs, with addresses written in *pinyin* and Chinese.

TV and radio

There is the occasional item of interest on Chinese **TV**, though you'd have to be quite bored to resort to it for entertainment. Domestic travel and wildlife programmes are common, as are song-and-dance extravaganzas, the most enjoyable of which feature dancers in weird fetishistic costumes. Soap operas and historical dramas are popular, and often feature a few foreigners, and talent and dating shows are currently all the rage.

CCTV, the state broadcaster, has an **English-language** rolling news channel, **CCTV International**. CCTV5 is a sports channel that often shows European football games. CCTV2, CCTV4 and local channel BTV1 all have English-language news programmes at 11pm. Satellite TV in English is available in the more expensive hotels.

On the **radio** you're likely to hear the latest ballads by pop-robots from the Hong Kong and Taiwan idol factories, or versions of Western pop songs sung in Chinese. Easy FM (91.5FM) is an expat-geared **English-language** station carrying music programmes and local information.

Public holidays and festivals

The rhythm of festivals and religious observances that used to mark the Chinese year was interrupted by the Cultural Revolution, and only now, more than forty years on, are old traditions beginning to re-emerge. The majority of festivals celebrate the turning of the seasons or propitious dates, such as the Double Ninth festival held on the ninth day of the ninth lunar month, and are times for gift-giving, family reunions and feasting.

Festivals and holidays calendar

Traditional festivals take place according to dates in the Chinese lunar calendar, in which the first day of the month is when the moon is a new crescent, with the middle of the month marked by the full moon; by the Gregorian calendar, these festivals fall on a different date every year.

January/February

New Year's Day (Jan 1).
Spring Festival (starts between late Jan and mid-Feb). The Chinese New Year celebrations extend over the first two weeks of the new lunar year (see box below).

Tiancang (Granary) Festival Chinese peasants celebrate with a feast on the twentieth day of the first lunar month, in the hope of ensuring a good harvest later in the year.

March

Guanyin's Birthday Guanyin, the goddess of mercy and China's most popular Buddhist deity, is celebrated on the nineteenth day of the second lunar month, most colourfully in Taoist temples.

April

Qingming Festival (April 4 & 5). This festival, Tomb Sweeping Day, is the time to visit the graves of ancestors, leave offerings of food, and burn ghost money – fake paper currency – in honour of the departed.

Spring Festival

The **Spring Festival**, usually falling in late January or the first half of February, is marked by two weeks of festivities celebrating the beginning of a new year in the lunar calendar (and thus also called Chinese New Year). In Chinese astrology, each year is associated with a particular animal from a cycle of twelve – 2012 is the Year of the Dragon, for example – and the passing into a new astrological phase is a momentous occasion. There's a tangible sense of excitement in the run-up to the festival, when China is perhaps at its most colourful, with shops and houses decorated with good luck messages and stalls and shops selling paper money, drums and costumes. However, the festival is not an ideal time to travel – everything shuts down, and most of the population is on the move, making travel impossible or extremely uncomfortable.

The first day of the festival is marked by a family feast at which *jiaozi* (dumplings) are eaten, sometimes with coins hidden inside. To bring luck, people dress in red clothes (red being regarded as a lucky colour) – a particularly important custom if the animal of their birth year is coming round again – and each family tries to eat a whole fish, since the word for fish (*yu*) sounds like the word for surplus. Firecrackers are let off to scare ghosts away and, on the fifth day, to honour Cai Shen, god of wealth. Another ghost-scaring tradition you may notice is the pasting up of images of door gods at the threshold. If you're in town at this time, make sure you catch a temple fair (see the colour insert, "Temple life").

Dragon Festival The fifth day of the fifth lunar month is a one-day public holiday. Traditionally, this is a time to watch dragon boat racing and eat treats wrapped in leaves.

May

Labour Day (May 1). Labour Day is a national holiday, during which all tourist sights are extremely busy.

Youth Day (May 4). Commemorates the student demonstrators in Tian'anmen Square in 1919, which gave rise to the nationalist "May Fourth" movement. It's marked in Beijing with flower displays in Tian'anmen.

June

Children's Day (June 1). Most school pupils are taken on excursions at this time, so if you're visiting a popular tourist site, be prepared for mobs of kids in yellow baseball caps.

September/October

Moon Festival Also known as the Mid-Autumn Festival, this is marked on the fifteenth day of the eighth lunar month (in 2011, this will be on September 12th). It's a time of family reunion, celebrated with fireworks and lanterns. Moon cakes, containing a rich filling of sweet bean paste, are eaten, and plenty of *maotai* – a strong white spirit distilled from rice – is consumed.

Double Ninth Festival Nine is a number associated with *yang*, or male energy, and on the ninth day of the ninth lunar month qualities such as assertiveness and strength are celebrated. It's believed to be a profitable time for the distillation (and consumption) of spirits.

Confucius Festival (Sept 28). The birthday of Confucius is marked by celebrations at all Confucian temples.

National Day (Oct 1). Everyone has three days off to celebrate the founding of the People's Republic.

Culture and etiquette

When Confucius arrives in a country, he invariably gets to know about its society. Does he seek this information, or is it given him? Confucius gets it through being cordial, good, respectful, temperate and deferential.

Confucius, *The Analects*, 1.10

Privacy is a luxury largely unheard of in China – indeed, Chinese doesn't have an exact translation of the word. Public toilets are built with low partitions, no one eats alone in restaurants, all leisure activities are performed in noisy groups, and a curiosity – such as a visiting Caucasian, or "big nose" as the Chinese like to say – can find him or herself the subject of frank stares and attention. The best thing to do in such situations is smile and say "*nǐhǎo*" – a simple hello. A desire to be left alone can baffle the Chinese, and is occasionally interpreted as arrogance. Conversely, behaviour seen as antisocial in the West, notably queue-jumping, spitting and smoking, is quite normal in China, though government campaigns to cut down on these are having some effect.

Skimpy **clothing** is fine (indeed fashionable), but looking scruffy will only induce disrespect: all foreigners are, correctly, assumed to be comparatively rich, so why they would want to dress like peasants is quite beyond the Chinese.

Shaking hands is not a Chinese tradition, though it is now fairly common between men. Businessmen meeting for the first time exchange business cards, with the offered card held in two hands as a gesture of respect – you'll see polite shop assistants doing the same with your change.

In a **restaurant**, the Chinese don't usually share the bill; instead, diners contest for the honour of paying it, with the most respected usually winning. You should make some effort to stake your claim but, as a visiting guest, you can pretty much guarantee that you won't get to pay a jiao.

Tipping is never expected, and though you might sometimes feel it's warranted, resist the temptation – you'll set an unwelcome precedent. A few upmarket places add a service charge, though it's highly unlikely that the serving staff ever see any of it.

If you visit a Chinese house, you'll be expected to present your hosts with a **gift**, which won't be opened in front of you (that would be impolite). Imported whisky and ornamental trinkets are suitable as presents, though avoid giving anything too practical, as it might be construed as charity.

Sex, sexuality and gender issues

Women travellers in Beijing usually find the incidence of sexual harassment much less of a problem than in other Asian countries. Chinese men are, on the whole, deferential and respectful. Being ignored is a much more likely complaint, as the Chinese will generally assume that any man accompanying a woman will be doing all the talking.

Prostitution, though illegal, has made a big comeback – witness all the new "hairdressers", saunas and massage parlours, almost every one a brothel. Single foreign men are likely to be approached inside hotels; it's common practice for prostitutes to phone around hotel rooms at all hours of the night – so unplug the phone if you don't want to be woken up. Bear in mind that China is hardly Thailand – consequences may be unpleasant if you are caught with a prostitute – and that AIDS is rife and much of the public largely ignorant of sexual health issues.

Beijing, and China as a whole, has become more tolerant of **homosexuality** in recent years; it's been removed from the list of psychiatric diseases and is no longer illegal. Still, the scene is fairly tame and low-key. See p.148 for a list of gay venues.

Travelling with children

Foreigners with kids can be expected to receive lots of attention from curious locals – and the occasional admonition that the little one should be wrapped up warmer.

Local kids don't use **nappies**, just pants with a slit at the back – and when baby wants to go, mummy points him at the gutter. Nappies and baby milk are available from modern supermarkets such as Carrefour (see p.144), though there are few public changing facilities. High-end hotels have **babyminding** services for around ¥150 an hour. **Breast-feeding** in public is acceptable, though more so outside the train station than in celebrity restaurants.

Sights that youngsters might enjoy are the zoo and aquarium (see p.94), pedal boating on Houhai (see p.87), the acrobat shows (see p.152) and the Puppet Theatre (see p.151), the Natural History Museum (see p.65) and the Goose and Duck Ranch (see p.104). If you're tired of worrying about them in the traffic, try taking them to **pedestrianized** Liulichang, the Olympic Green, the 798 Art District, or the parks – Ritan Park has a good playground (see p.80) and Chaoyang Park has boating. Note that most Beijing attractions are free for children under 1.2m high.

Check ⓦwww.beijing-kids.com for more suggestions and advice.

Travel essentials

Costs

In terms of **costs**, Beijing is a city of extremes. You can, if you wish to live it up, spend as much here as you would visiting any Western capital; on the other hand, it's also quite possible to live extremely cheaply – most locals survive on less than ¥2000 a month.

Generally, your biggest expense is likely to be **accommodation**. **Food** and **transport**, on the other hand, are relatively cheap. The minimum you can live on comfortably is about £15/US$20/¥150 a day if you stay in a dormitory, get around by bus and eat in simple restaurants. On a budget of £40/US$55/¥400 a day, you'll be able to stay in a modest hotel, travel in taxis and eat in good restaurants. To stay in an upmarket hotel, you'll need to have a budget of around £100/US$130/¥1000 a day.

Discounts on admission prices are available to students in China on production of the red Chinese student identity card. A youth hostel card gets a small discount at hostels (and can be bought at the front desk).

Crime and personal safety

With all the careful showcasing of modernity and rampant consumerism, it's easy to forget that Beijing is the heart of an **authoritarian** state that has terrorized its subjects for much of its short, inglorious history. Not that this should physically affect visitors too much; the state is as anxious to keep tourists happy as it is to incarcerate democracy activists, bloggers and the like. Indeed, Chinese who commit crimes against foreigners are treated much more harshly than if their victims had been compatriots.

Crime is a growth industry in China, partly thanks to appalling disparities in income, and the prevailing get-rich-quick ideology. Official corruption is rampant, and the state sometimes shoots scapegoats in an effort to cut it down (it's called "killing the chicken to frighten the monkeys").

Emergency numbers

Police ☎110
Fire ☎119
Ambulance ☎120

Con artists

Getting **scammed** is by far the biggest threat to foreign visitors, and there are now so many professional con artists targeting tourists that you can expect to be approached many times a day at places such as Wangfujing and on Tian'anmen Square. A sweet-looking young couple, a pair of girls, or perhaps a kindly old man, will ask to practise their English or offer to show you round. After befriending you – which may take hours – they will suggest some refreshment, and lead you to a tea house. After a traditional-looking tea ceremony you will be presented with a bill for thousands of yuan, your new "friends" will disappear or pretend to be shocked, and some large gentlemen will appear. In another variation, you will be coaxed into buying a painting (really a print) for a ridiculous sum. Never drink with a stranger if you haven't seen a price list.

While there is no need for obsessive paranoia – Beijing is still safer than most Western cities – you do need to take care. Tourists are an obvious target for petty **thieves**. Passports and money should be kept in a concealed money belt; a bum bag offers much less protection and is easy for skilled pickpockets to get into. It's a good idea to keep around £400/US$500 separately from the rest of your cash, together with copies of all your important documents. Be wary on buses, the favoured haunt of pickpockets, and trains, particularly in hard-seat class and on overnight journeys.

Take a chain and padlock to secure your luggage in the rack.

Hotel rooms are on the whole secure, dormitories much less so – in the latter case it's often fellow travellers who are the problem. Most hotels should have a safe, but it's not unusual for things to go missing from these.

On the **street**, flashy jewellery and watches will attract the wrong kind of attention, and try to be discreet when taking out your cash. Not looking obviously wealthy also helps if you want to avoid being ripped off by street traders and taxi drivers, as does telling them you are a student – the Chinese have a great respect for education, and more sympathy for foreign students than for tourists.

The police

If you do have anything stolen, you'll need to get the police, known as the **Public Security Bureau** or PSB, to write up a loss report in order to claim on your insurance. Their main office is at 2 Andingmen Dong Dajie, 300m east of Yonghe Gong subway stop (Mon–Fri 8am–4.30pm; ⓣ010/84015292).

The **police** are recognizable by their dark blue uniforms and caps, though there are a lot more around than you might at first think, as plenty are undercover. They have much wider powers than most Western police forces, including establishing the guilt of criminals – trials are often used only for deciding the sentence of the accused, though China is beginning to have the makings of an independent judiciary. Laws are harsh, with execution – a bullet in the back of the head – the penalty for a wide range of serious crimes, from corruption to rape, though if the culprit is deemed to show proper remorse, the result can be a more lenient sentence.

While individual police often go out of their way to help foreigners, the institution of the PSB is, on the whole, tiresomely officious.

Electricity

The electrical supply is 220V. **Plugs** come in four types: three-pronged with angled pins, three-pronged with round pins, two flat pins and two narrow round pins. Adaptor plugs are available from hardware and electronic stores; try the Hi-Tech Mall (see p.165).

Entry requirements

To enter China, all foreign nationals require a **visa**, available worldwide from Chinese embassies and consulates and through specialist tour operators and visa agents. **Single-entry tourist visas** (called "L" visas) must be used within three months of issue, and cost US$30–50, or the local equivalent. They are valid for a month, but the authorities might well grant a request for a two- or three-month visa if asked (which costs the same) though there is no certainty about this.

To **apply** for a visa you have to submit an application form, one or two passport-size photographs, your passport (which must be valid for at least another six months from your planned date of entry into China, and have at least one blank page for visas) and the fee. If you apply in person, processing should take between three and five working days. Postal applications take three weeks.

You'll be asked your occupation – don't admit to being a journalist or writer as you might be called in for an interview and made to get the annoying **journalist visa** (J), which means you'll have to report to police stations in China. At times of political sensitivity you may be asked for a copy of any air tickets and hotel bookings in your name.

A **business visa** (F) costs US$100–150 and is valid for six months and multiple journeys; you'll need an official invitation from a government-recognized Chinese organization to apply for one (except in Hong Kong, where you can simply buy one). Twelve-month **work visas** (Z) cost US$300 and again require an invitation, plus a health certificate from your doctor. Students intending to study in Beijing for less than six months need an invitation or letter of acceptance from a college there in order to apply for **student visas** (US$150). If you're intending to go on a longer course, you have to fill in an additional form, available from Chinese embassies, and will also need a health certificate; then you'll be issued with an X visa, valid for a year, and renewable.

Chinese embassies

Australia ⓦau.china-embassy.org/eng
Canada ⓦwww.chinaembassycanada.org
India ⓦwww.chinaembassy.org.in
Republic of Ireland ⓦie.china-embassy.org/eng
Laos ⓔchinaemb_la@mfa.gov.com
New Zealand ⓦwww.chinaembassy.org.nz
Russia ⓦwww.chinaembassy.ru
South Africa ⓦwww.chinese-embassy.org.au.za
UK ⓦwww.chinese-embassy.org.uk
US ⓦwww.china-embassy.org
Vietnam ⓦwww.fmprc.gov.cn/eng

Visa extensions

Once in China, a **first extension** to a tourist visa, valid for a month, is easy to obtain; most Europeans pay ¥160 for this, Americans a little more. To apply for an extension, go to the "Aliens Entry Exit Department" of the PSB at 2 Andingmen Dong Dajie, 300m east of Yonghe Gong subway stop (Mon–Fri 8am–4.30pm; ⓣ010/84015292). The staff will **keep your passport** for three working days; note that you can't change money, or even book into a new hotel, while they've got it. Subsequent applications for extensions will be refused unless you have a good reason to stay, such as illness. They'll reluctantly give you a couple of extra days if you have a flight out of the country booked; otherwise, you'll be brusquely ordered to leave the country. Don't; simply go to Chengde (see p.114), where the friendlier PSB office will grant month-long second extensions on the spot.

Don't **overstay** your visa even for a few hours – the fine is ¥500 per day, and if you're caught at the airport with an out-of-date visa the hassle that will follow may mean you'll miss your flight.

Customs allowances

You're allowed to **import** into China up to four hundred cigarettes, two litres of alcohol, twenty fluid ounces (590ml) of perfume and up to fifty grams of gold or silver. You can't take in more than ¥6000, and foreign currency in excess of US$5000 or the equivalent must be declared. It's illegal to import printed or filmed matter critical of the country, but confiscation is rare in practice.

Export restrictions apply on any items over 100 years old that you might buy in China. Taking these items out of the country requires an export form, available from the Friendship Store (see p.144); ask at the information counter for a form, take along the item and your receipt, and approval is given on the spot. You needn't be unduly concerned about the process – the "antiques" you commonly see for sale are all fakes anyway.

Embassies in Beijing

Most **embassies** are either around Sanlitun, in the northeast, or in the Jianguomenwai compound, north of and parallel to Jianguomenwai Dajie. You can get passport-size photos for visas from an annex just inside the front entrance of the Friendship Store. Visa departments usually open for a few hours every weekday morning (phone for exact times and to see what you'll need to take). During the application process they might take your passport for as long as a week; remember that you can't change money or your accommodation without it.

Australia 21 Dongzhimenwai Dajie, Sanlitun ⓣ010/51404111.
Azerbaijan 7-2-5-1 Tayuan Building ⓣ010/65324614.
Canada 19 Dongzhimenwai Dajie, Sanlitun ⓣ010/51394000.
France 3 Dong San Jie, Sanlitun ⓣ010/85328080.
Germany 17 Dongzhimenwai Dajie, Sanlitun ⓣ010/85329000.
India 1 Ritan Dong Lu, Sanlitun ⓣ010/65321908.
Ireland 3 Ritan Dong Lu, Sanlitun ⓣ010/65322691.
Italy 2 Dong'er Jie, Sanlitun ⓣ010/85327600.
Japan 7 Ritan Lu, Jianguomenwai ⓣ010/65322361.
Kazakhstan 9 Dong Liu Jie, Sanlitun ⓣ010/65326183.
Kyrgyzstan 2-4-1 Tayuan Building ⓣ010/65326458.
Laos 11 Dongsi Jie, Sanlitun ⓣ010/65321224.
Mongolia 2 Xiushui Bei Jie, Jianguomenwai ⓣ010/65321203.
Myanmar (Burma) 6 Dongzhimenwai Dajie, Sanlitun ⓣ010/65321425.
New Zealand 1 Ritan Dong'er Jie, Sanlitun ⓣ010/65327000.
North Korea Ritan Bei Lu, Jianguomenwai ⓣ010/65321186.

Pakistan 1 Dongzhimenwai Dajie, Sanlitun ⓣ010/65322660.
Russian Federation 4 Dongzhimen Bei Zhong Jie ⓣ010/65321381.
South Africa 5 Dongzhimenwai Dajie ⓣ010/65320171.
South Korea 20 Dongfang Dong Lu ⓣ010/85310700.
Thailand 40 Guanghua Lu, Jianguomenwai ⓣ010/65321749; visa and consular section, 15th floor, Building D, Twin Tower, Jianguomenwai Da Jie ⓣ010/85664469.
UK 11 Guanghua Lu, Jianguomenwai ⓣ010/51924000; visa and consular section, 21st floor, Kerry Centre, 1 Guanghua Lu ⓣ010/85296600.
Ukraine 11 Dong Lu Jie, Sanlitun ⓣ010/65324014.
US 55 Anjialou (entrance on Tianze Lu), ⓣ010/85313333; visa call centre ⓣ4008872333.
Uzbekistan 7 Beixiao Jie, Sanlitun ⓣ010/65326305.
Vietnam 32 Guanghua Lu, Jianguomenwai ⓣ010/65321155.

Health

The most common health hazard in Beijing is the host of **cold and flu infections** that strike down a large proportion of the population, mostly in the winter months. The problem is compounded by the overcrowded conditions, chain-smoking, pollution and the widespread habit of spitting, which rapidly spreads infection. Initial symptoms are fever, sore throat, chills and a feeling of malaise, sometimes followed by a prolonged bout of bronchitis. If you do come down with something like this, drink lots of fluids and get plenty of rest, and seek medical advice if symptoms persist.

Diarrhoea is another common illness to affect travellers, usually in a mild form, while your stomach gets used to unfamiliar food. The sudden onset of diarrhoea with

Healing hands

Beijing's massage centres and **spas** are a great way to unwind from the stresses of city life, and not expensive. Try one of the following:

Aibosen 11 Liufang Bei Lu ⓣ010/64652044. The staff at this clinic are trained in Chinese medical massages; ¥88/70min foot massage.

Bodhi 17 Gongti Bei Lu, close to the Workers' Stadium ⓣ010/64179595. Ayurvedic and Thai massages are among the many options available at this clinic. Daily 11am–12.30pm; prices begin at ¥158/hr, but it's half-price Mon–Thurs before 5pm.

Chi *Shangri-La Hotel*, 29 Zizhuyuan Rd ⓣ010/88826748. Therapies at this luxurious New Age spa claim to use the five Chinese elements – metal, fire, wood, water and earth – to balance your *yin* and *yang*. It might look like a Tibetan temple, but there can't be many real Tibetans who could afford to darken its doors; a Chi Balance massage costs ¥1350, a Himalayan Healing Stone Massage ¥1600 (and there's a fifteen percent service charge). Daily 10am–midnight.

Dragonfly First Floor/*Eastern Inn*, Sanlitun Nan Lu ⓣ010/65936066; 60 Donghuamen Dajie, outside the east gate of the Forbidden City ⓣ010/65279368, ⓦwww.dragonfly.net.cn. This well-reputed Shanghai chain has opened a couple of conveniently located centres in the capital. Their two-hour hangover release special (¥288) is always popular. Daily 10am–1am.

St Regis Spa Centre *St Regis Hotel*, 21 Jianguomenwai Dajie ⓣ010/64606688. Traditional Chinese massage, aromatherapy and facials are among the treatments on offer at this very upscale hotel. Prices start at ¥250 for a head and shoulders massage.

Taipan 6 Ritan Lu ⓣ010/65025722, ⓦwww.taipan.com.cn. A popular chain – no frills, but clean and cheap. Around ¥168 for a 90min foot massage or a 60min body massage.

Zen Spa House 1, 8A Xiaowuji Lu ⓣ010/87312530, ⓦwww.zenspa.com.cn. This spa, in a courtyard house full of antique furniture, offers Thai and Chinese massages as well as all sorts of scrub and detox treatments. A full 2 hour 30 minutes treatment costs ¥2100, but there are cheaper options. Daily 11am–11pm; you have to book at least a day in advance.

stomach cramps and vomiting indicates food poisoning. In both instances, get plenty of rest, drink lots of water, and in serious cases replace lost salts with oral rehydration solution (ORS); this is especially important with young children. Take a few sachets with you, or make your own by adding half a teaspoon of salt and three of sugar to a litre of cool, previously boiled water. While down with diarrhoea, avoid milk, greasy or spicy foods, coffee and most fruit, in favour of bland food such as rice, plain noodles and soup. If symptoms persist, or if you notice blood or mucus in your stools, consult a doctor.

To avoid stomach complaints, eat at places that look busy and clean and stick to fresh, thoroughly cooked food. Beware of food that has been pre-cooked and kept warm for several hours. Shellfish are a potential hepatitis A risk, and best avoided. Fresh fruit you've peeled yourself is safe; other uncooked foods may have been washed in unclean water. You may be advised not to drink **tap water**, and to avoid locally made ice drinks.

Hospitals, clinics and pharmacies

Medical facilities in Beijing are adequate: there are some high-standard international clinics, most big hotels have a resident doctor, and for minor complaints there are plenty of pharmacies that can suggest remedies. Most doctors will treat you with Western techniques first, but will also know a little Traditional Chinese Medicine (TCM).

If you don't speak Chinese, you'll generally need to have a good phrasebook or be accompanied by a Chinese-speaker. However, the following two **hospitals** have **foreigners' clinics** where some English is spoken (you will have to pay a **consultation fee** of around ¥200): Peking Union Medical College Hospital, 1 Shuaifuyuan, Wangfujing (Mon–Fri 8am–4.30pm; the foreigner unit is south of the inpatient building; ⓣ010/65295284, ⓦwww.pumch.ac.cn); and the Sino Japanese Friendship Hospital, in the northeast of the city just beyond Beisanhuan Dong Lu (daily 8–11.30am & 1–4.30pm with a 24hr emergency unit; ⓣ010/64221122, ⓦwww.zryhyy.com.cn).

For **services run by and for foreigners**, try the Beijing International SOS Clinic at Suite 105, Kunsha Building, 16 Xin-yuan-li (daily 24hr; ⓣ010/64629112, ⓦwww.internationalsos.com); the International Medical and Dental Centre at S111 in the Lufthansa Centre, 50 Liangmaqiao Lu (ⓣ010/64651384) or the Hong Kong International Clinic on the 3rd floor of the *Swissôtel Hong Kong Macau Centre*, Dongsi Shitiao Qiao (daily 9am–9pm; ⓣ010/65012288 ext 2346); or the United Family Hospital, the only completely foreign-operated clinic, at 2 Jingtai Lu (appointment ⓣ010/59277000; emergency ⓣ010/59277120, ⓦwww.unitedfamilyhospitals.com). Expect to pay at least ¥500 for a consultation at any of these places.

For **emergencies**, the AEA International Clinic has English-speaking staff and offers a comprehensive (and expensive) service at 14 Liangmahe Lu, not far from the Lufthansa Centre (clinic ⓣ010/64629112, emergency calls ⓣ010/64629100). **Ambulances** can be called on ⓣ120, but taking a taxi will be cheaper and probably quicker.

Pharmacies are marked by a green cross. There are large ones at 136 Wangfujing and 42 Dongdan Bei Dajie (daily 9am–8pm) or you could try the well-known Tongrentang Pharmacy on Dazhalan for traditional remedies (see p.164). For imported non-prescription medicines, try Watsons (daily 9am–9pm) at the *Holiday Inn Lido*, Shoudujichang Lu, in the northeast of the city, or at the Full Link Plaza on Chaoyangmenwai Dajie (daily 10am–9pm), or in the basement of Raffles Mall, Dongzhimen.

Insurance

You'd do well to take out an **insurance policy** before travelling, to cover against theft, loss and illness or injury. Before paying for a new policy, however, it's worth checking whether you are already covered: some all-risks home insurance policies may cover your possessions when overseas, and many private medical schemes include cover when abroad.

There's little opportunity for dangerous sports in Beijing (unless crossing the road counts) so a standard policy should be sufficient.

Rough Guides travel insurance

Rough Guides has teamed up with WorldNomads.com to offer great **travel insurance** deals. Policies are available to residents of over 150 countries, with cover for a wide range of **adventure sports**, 24hr emergency assistance, high levels of medical and evacuation cover and a stream of **travel safety information**. Roughguides.com users can take advantage of their policies online 24/7, from anywhere in the world – even if you're already travelling. And since plans often change when you're on the road, you can extend your policy and even claim online. Roughguides.com users who buy travel insurance with WorldNomads.com can also leave a positive footprint and donate to a community development project. For more information go to ⓦ**www.roughguides.com/shop**.

Internet

Smoky **internet cafés** full of kids playing Counterstrike and MMUDs are legion, and looked on with some disquiet – Beijing's vice mayor has called them the new opium dens, and internet addiction clinics have opened to deal with young adults whose online use has become excessive. At these "vice dens", you'll be asked to show your passport before being allowed near a computer. They're on every back street, but are particularly prevalent close to colleges. There's never an English sign; look out for the character for "net", *wang* – two crosses inside an "n" (see p.192).

There's a handy internet café on the 3rd floor of The Station, the shopping centre on the east side of Qianmen; note that there's one section for locals at ¥7 per hour, and one for foreigners that charges ¥20 per hour. Another large café is on Dianamen Dajie, opposite the south entrance to Nanluogu Xiang (24hr; ¥3/hr). In addition, all but the smallest hotels have business centres where you can get online, generally for about ¥30 an hour. Better value are the hostels, where getting online is usually free. **Free wi-fi** is widespread, and it's safe to assume that cafés will have it – they even have it at *McDonald's*.

Laundry

You might have a tough time finding a self-service **laundry**; it's said that Chinese housewives wouldn't trust a stranger with the family's clothes. **Hotels** all offer a laundry service.

Left luggage

The main **left-luggage office** at Beijing Zhan is on the east side of the station (daily 5am–midnight; ¥10/day). There's also a

The new Great Wall of China

Tireless as ever in controlling what its citizens learn and know about, the Chinese government has built a sophisticated **firewall** – nicknamed the new Great Wall of China – that blocks access to undesirable websites. The way this is administered shifts according to the mood of the powers that be – restrictions were loosened, for example, while Beijing was campaigning to be awarded the 2008 summer Olympics (the government was anxious to be seen not to be oppressing its subjects). Now they've slammed the gate firmly back down again.

In general, you can be pretty sure you won't be able to access stories deemed controversial from sites such as BBC or CNN, anything about Tibetan freedom or democracy, and **Facebook**, YouTube and **Twitter** are all blocked. The firewall isn't impenetrable, it's simply meant to make getting information deemed controversial enough of a hassle that most Chinese people won't bother. You can **get around it** simply by subscribing to a Virtual Private Network, or VPN, such as WiTopia, Hotspot Shield or UltraSurf (just about every foreign business in China does this) all of which cost a few pounds a month and offer a free limited period trial.

left-luggage office in the foreigners' waiting room, signposted at the back of the station, with lockers for ¥20 (daily 5am–midnight). The left-luggage office at Xi Zhan is downstairs on the left as you enter (daily 5am–midnight; ¥15/day). There are 24hr left-luggage offices at each terminal at Pudong; follow the signs. Price depends on size, but all but the biggest suitcase will cost a reasonable ¥20 per day.

Libraries

The **Beijing National Library**, 39 Baishiqiao Lu (Mon–Fri 8am–5pm; ⓣ010/68415566), just north of Zizhuyuan Park, is one of the largest in the world, with more than ten million volumes, including ancient manuscripts and a Qing-dynasty encyclopedia; the very oldest of its texts are Shang-dynasty inscriptions on bone. To take books out, you need to be resident in the city, but you can turn up and get a day pass that lets you browse (apply in the office on the south side; ¥5). The **Capital Library**, 88 Dongsanhuan Nan Lu (ⓣ010/67358114) is smaller, but will let foreign visitors borrow books, though you have to pay a deposit of ¥250. They hold some foreign magazines and newspapers. The library of the **British Embassy**, on the fourth floor of the Landmark Building, 8 Dongsanhuan Bei Lu (Mon–Fri 9am–5pm; ⓦwww.britishcouncil.org.cn), has a wide selection of books and magazines and is open to all.

Living in Beijing

Foreigners are allowed to reside anywhere in the city, though most live in **expat housing**, often in **Chaoyang** in the east of the city. Rent in these districts is expensive, usually at least £1000/US$1500/¥1000 a month, which gets you a rough imitation of a Western apartment. Living in **ordinary neighbourhoods** is much cheaper: a furnished two-bedroom apartment can cost around £250/US$300/¥2500 a month.

The easiest way to find an apartment is through a **real estate agent**, who will usually take a month's rent as a fee. There are plenty of agents, and many advertise in the expat magazines – an example is *Wo Ai Wo Jia* (44 Chengfu Lu; ⓣ010/62557602, ⓦwww.5i5j.com). **Homestays** can be cheap, but you won't get much privacy; check ⓦwww.chinahomestay.org. For anywhere, as soon as you move in, you and the landlord should register with the local PSB office.

Anyone intending to live in Beijing should get hold of the fat **Insider's Guide to Beijing** published by Middle Kingdom Press, which includes information on finding housing and doing business. It's available in the Friendship Store.

Working in Beijing

There are plenty of **jobs** available for foreigners in mainland China, with a whole section of expat society surviving as actors, cocktail barmen, models and so on. Many foreign workers are employed as English-language teachers – most universities and many private colleges now have a few foreign teachers.

There are schemes to place foreign **teachers** in Chinese educational institutions – contact your nearest Chinese embassy (see p.35) for details, or check the list of organizations given below. Teaching at a university, you'll earn about ¥3000 a month, more than your Chinese counterparts do, though your workload of between ten and twenty hours a week is correspondingly a lot heavier. The pay isn't enough to allow you to put much aside, but is bolstered by on-campus accommodation. Contracts are generally for one year. Most teachers find their students keen, hard-working, curious and obedient, and report that it was the contact with them that made the experience worthwhile. That said, avoid talking about religion or politics in the classroom, as this could get you into trouble.

You'll earn more – up to ¥150 per hour – in a **private school**, though be aware of the risk of being ripped off (you might be given more classes to teach than you'd signed up for, for example).

Studying in Beijing

There are plenty of opportunities to **study** in Beijing but note that most courses are in Chinese (for details of courses on the Chinese language itself, see below). Beijing Daxue (usually referred to as Beida, see p.97; ⓦwww.pku.edu.cn) and Tsinghua

Daxue (Ⓦwww.tsinghua.edu.cn), both in Haidian in the northwest of the city, are the most famous **universities** in China.

Studying Chinese

You can do **short courses** (from two weeks to two months) in Mandarin Chinese at Beijing Foreign Studies University, 2 Xi Erhuan Lu (Ⓣ010/68468167, Ⓦwww.bfsu.edu.cn); at Berlitz, 6 Ritan Lu (Ⓣ010/65930478, Ⓦwww.berlitz.com); at the Bridge School in Jianguomenwai Dajie (Ⓣ010/64940243), which offers evening classes; or at the Cultural Mission at 7 Beixiao Jie in Sanlitun (Ⓣ010/65323005), where most students are diplomats. For **longer courses** in Chinese, lasting six months to a year, apply to the Beijing International School at Anzhenxili, Chaoyang (Ⓣ010/64433151, Ⓦwww.isb.bj.edu.cn), Beida in Haidian (see p.97), or Beijing Normal University (Ⓦwww.bnu.edu.cn/bnueng).

Useful resources

Chinatefl Ⓦwww.chinatefl.com. A good overview of English-teaching opportunities in the Chinese public sector.

Council on International Educational Exchange Ⓦwww.ciee.org. Exchange programmes for US students of Mandarin or Chinese studies, with placements in Beijing.

Teach Abroad Ⓦwww.teachabroad.com. A website where you can post your CV.

Zhaopin Ⓦwww.zhaopin.com. A huge jobs site, in Chinese and English.

Mail

Main **post offices** are open Monday to Saturday between 9am and 5pm; smaller offices may close for lunch or at weekends. Offices in the *New Otani Hotel* (daily 8am–6pm) and at L115, China World Trade Centre (daily 8am–8pm) keep longer hours.

The **International Post Office** is on Chaoyangmen Dajie, just north of the intersection with Jianguomen Dajie (Mon–Sat 8am–7pm; Ⓣ010/5128114). Here you can rent a PO box, use their packing service for parcels, and buy a wide variety of collectable stamps, but staff are not very helpful. This is where poste restante letters end up, dumped in a box; you'll have to rifle through them all to find your mail – bring your passport as identification. Have letters addressed to you c/o Poste Restante, GPO, Beijing. Letters are only kept for a month and are then sent back. You can also leave a message for someone in the poste restante box, but you'll have to buy a stamp at the post office. There are other post offices in the basement of the World Trade Centre; on Xi Chang'an Jie, just east of the Concert Hall; on Wangfujing Dajie; and at the north end of Xidan Dajie (all Mon–Sat 9am–5pm).

The Chinese **postal service** is, on the whole, fast and reliable. A postcard costs ¥4.2, while a standard letter is ¥6 or more, depending on the weight.

An **Express Mail Service** (**EMS**) operates to most countries and to most destinations within China and is available from all post offices. Besides cutting delivery times, the service ensures the letter or parcel is sent by registered delivery – though note that the courier service of **DHL** (24hr office at 2 Jiuxian Qiao in the Chaoyang district, Ⓣ010/64662211) is rather faster, and costs about the same.

To send **parcels**, turn up at a post office with the goods you want to send and the staff will sell you a box to pack them in for ¥15 or so. Once packed, but before the parcel is sealed, it must be checked at the customs window in the post office. A one-kilogram parcel should cost upwards of ¥70 to send surface mail, ¥120 by airmail to Europe; the largest box available holds 30kg and costs about ¥750 to send. If you are sending valuable goods bought in China, put the receipt or a photocopy of it in with the parcel, as it may be opened for customs inspection farther down the line.

Maps

A large fold-out **map** of the city is vital. In general, the free tourist maps – available in large hotels and printed inside tourist magazines – don't show enough detail. A wide variety of city maps are available at all transport hubs and from street vendors, hotels and bookshops. The best is widely available *Beijing Tourist Map* (¥8), which is labelled in English and Chinese and has bus routes, sights and hotels marked.

Worth seeking out before you go is the *Berndtson and Berndtson* map, which is laminated, and the *Periplus Beijing* map, which has all the street names, including those of many *hutongs* (alleyways), in English. Whatever map you get, you can gauge if it's really up to date by whether it includes the newer subway lines.

Money

Chinese **currency** is formally called the **yuan** (¥), more colloquially known as renminbi (RMB) or kuai; a yuan breaks down into units of ten **jiao** (also called mao). One jiao is equivalent to ten **fen**, though these are effectively worthless – you'll only ever be given them in official currency transactions, or see the tiny notes folded up and used to build model dragons or boats. Paper money was invented in China and is still the main form of exchange, available in ¥100, ¥50, ¥20, ¥10, ¥5, and ¥1 notes, with a similar selection of jiao. At the time of writing the exchange rate was approximately ¥15 to £1, ¥8 to $1 and ¥10 to €1.

China is suffering from a rash of **counterfeiting**. Check your change carefully, as the locals do – hold 100s and 50s up to the light and rub them; fakes have no watermarks and the paper feels rougher.

Banks and ATMs

Most **ATMs** accept foreign bankcards, connected to the Cirrus, AmEx, Visa, Plus and Mastercard networks. Some banks charge transaction fees (highest is the Bank of China, at ¥25), but most do not. There's usually a maximum of ¥2000 in a single withdrawal, and a maximum per day limit of between ¥3000 and ¥5000, depending on your card. For a list of ATMs in Beijing, see Ⓦ www.moveandstay.com/beijing/guide_banks.asp.

Banks are usually open from Monday to Friday (9am–5pm), though some branches open on weekends too. All are closed on New Year's Day, National Day, and for the first three days of the Chinese New Year, with reduced hours for the following eleven days. The Commercial Bank (Mon–Fri 9am–noon & 1–4pm) in the CITIC Building, 19 Jianguomenwai Dajie, next to the Friendship Store, offers the most comprehensive **exchange** service: here, you can change money and travellers' cheques, or use most credit cards to obtain cash advances or buy American dollars (if you present exchange certificates).

All branches of the Bank of China will give cash advances on Visa cards. Their main branch is at 108 Fuxingmennei Dajie (Mon–Fri 9am–noon & 1.30–5pm), off Chaoyangmen Dajie, just north of the International Post Office. You'll find other branches in the SCITECH Plaza (Mon–Fri 9am–noon & 1–6.30pm), the China World Trade Centre (Mon–Fri 9am–5pm, Sat 9am–noon), the Sun Dong'an Plaza (Mon–Fri 9.30am–noon & 1.30–5pm) and the Lufthansa Centre (Mon–Fri 9am–noon & 1–4pm), among others.

Credit cards and wiring money

Major credit cards, such as Visa, American Express and MasterCard, are accepted only at big tourist hotels and restaurants, and by a few tourist-oriented shops. It's possible to **wire money** to Beijing through **Western Union** (Ⓦ www.westernunion.com); funds can be collected from one of their agents in the city, in post offices and the Agricultural Bank of China.

Opening hours and public holidays

Offices and **government agencies** are open from Monday to Friday, usually from 8am to noon and then from 1pm to 5pm; some open on Saturday and Sunday mornings, too. **Shops** are generally open from 9am to 6pm or 7pm Monday to Saturday, with shorter hours on Sunday; large shopping centres are open daily and don't close till around 9pm. **Museums** are either open all week or are shut on one day, usually Monday.

Public holidays (see p.30) have little effect on business, with only government departments and certain banks closing. However, on New Year's Day, during the first three days of the Chinese New Year, and on National Day, most businesses, shops and sights will be shut, though some restaurants stay open.

The best time to sightsee is during the week, as all attractions are swamped with local tourists at weekends. Some **attractions** have separate low- and high-season opening times and prices; in high season (end March to early November), places open usually half an hour earlier, and close half an hour later, while prices rise by ¥5 or ¥10.

Phones

Local calls are free from landlines, and **long-distance China-wide calls** are fairly cheap. Note that everywhere in China has an **area code** that must be used when phoning from outside that locality; Beijing's is 010, and is given throughout the Guide. **International calls** cost at least ¥8 a minute (cheaper if you use an IC card and even cheaper with an Internet Phone/IP card – see below).

The most prevalent **public phones** are attached to small stores; simply pick up, dial and pay the amount on the meter afterwards. Most of these however, will not handle international calls. The cheapest way to make long-distance and international calls is with **card phones** (¥0.2 for 3min). They take **IC Cards** (I-C kǎ in Mandarin), which are sold at every little store and in hotels, in units of ¥20, ¥50 and ¥100. There's a fifty percent discount after 6pm and at weekends. You will be cut off when the credit left on the card drops below the amount needed for the next minute. You'll find a card phone in every hotel lobby, and there are many booths on the street.

Another option is the **IP (Internet Phone) card**, which can be used from any phone, and comes in ¥50 and ¥100 denominations (though the card is always discounted). You dial the number on the card, then instructions in Chinese and English ask you to dial a PIN printed under a silver strip on the card, which activates the account; finally you call the number you want. Rates are as low as ¥2.4 per minute to the US and Canada, ¥3.2 to Europe. The cards are widely available, but check that you are buying a card that can be used for international calls, as some are China only (ask for a *guójì* card).

Note that calling from **tourist hotels**, whether from your room or from their business centres, will attract a surcharge and may well be extortionate.

Mobile phones

Your **home mobile phone** may already be compatible with the Chinese network (visitors from North America should ensure their phones are GSM/Triband), though you will pay a premium to use it abroad, and callers within China have to make an

Useful dialling codes

To **call mainland China from abroad**, dial:

from Australia ⓣ0011 + 86 + number (minus the initial zero)
from New Zealand ⓣ00 + 86 + number (minus the initial zero)
from Republic of Ireland ⓣ00 + 86 + number (minus the initial zero)
from South Africa ⓣ00 + 86 + number (minus the initial zero)
from the UK ⓣ00 + 86 + number (minus the initial zero)
from the US and Canada ⓣ011 + 86 + number (minus the initial zero)

To **call abroad from mainland China**, dial:

to Australia ⓣ00 + 61 + area code (if any, omitting the initial zero)
to New Zealand ⓣ00 + 64 + area code (if any, omitting the initial zero)
to Republic of Ireland ⓣ00 + 353 + area code (if any, omitting the initial zero)
to South Africa ⓣ00 + 27 + area code (if any, omitting the initial zero)
to the UK ⓣ00 + 44 + area code (if any, omitting the initial zero)
to the US and Canada ⓣ00 + 1 + area code (if any, omitting the initial zero)

international call to reach you. For more information, check with the manufacturer and/or your telephone service provider. It's also worth contacting your phone company to ask whether they do calling cards that can be charged to your home bill. Alternatively, once in Beijing you can buy a GSM SIM card from any China Mobile shop or street kiosk, which allows you to use your phone as though it's a local mobile, with a new number, as long your phone is unlocked. The SIM card costs around ¥100, with some variation according to how lucky the digits are – favoured sixes and eights bump up the price, while unlucky fours make it cheaper. Additionally, you'll need to buy prepaid cards to pay for the calls. Making and receiving domestic calls this way costs ¥0.6 per minute; international calls will cost considerably more.

The cheapest phones **to buy** will cost around ¥400; make sure the staff change the operating language into English for you. You can also **rent mobile phones** from China Mobile, which is most conveniently arranged online at ⓦwww.china-mobile-phones.com. The phone can be picked up from your hotel and left there when you leave. Phones cost ¥80, with an ¥8 per day charge, and all calls are at the local rate.

Time

Beijing, like the rest of China, is eight hours ahead of GMT, thirteen hours ahead of US Eastern Standard Time, sixteen hours ahead of US Pacific Time and two hours behind Australian Eastern Standard Time. It does not have **daylight saving time**.

Tourist information

For details of the government-run CITS and CYTS offices, see p.25. For the locations of Chinese tourist offices abroad, which can book tours and tickets, see ⓦwww.cnto.org/offices.htm, and for details of **English-language listings magazines**, see p.29.

Online resources

There's plenty of **online information** about China in general and Beijing specifically, though as a general rule, avoid websites run by official agencies such as CITS; they're dry as dust. Here's a selection of sites to start you off:

The Beijing Page ⓦwww.beijingpage.com. A comprehensive and well-organized page of links, with sections on tourism, entertainment and industry.

CCTV 9 ⓦwww.cctv-9.com. Featuring a live video stream plus other programmes available to watch on demand, this is the website of the Chinese state television's English-language channel.

China Business World ⓦwww.cbw.com. A corporate directory site with a useful travel section, detailing tours and allowing you to book flights and hotels.

China Vista ⓦwww.chinavista.com. China-based website with snippets about Chinese culture, history, attractions and food.

Danwei ⓦwww.danwei.org. English commentary and reporting on what's hot in the Chinese media; very informative, but usually blocked in China.

Friends of the Great Wall ⓦwww.friendsofgreatwall.org. Covers efforts to maintain and clean up the Great Wall, with useful links.

Sinomania ⓦwww.sinomania.com. A California-based site with links to current Chinese news stories and a good popular music section, with MP3 downloads available.

Yesasia ⓦwww.yesasia.com. Online shopping for Chinese movies, CDs, books, collectables, etc.

Youku ⓦwww.youku.com. With YouTube blocked, this popular site fills the gap, with millions of clips and home videos. In Chinese, but easy enough to navigate.

Zhongwen.com ⓦwww.zhongwen.com. Especially interesting if you're a student of Chinese, this site includes background on the Chinese script, several classic texts (with links to some English translations) and even a bunch of suggested renderings into Chinese of common first names.

Travellers with disabilities

Beijing makes **few provisions** for **disabled** people. Undergoing an economic boom, the city resembles a building site, with uneven, obstacle-strewn paving, intense crowds and vehicle traffic, and few access ramps. Public transport is generally inaccessible to wheelchair users, though a few of the upmarket hotels are equipped to assist disabled visitors; in particular, Beijing's several *Holiday Inns* (*Holiday Inn Downtown* at 98 Beilishi Lu ⓣ010/68132299) and *Hiltons* (there's one at 1 Dongfang Lu ⓣ010/58655000) have rooms designed for wheelchair users.

The disabled in Chinese are usually kept hidden away; attitudes are not, on the whole, very enlightened, and disabled visitors should be prepared for a great deal of staring. Given the situation, it may be worth considering an **organized tour**. Make sure you take spares of any specialist clothing or equipment, extra supplies of drugs (carried with you if you fly), and a prescription including the generic name – in English and Chinese characters – in case of emergency. If there's an association representing people with your disability, contact them early on in the planning process.

Visas

See "**Entry requirements**" on p.34.

The City

The City

1

Tian'anmen Square and the Forbidden City

The first stop for any visitor to Beijing is **Tian'anmen Square**, which at over 400,000 square metres is the greatest public space on earth. Right in the city centre, the square is symbolically the heart of China, and the events it has witnessed have shaped the history of the People's Republic from its inception. Laid out in 1949, it is a modern creation in a city that traditionally had no places where crowds could gather. As one of the square's architects put it: "Beijing was a reflection of a feudal society… We had to transform it, we had to make Beijing into the capital of socialist China". So they created a vast concrete plain dotted with worthy statuary and bounded by stern, monumental buildings: the **Great Hall of the People** to the west and the **National Museum of China** to the east. To the north you'll see Tian'anmen, a gateway of great significance to both imperial and communist China.

Beyond it, and in its luxury and ornament a complete contrast to the square's austerity, is the Gugong, or Imperial Palace, better known in the West by its unofficial title, the **Forbidden City** – a reference to its exclusivity. Indeed, for the five centuries of functioning, through the reigns of 24 emperors of the Ming and Qing dynasties, civilian Chinese were forbidden from even approaching the walls. With its maze of eight hundred buildings and nine thousand chambers, it was the core of the capital, the empire, and (so the Chinese believed) the universe. From within, the emperors – the **Sons of Heaven** – issued commands with absolute authority to their millions of subjects. It remains an extraordinary place today, unsurpassed in China for monumental scale, harmonious design and elegant grandeur.

Tian'anmen Square

For many Chinese tourists, **Tian'anmen Square** (天安门广场, *tiānānmén guǎngchǎng*) is a place of pilgrimage. Crowds flock to see the corpse of Chairman Mao in his **mausoleum** and to see the most potent symbols of power in contemporary China:

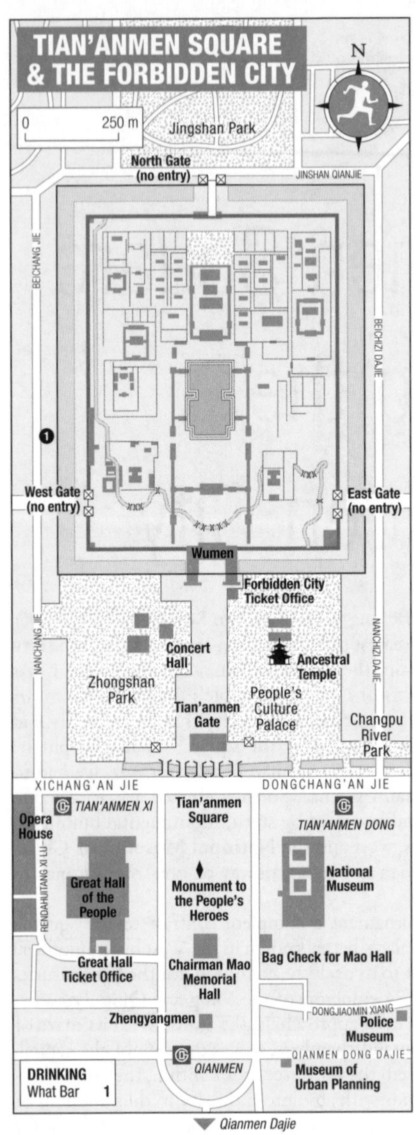

the Great Hall of the People and Tian'anmen Gate. Some quietly bow their heads before the **Monument to the People's Heroes**, a 30m-high obelisk commemorating the victims of the revolutionary struggle. Its foundations were laid on October 1, 1949, the day that the establishment of the People's Republic was announced. Bas-reliefs illustrate key scenes from China's revolutionary history; one of these, on the east side, shows the Chinese burning British opium (see p.174) in the nineteenth century. The calligraphy on the front is a copy of Mao Zedong's handwriting and reads "Eternal glory to the Heroes of the People". The platform on which the obelisk stands is guarded, and a prominent sign declares that commemorative gestures, such as the laying of wreaths, are banned. In 1976, riots broke out when wreaths honouring the death of the popular politician Zhou Enlai were removed; the demonstrations of 1989 began here with the laying of wreaths to a recently deceased liberal politician.

For a great view over the square head to the south gate, **Zhengyangmen** (正阳门, *zhèngyáng mén*; daily 8.30am–4pm; ¥20). Similar to Tian'anmen (North Gate), this squat, 40m-high structure with an arched gateway through the middle once marked the boundary between the imperial city and the commoners outside. Avoid the tacky souvenir stores on the first two floors and head to the top; you'll get a good idea of how much more impressive the square looked before Mao's mausoleum was stuck in the middle of it.

At dawn, the flag at the northern end of the square is raised in a military ceremony. It's lowered again at dusk, which is when most people come to watch, though some complain that the regimentation of the crowds is oppressive. After dark, the square is at its most appealing and, with its sternness softened by mellow lighting, it becomes the haunt of strolling families and lovers.

Dissent in Tian'anmen Square

Though it was designed as a space for mass declarations of loyalty, Tian'anmen Square has as often been a venue for expressions of popular **dissent**. The first mass protests here occurred on May 4, 1919, when students gathered in the area to demonstrate against the disastrous terms of the Treaty of Versailles, under which the victorious Allies granted several former German concessions in China to the Japanese. The protests, and the movement they spawned, marked the beginning of the painful struggle for Chinese modernization. In 1925, the inhabitants of Beijing again occupied the square, to protest over the massacre in Shanghai of Chinese demonstrators by British troops. The following year, protesters angered at the weak government's capitulation to the Japanese marched on government offices and were fired on by soldiers.

The first time the square became the focus of outcry in the communist era was in 1976, when thousands assembled here, without government approval, to voice their dissatisfaction with their leaders; in 1978 and 1979, large numbers came to discuss new ideas of democracy and artistic freedom, triggered by writings posted along "Democracy Wall" on the edge of the Forbidden City. People gathered again in 1986 and 1987, demonstrating against the Party's refusal to allow limited municipal elections to be held. But it was in **1989** that Tian'anmen Square became the venue for the largest expression of popular dissent in China in the twentieth century; from April to June of that year, nearly a million protesters demonstrated against the slow reform, lack of civil liberties and widespread corruption. The government, infuriated at being humiliated by their own people, declared martial law on May 20, and on June 4 the military moved into the square. The ensuing **killing** was indiscriminate; tanks ran over tents and machine guns strafed the avenues. No one knows exactly how many demonstrators died in the massacre – probably thousands; hundreds were arrested afterwards and some remain in jail (though others have since joined the administration).

These days the square is occasionally the venue for small protests by foreigners or members of the cultish, religious sect Falun Gong – hence the many closed-circuit TV cameras and large numbers of Public Security men, not all in uniform; look out, for example, for the plainclothes bruisers who stand either side of Tian'anmen's Mao painting.

As a **transport hub**, the square is easy to get to: Qianmen subway stop is just south of the square, with Tian'anmen Xi and Tian'anmen Dong stops nearby to the west and east respectively; you can also get here on buses #1, #4, #10, #22, #52 or #57.

The Museum of Urban Planning

The **Museum of Urban Planning** (规划博物馆, *guīhuà bówùguǎn*; Tues–Sun 9am–5pm; ¥30), just off Qianmen Dong Dajie, is little visited; for some reason, displays on solid waste management, air quality, and the eleventh five year plan have failed to galvanise the public. Staff are so bored they stand by the motion-sensitive escalators and wave their hands to start the things for you. Still, the showcase is worth a poke around if you ignore the tedious displays on the first two floors. On the third floor you'll find, on the wall, a fascinating bronze model showing the city as it used to look in imperial times, back when every significant building was part of an awesome, grand design. The star attraction, though, is an enormous and fantastically detailed underlit model of the city that takes up the entire top floor. At a scale of 1m:1km it covers more than three hundred square metres, and illustrates what the place will look like once it's finished being ripped up and redesigned by 2020 – with lots of office blocks and few *hutongs*.

The Chairman Mao Memorial Hall

Mao's **mausoleum** (毛主席纪念堂, *máozhǔxí jìniàntáng*; daily 8.30–11.30am, plus April–Oct Mon, Wed & Fri 2–4pm; free), constructed in 1977 by an estimated million volunteers, is an ugly building that looks like a drab municipal facility. It contravenes the principles of *feng shui* (see box, p.53) – presumably deliberately – by interrupting the line from the palace to Qianmen and by facing north. Mao himself wanted to be cremated, and the erection of the mausoleum was apparently no more than a power assertion by his would-be successor, Hua Guofeng. In 1980 Deng Xiaoping, then leader, said it should never have been built, although he wouldn't go so far as to pull it down.

After depositing your bag and camera at the bag check across the road to the east (¥10), join the orderly queue of Chinese – almost exclusively working-class out-of-towners – on the northern side. The queue advances surprisingly quickly, and takes just a couple of minutes to file through the chambers. Mao's pickled **corpse**, draped with a red flag within a crystal coffin, looks unreal, which it may well be; a wax copy was made in case the preservation went wrong. Mechanically raised from a freezer every morning, it is said to have been embalmed with the aid of Vietnamese technicians who had previously worked on the body of Ho Chi Minh. Apparently, 22 litres of formaldehyde went into preserving his body;

Chairman Mao

A revolution is not a dinner party.

Mao Zedong

Mao Zedong, the son of a well-off Hunnanese farmer, believed social reform lay in the hands of the peasants. Having helped found the Chinese Communist Party, on the Soviet model, in Shanghai in 1921, he quickly organized a peasant workers' militia – the Red Army – to take on the Nationalist government. A cunning guerrilla leader, Mao was said to have learnt his tactics from studying the first tyrant Emperor Qin Shihuang, Sun Tzu's *Art of War*, and from playing the East Asian game of Go. In 1934 Mao's army was encircled; the epic retreat that followed, the **Long March** – eighty thousand men walking ten thousand kilometres over a year – solidified Mao's reputation and spread the message of the rebels through the countryside. They joined another rebel force at Yan'an, in northern China, and set up the first soviets, implementing land reform and educating the peasantry.

In 1949, now at the head of a huge army, Mao finally vanquished the Nationalists and became the "Great Helmsman" of the new Chinese nation – and here the trouble started. The chain-smoking poet rebel indulged what appeared to be a personal need for permanent revolution in catastrophes such as the **Great Leap Forward** of the Fifties and the **Cultural Revolution** of the Sixties. His policies caused enormous suffering; some estimate Mao was responsible for the deaths of over 38 million people – mostly from famine as a result of incompetent agricultural policies. Towards the end of his life Mao became increasingly paranoid and out of touch, surrounded by sycophants and nubile dancers – a situation vividly described by his physician, Zhisui Li, in his book *The Private Life of Chairman Mao*.

Today the official Chinese position on Mao is that he was "seventy percent right". Although public images of him have largely been expunged, the personality cult he fostered lives on, particularly in taxis where his image is hung like a lucky charm from the rear-view mirror, and he's often included among the deities in peasant shrines. Today his **Little Red Book**, source of political slogans such as "power grows from the barrel of a gun", is no longer required reading but English translations are widely available in Beijing – though from souvenir vendors rather than bookshops. His poetry is highly regarded; check it out at Ⓦwww.mzdthought.com.

rumour has it that not only did the corpse swell grotesquely when too much fluid was used, but that Mao's left ear fell off during the embalming process, and had to be stitched back on.

Much of the interest of a visit here lies in witnessing the sense of awe of the Chinese confronted with their former leader, the architect of modern China who was accorded an almost god-like status for much of his life. The atmosphere is one of reverence, though once through the marble halls, you're herded past a splendidly wide-ranging array of tacky Mao souvenirs; the flashing Mao lighter that plays the national anthem is a perennial favourite (¥10).

The Great Hall of the People

Taking up almost half the west side of the square is the monolithic **Great Hall of the People** (人民大会堂, *rénmín dàhuìtáng*; daily 8.30am–3pm when not in session; ¥30; buy tickets and leave bags at the office on the southern side), one of ten Stalinist wedding-cake-style buildings constructed in 1959 to celebrate "ten years of liberation" (others include Beijing Zhan and the Military Museum – see p.24 and p.71). This is the venue of the National People's Congress (the Chinese legislature), and the building is closed to the public when the Congress is in session – you'll know by the hundreds of black limos with darkened windows parked outside. It's not really a sight as such, but you can take a turn around the building; what you see on the roped-off route through is a selection of the 29 cavernous, dim reception rooms, decorated in the same pompous but shabby style seen in the lobbies of cheap Chinese hotels – badly fitted red carpet, lifeless murals and armchairs lined up against the walls and draped with antimacassars.

Each room is named after a part of China; one is called "Taiwan Province". The route ends at the massive five-thousand-seater banqueting hall where you can buy a bland canteen lunch (¥10). When Mrs Thatcher came here in 1982 she tripped on the steps – this was regarded in Hong Kong as a terrible omen for the negotiations she was having over the territory's future. In 1989, the visiting Mikhail Gorbachev had to be smuggled in through a side entrance to avoid the crowds of protesters outside (see p.49). If you're not a national leader on a meet-and-greet, you'll be better rewarded elsewhere; the Russian-built Exhibition Hall (see p.94) is a more pleasing example of monumental communist architecture.

The National Museum of China

On the east side of the square is a giant digital clock. It was used to count down the seconds till the start of the Olympic Games, and before that, till the handovers of Hong Kong and then Macau. At the time of writing it counted down to the opening of the Shanghai Expo; who knows what event they'll use it to celebrate next.

The monumental building behind it once held a couple of shabby history museums, but at the time of writing the whole place was closed down for an enormous refit. It should be open, as the **National Museum of China** (自然博物馆, *zìrán bówùguǎn*), by the time you read this. Expect it to be aimed more at the education of the Chinese masses than foreign tourists – it will be interesting to see whether exhibits are still divided according to a Marxist reading of history, into "primitive", "slave", "feudal" and "semi-colonial".

Tian'anmen

Tian'anmen (天安门, *tiānānmén*; daily 8.30am–4.30pm; ¥15), the Gate of Heavenly Peace, is the main entrance to the Forbidden City (buy tickets from the Forbidden

The emperor speaks to his people

In the Ming and Qing dynasties, Tian'anmen was where the **ceremony** called "the golden phoenix issues an edict" took place. The minister of rites would receive an imperial edict inside the palace, and take it to Tian'anmen on a silver "cloud tray", he and his charge under a yellow umbrella. Here, the edict was read aloud to the officials of the court who knelt below, lined up according to rank. Next, the edict was placed in the mouth of a gilded wooden phoenix, which was lowered by rope to another cloud tray below. The tray was then put in a carved, wooden dragon and taken to the Ministry of Rites to be copied out and sent around the country.

Mao too liked to address his subjects from here; on October 1, 1949, he delivered the **liberation speech** to jubilant crowds below, declaring that "the Chinese people have now stood up"; in the 1960s, he spoke from this spot to massed ranks of Red Guards and declared that it was time for a "cultural revolution" (see p.176).

City ticket office, further north on the right). An image familiar across the world, Tian'anmen occupies an exalted place in Chinese iconography, appearing on policemen's caps, banknotes, coins, stamps and most pieces of official paper. As such it's a prime object of pilgrimage, with many visitors milling around and taking pictures of the large **portrait of Mao** (the only one still on public display), which hangs over the central passageway. Once reserved for the sole use of the emperor, but now standing wide open, the entrance is flanked by the twin slogans "Long Live the People's Republic of China" and "Long Live the Great Union between the Peoples of the World".

The entry ticket allows you to climb up onto the **viewing platform** above the gate. Security is tight: all visitors have to leave their bags and go through a metal detector before they can ascend. Inside, the fact that most people cluster around the souvenir stall – which only sells official certificates to anyone who wants their visit here documented – reflects the fact that there's not much to look at.

The parks

The two parks either side of Tian'anmen, **Zhongshan** (中山公园, *zhōngshān gōngyuán*; daily 6am–9pm; ¥10) to the west and the grounds of the **People's Culture Palace** (劳动人民文化宫, *láodòng rénmín wénhuàgōng*; daily 6am–9pm; ¥2) to the east, are great places to escape the square's rigorous formality.

Zhongshan park boasts the ruins of the Altar of Land and Grain, a site of biennial sacrifice during the Qing and Ming dynasties, with harvest-time events closely related to those of the Temple of Heaven (see p.63). There's a concert hall here too (see p.153). The People's Culture Palace – symbolically named in deference to the fact that only after the communist takeover in 1949 were ordinary Chinese allowed within this central sector of their city – has a number of modern exhibition halls, often worth checking out for their temporary art shows, and a scattering of original fifteenth-century structures, most of them Ming or Qing ancestral temples.

The Forbidden City

Lying at the heart of the city, the **Imperial Palace** (故宫, *gùgōng*), or, most evocatively, the **Forbidden City**, is Beijing's finest monument. To do it justice, you should plan to spend at least a whole day here; you could wander the complex for a week and keep discovering new aspects, especially now that many of the halls are doubling as museums of dynastic artefacts. The central halls, with their wealth of imperial pomp, may be the most magnificent buildings, but for many visitors it's the side rooms, with their displays of the more intimate accoutrements of court life, that bring home the realities of life for the inhabitants in this, the most gilded of cages.

Although the earliest structures (none of which survive today) on the site of the Forbidden City began with Kublai Khan during the Mongol dynasty, the **plan** of the palace buildings is essentially Ming. Most date back to the fifteenth century and the ambitions of the **Emperor Yongle**, the monarch responsible for switching the capital from Nanjing back to Beijing in 1403 (see p.173). His programme to construct a complex worthy enough to house the Son of Heaven was concentrated between 1407 and 1420, involving up to ten thousand artisans and perhaps a million labourers.

All the halls of the Forbidden City were laid out according to geomantic theories – the balance between *yin* and *yang*, or negative and positive energy. The buildings, signposted in English, face south in order to benefit from the invigorating advantages of *yang* energy, and as a protection against harmful *yin* elements from the north, both real and imagined – cold winds, evil spirits and steppe barbarians. Ramparts of compacted earth and a 50m-wide moat isolated the complex from the commoners outside, with the only access being through four monumental gateways in the four cardinal directions. The layout is the same as that of any grand Chinese house of the period; pavilions are arranged around courtyards, with reception rooms and official buildings at the front (south), set out with rigorous symmetry, and a labyrinthine set of private chambers to the north.

Visiting the Forbidden City

You can **get to the Forbidden City** (daily: April–Sept 8.30am–4.30pm; Oct–March 8.30am–3.30pm; last admission 30min before closing; ¥40 Nov–March, ¥60 April–Oct, including special exhibitions) on **bus** #5 from Qianmen; #54 from Beijing Zhan; or #1, which passes the complex on its journey along Chang'an Jie. All three buses drop you at the north end of Tian'anmen Square. The nearest **subways** are Tian'anmen Xi and Tian'anmen Dong, each about 300m away. Once through Tian'anmen, you find yourself on a long walkway, with the moated palace complex and massive main gate, Wumen, directly ahead; this is where you buy your ticket. If you're in a taxi, you can be dropped right outside the ticket office.

Visitors have freedom to wander most of the one-square-kilometre site, though not all of the buildings. If you want detailed explanations of everything you see,

Feng shui

Feng shui, literally "wind and water", is a form of geomancy, which assesses how objects must be positioned so as not to disturb the spiritual attributes of the surrounding landscape. This reflects Taoist cosmology, which states that the inner harmonies of the landscape must be preserved to secure all other harmonies. Buildings should be favourably oriented according to the compass – tombs, for example, should face south – and protected from unlucky directions by other buildings or hills.

Even the minutiae of interior **decor** are covered by *feng shui*. Some of its handy rules for the modern home include: don't have a mirror at the foot of the bed; don't have sharp edges pointing into the room; cover the television when it's not in use; and don't leave the lavatory seat up.

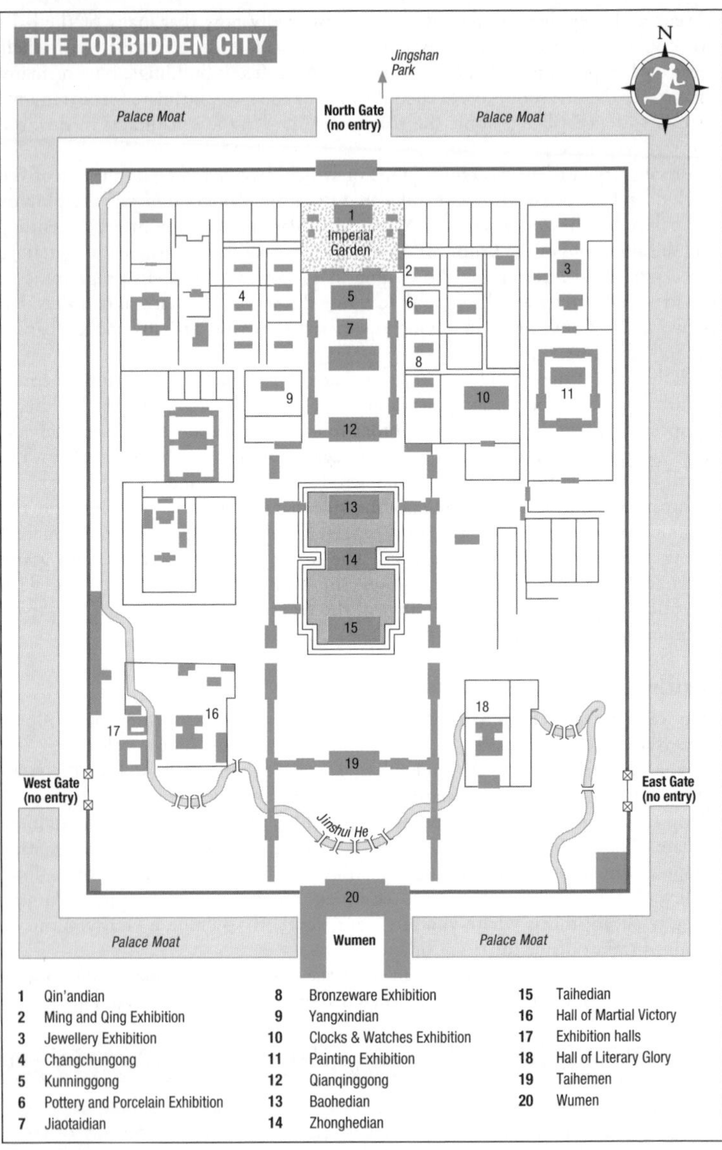

you can tag along with one of the numerous tour groups, buy one of the many specialist books on sale at Wumen, or take the **audio tour** (¥40), available at the main gate. If you take this option, it's worth retracing your steps afterwards for an untutored view, and heading off to the side halls that aren't included on the tour. There are plenty of clean toilets inside the complex, a few places to get a coffee (though *Starbucks* were kicked out of here recently after a public campaign), and even an ATM.

From Wumen to Taihemen

A huge building, whose central archway was reserved for the emperor's sole use, **Wumen** (Meridian Gate) is the largest and grandest of the Forbidden City gates. From a vantage point at the top, each new lunar year the Sons of Heaven would announce to their court the details of the forthcoming calendar, including the dates of festivals and rites, and, in times of war, inspect the army. It was customary for victorious generals returning from battle to present their prisoners here for the emperor to decide their fate. He would be flanked, as on all such imperial occasions, by a guard of elephants, the gift of Burmese subjects. In the Ming dynasty, this was also where disgraced officials were flogged or executed.

In the wings on either side of the Wumen are two drums and two bells; the drums were beaten whenever the emperor went to the Temple of the Imperial Ancestors, the bells rung when he visited the temples of Heaven (see p.63) and Earth (see p.92).

Passing through Wumen, you find yourself in a vast paved court, cut east–west by the **Jinshui He**, or Golden Water Stream, with its five marble bridges, one for each Confucian virtue (see p.91). They're decorated with carved torches, a symbol of masculinity. Beyond is another ceremonial gate, **Taihemen**, the Gate of Supreme Harmony, its entrance guarded by a magisterial row of lions, and further on a larger courtyard where the principal imperial audiences were held. Within this space the entire court – up to 100,000 people – could be accommodated. They made their way in through the lesser side gates – military men from the west, civilian officials from the east – and waited in total silence as the emperor ascended his throne. Then, with only the Imperial Guard remaining standing, they prostrated themselves nine times.

The galleries running round the courtyard housed the imperial storerooms. The buildings either side are the Hall of Martial Victory to the west and Hall of Literary Glory to the east; the latter, under the Ming emperors, housed the 11,099 volumes of the encyclopedia Yongle commissioned.

The ceremonial halls

The three main **ceremonial halls** stand directly north of Taihemen, dominating the court. The main halls, made of wood, are traditionally built all on the same level, on a raised stone platform. Their elegant roofs, curved like the wings of a bird, are supported entirely by pillars and beams; the weight is cleverly distributed by ceiling consoles, while the walls beneath are just lightweight partitions. Doors,

Imperial symbolism

Almost every colour and image in the Imperial Palace is richly **symbolic**. Yellow was the imperial colour; only in the palace were yellow roof tiles allowed. Purple was just as important, though used more sparingly; it symbolized joy and represented the pole star, centre of the universe according to Chinese cosmology (the implication of its use – usually on wall panels – was that the emperor resided in the earthly equivalent of the celestial zenith). The sign for the emperor was the dragon and for the empress, the phoenix; you'll see these two creatures represented on almost every building and stairway. The crane and turtle, depicted in paintings, carved into furniture or represented as freestanding sculptures, represent longevity of reign. The numbers nine and five crop up all over the complex, manifested in how often design elements are repeated; nine is lucky and associated with *yang*, or male energy, while five, the middle single-digit number, is associated with harmony and balance. Nine and five together – power and balance – symbolize "the heavenly son" – the emperor.

steps and access ramps are always odd in number, with the middle passageway reserved for the emperor's palanquin.

Raised on a three-tiered marble terrace is the first and most spectacular of the halls, the **Taihedian**, Hall of Supreme Harmony. The vast hall, nearly 38m high, was the tallest in China during the Ming and Qing dynasty – no civilian building was permitted to be taller. Taihedian was used for the most important state occasions: the emperor's coronation, birthday or marriage; ceremonies marking the new lunar year and winter solstice; proclamations of the results of the imperial examinations; and the nomination of generals at the outset of a military campaign. During the Republic, it was proposed that parliament should sit here, though the idea wasn't put into practice.

Decorated entirely in red and gold, Taihedian is the most sumptuous building in the complex. In the central coffer, a sunken panel in the ceiling, two gold-plated dragons play with a huge pearl. The gilded rosewood chair beneath, the dragon throne, was the exact centre of the Chinese universe. A marble pavement ramp, intricately carved with dragons and flanked by bronze incense burners, marks the path along which the emperor's sedan chair was carried whenever he wanted to be taken somewhere. The grain measure and sundial just outside are symbols of imperial justice.

Moving on, you enter the **Zhonghedian**, Hall of Middle Harmony, another throne room, where the emperor performed ceremonies of greeting to foreign dignitaries and addressed the imperial offspring (the progeny of his several wives and numerous concubines). It owes its name to a quote from the *I-Ching*, a Chinese tome dating back to 200 BC: "avoiding extremes and self control brings harmony" – the idea being that the middle course would be a harmonious one. The emperor also examined the seed for each year's crop in the hall, and it was used, too, as a dressing room for major events held in the Taihedian.

The third of the great halls, the **Baohedian**, or Preserving Harmony Hall, was the venue for state banquets and imperial examinations; graduates from the latter were appointed to positions of power in what was the world's first recognizably bureaucratic civil service. Huge ceremonies took place here to celebrate Chinese New Year; in 1903, this involved the sacrifice of 10,000 sheep. The hall's galleries, originally treasure houses, display various finds from the site, though the most spectacular, a vast marble block carved with dragons and clouds, stands at the rear of the hall. A Ming creation, reworked in the eighteenth century, it's among the finest carvings in the palace and certainly the largest – the 250-tonne chunk of marble was slid here from well outside the city by flooding the roads in winter to form sheets of ice.

Dining, imperial style

The **emperor** ate twice a day, at 6.30am and around noon. Often **meals** consisted of hundreds of dishes, with the emperor eating no more than a mouthful of each – to eat more would be to express a preference, and that information might reach a potential poisoner. According to tradition, no one else was allowed to eat at his table, and when banquets were held he sat at a platform well above his guests. Such occasions were extremely formal and not to everyone's liking; a Jesuit priest invited to such a feast in 1727 complained, "A European dies of hunger here; the way in which he is forced to sit on the ground on a mat with crossed legs is most awkward; neither the wine nor the dishes are to his taste... Every time the emperor says a word which lets it be known he wishes to please, one must kneel down and hit one's head on the ground. This has to be done every time someone serves him something to drink."

The imperial living quarters

To the north, repeating the hierarchy of the ceremonial halls, are the three principal palaces of the **imperial living quarters**. Again, it's the first of these, the **Qianqinggong**, or Palace of Heavenly Purity, that's the most extravagant. Originally the imperial bedroom, its terrace is surmounted by incense burners in the form of cranes and tortoises. It was here in 1785 that Qianlong presided over the famous "banquet of old men" that brought together three thousand men of over sixty years of age from all corners of the empire. Used for the lying in state of the emperor, the hall also played a role in the tradition that finally solved the problem of **succession** (hitherto fraught with intrigue and uncertainty, as the principle of primogeniture was not used). The practice was begun by Qing Emperor Yongzheng: keeping an identical document on his person, Yongzheng and his successors deposited the name of his chosen successor in a sealed box hidden in the hall. When the emperor died, it was sufficient to compare the two documents to proclaim the new Son of Heaven.

Beyond is the **Jiaotaidian**, Hall of Union, the empress's throne-room, where the 25 imperial document seals were kept. The ceiling here is possibly the finest in

Eunuchs and concubines

For much of the imperial period, the Forbidden City was home to members of the royal household. Around half of these were **eunuchs**, introduced into the imperial court as a means of ensuring the authenticity of the emperor's offspring and, as the eunuchs would never have any family, an extreme solution to the problem of nepotism. As virtually the only men allowed into the palace, they came into close contact with the emperor and often rose to positions of considerable power. Their numbers varied greatly from one dynasty to the next – the Ming court is supposed to have employed 20,000, but this is probably an overestimate; the relatively frugal Qing Emperor Kangxi reduced the number to nine thousand.

Most of the eunuchs (or "bob-tailed dogs" as they were nicknamed) came from poor families, and volunteered for their emasculation as a way of acquiring wealth and influence. The operation cost six silver pieces and was performed in a hut just outside the palace walls. Hot pepper-water was used to numb the parts, then after the blade had flashed the wound was sealed with a solder plug. The plug was removed three days later – if urine gushed out, the operation was a success. If it didn't, the man would die soon, in agony. Confucianism held that disfiguration of the body impaired the soul, so in the hope that he would still be buried "whole", the eunuch carried his severed genitalia in a bag hung on his belt. One problem eunuchs were often plagued with was bed-wetting; hence the old Chinese expression, "as stinky as a eunuch". Eunuchry was finally banned in 1924, and the remaining 1500 eunuchs were expelled from the palace. An observer described them "carrying their belongings in sacks and crying piteously in high pitched voices".

Scarcely less numerous than the eunuchs were the **concubines**, whose role varied from consorts to whores. At night, the emperor chose a girl from his harem by picking out a tablet bearing her name from a pile on a silver tray – though the court astrologer had to OK the decision. She would be delivered to the emperor's bedchamber naked but for a yellow cloth wrapped around her, and carried on the back of one of the eunuchs, since she could barely walk with her bound feet. Eunuchs would be on hand for the event, standing behind a screen and shouting out cautions for the emperor not to get too carried away and risking harming the imperial body. Favoured wives and concubines were the only women in dynastic China with power and influence; see the box on Cixi (p.100) for a telling example of just how successful a wily concubine could be.

the complex, a gilt confection with a dragon surrounded by phoenixes at the centre; also here is a fine, and very hefty, water clock. The two characters *wu wei* at the back of the hall mean "no action" – a reference to the Taoist political ideal of not disturbing the course of nature or society.

Lastly, the **Kunninggong**, or Palace of Earthly Tranquillity, was where the emperor and empress traditionally spent their wedding night. By law the emperor

Exhibitions in the Forbidden City

The Imperial Palace is increasingly being devoted to museum space – 50,000 square metres today and due to increase eightfold in a few years. It's becoming arguably the best museum in China, and after appreciating the palace itself it's worth visiting a second time just to take in the exhibits. There's a strip of exhibition halls on the western side of the complex and a few more in the northeast; you'll find a map showing the location of the exhibitions on the back of your entrance ticket. Check out what's on at ⓦwww.dpm.org.cn; new exhibitions are opening all the time. All are free unless specified otherwise. Exhibitions listed below are in approximate geographical order, south to north.

Insignia of the Qing Court Lots of fans and canopies.

Qing Dynasty Weapons Most of the exhibits here reflect the Qing armies' mounted archers, with plenty of bows and saddles. There are also some early firearms.

Qing Dynasty Musical Instruments As well as displaying lots of instruments, you can listen to extracts of imperial music.

Qing Treasures Exquisite lacquerware, and carvings of jade, wood, bamboo and ivory.

History of the Qing Council A rather dry show of bureaucratic accoutrements.

Imperial Birthday Celebrations The emperor's birthday was an occasion for spectacle; check out the sumptuous gifts that he received here.

Qing Dynasty Imperial Weddings Dowry gifts and extravagant costumes.

Gifts Presented to the Museum Qing dynasty finery and oddments.

The Life of Qing Concubines Costumes and accessories for the court ladies.

Empress Dowager Cixi Formal costumes and fine objects.

Life of the Last Emperor Pu Yi Mostly photos and the emperor's personal possessions.

Pottery and porcelain Seven hundred pieces of pottery and porcelain from the Stone Age to the Qing dynasty.

Bronzeware Five hundred pieces of bronzeware from the Shang dynasty to the Warring States period (sixteenth century BC to 200 BC).

Painting Thousands of magnificent paintings from the Jin to the Qing dynasties, with displays changing monthly.

Jewellery (¥10) In Yangxindian and Leshoutang, north of the painting exhibition. The first hall houses mostly gold, silver and jade tableware and tea and wine utensils. There are also gold chimes, seals, books and a pagoda that was used to store any hair that fell out, on brushing, from the imperial head of Emperor Qianlong's mother. The second hall holds the costumes and utensils the emperor and empress used. Particularly impressive is a huge jade carving illustrating a Taoist immortal taming the waves. It weighs over five tonnes and reputedly took ten years to carve.

Clocks and watches (¥10). In Fengxiandian, the eastern palace quarters. This hall, always a favourite, displays the result of one Qing emperor's passion for liberally ornamented Baroque timepieces, most of which are English and French, though the rhino-sized water clock by the entrance is Chinese. There's even one with a mechanical scribe who can write eight characters. Some clocks are wound to demonstrate their workings at 11am and 2pm.

had to spend the first three nights of his marriage, and the first day of the Chinese New Year, with his new wife. On the left as you enter is a large sacrificial room, its vats ready to receive offerings (1300 pigs a year during the Ming dynasty). The wedding chamber is a small room off to one side, painted entirely in red and covered with decorative emblems symbolizing fertility and joy. It was last pressed into operation in 1922 for the wedding of 12-year-old Pu Yi, the last emperor, who, finding it "like a melted red wax candle", decided that he preferred the Mind Nurture Palace and went back there.

One of a group of palaces to the west, the Mind Nurture Palace, or **Yangxindian**, was where the emperors spent most of their time. Several of these palaces retain their furniture from the Manchu times, most of it eighteenth-century; in one, the **Changchungong** (Palace of Eternal Spring), is a series of paintings illustrating the Ming novel, *The Story of the Stone*.

The northern museums

To the east of the **Kunninggong** is a group of palaces, once residences of the emperor's wives and now adapted as **museum galleries** (see box opposite). The atmosphere here is much more intimate than in the state buildings, and you can peer into well-appointed chambers full of elegant furniture and ornaments, including English clocks decorated with images of English gentlefolk, looking very out of place among the jade trees and ornate fly whisks.

The Imperial Garden

From the Inner Court, the Kunningmen (Gate of Terrestrial Tranquillity) opens north onto the **Imperial Garden**, by this stage something of a respite from the elegant buildings. There are a couple of **cafés** here (and toilets) amid a pleasing network of ponds, walkways and pavilions, designed to be reminiscent of southern Chinese landscapes. In the middle of the garden, the **Qin'andian**, or Hall of Imperial Tranquillity, was where the emperor came to worship a Taoist water deity, Xuan Wu, who was responsible for keeping the palace safe from fire. You can exit here into Jingshan Park, which provides an overview of the complex – see p.83.

2

South of the centre

Most visitors head **south of the centre** to sample the glorious Temple of Heaven, but there's plenty to distract you on your way: just south of Tian'anmen Square, the **Qianmen district** offers a tempting antidote to the square's formality and grandeur – and a dramatic change of scale. This has always been an area to browse, with small, specialist stores, and, despite a recent massive redevelopment, that's still largely the case. It's a part of the city that lends itself to browsing, snacking and wandering.

Down Qianmen Dajie, once the Imperial Way, lies ravishing **Tiantan**, the **Temple of Heaven**. An example of imperial architecture at its best, it's perfectly set in one of Beijing's prettiest parks. Another site of imperial ritual nearby, the Temple of Agriculture, has become an engrossing **Museum of Ancient Architecture**. West of here, **Niu Jie** – at the heart of the city's Muslim quarter – and the **Fayuan Temple** are both worth a look. A very different sort of large-scale project is on show back near Qianmen in the **Underground City**, a shabby relic of communist paranoia.

Qianmen and around

The northern entrance to the Qianmen district is marked by the imposing, fifteenth-century, double-arched **Qianmen** 前门, *qiánmén*), the gate just south of Tian'anmen Square. Before the city's walls were demolished, this controlled the entrance to the inner city from the outer, suburban sector, and in imperial days the shops and places of entertainment banned from the interior city were concentrated around here. The quarter's biggest street, **Qianmen Dajie** (前门大街, *qiánmén dàjiē*), runs immediately south from the gate. Today it's a rather quaint pedestrianized Chinatown-style street – an open air mall of international brands, basically, with a handy sinified *Starbucks* at the northern end (see p.137) and an *Element Fresh* opposite (see p.140). A little tourist tram runs for about 1km the length of the street, though you'd have to be very lazy to consider it (¥2). The area south and off to either side of Qianmen Dajie was until recently the city's liveliest *hutong* district; though the street plan has been largely preserved, the buildings have been comprehensively bulldozed.

Dazhalan Street

The famous shopping street **Dazhalan** (大栅栏, *dà zhàlán*), leading west off Qianmen Dajie, has mercifully been spared the wrecking ball. Where theatres were once concentrated, it's now a hectic, pedestrianized shopping district, its genteel old buildings mostly occupied by tea merchants and clothing stores. It's a good place to pick up tea, silk clothes and souvenirs. Just beyond the entrance on the right you'll find the **Ruifuxiang** (瑞蚨祥绸布店, *ruìfúxiáng chóubùdiàn*), a venerable **fabric shop** – look for the storks on its facade, above the arched entrance – that's an excellent place to get silk and satin fabrics and *qipaos*. Even if you're not buying, take a look at the top-floor exhibition of vintage photos of the street. On the other side of the road at no. 24, the **Tongrengtang** (同仁堂, *tóngréntáng*) is a famous **traditional Chinese pharmacy** whose reputation has spread as far as Korea and Japan. The place even has its own foreign-exchange counter and a booth where a resident pharmacist offers on-the-spot diagnoses. Head upstairs for the weird stuff – aphrodisiacs, deer antlers and ginseng "children" (the more the root looks like a person, the more efficacious it's said to be). Finally, check in at no. 34 for handmade shoes and slippers (see p.164).

At the end of the pedestrianized area, the street narrows and you enter a district of **hutongs**, many destined for the wrecking ball. A stroll here offers a glimpse of the bustle and shabbiness that remains typical of Chinese metropolitan life but is vanishing from Beijing; you'll come across cobblers and knife sharpeners and dubious masseurs, stone lions flanking sagging courtyard doors, and furtive fruit vendors keeping an eye out for the police. The prevalence of public toilets hints at one reason why the locals don't necessarily worry about the *hutongs* being ripped up – the buildings have terrible plumbing. If you keep going straight, you'll eventually rejoin the traffic at Nanxinhua Jie. Head off either side and you're likely to get lost – not an unpleasant experience if you're not in a hurry; Liulichang (see below) is a good destination to ask for.

Liulichang Street

Liulichang Street (琉璃厂, *liúlíchǎng*) – split into "dong" (east) and "xi" (west) – lies west of Dazhalan Jie. If you're approaching from Hepingmen subway stop, you can get here by heading south down Nanxinhua Jie, which cuts Liulichang Jie at right angles – look for the marble bridge over the road. Liulichang – whose name literally means "glaze factory street", after the erstwhile factories here making glazed tiles for the roofs of the Forbidden City – has been rebuilt as a heritage street, using Ming-style architecture; today it's full of curio stores (remember to bargain hard, and that every antique is fake). Though there is nothing to distinguish it outwardly from the shops, no. 14 is a small and rather charming **museum** of folk carving (daily 9am–6pm; free), full of screen doors, woodblocks and the like, with some very skilfully crafted pieces. The **Ji Guge teahouse** at no. 136 offers a welcome respite for shoppers.

The Underground City

In response to the perceived nuclear threat from the Soviet Union in the 1960s, Chairman Mao charged "volunteers" to construct a warren of bunkers under the city. The tunnel network known as the **Underground City** (地下城, *dìxià chéng*) had entrances all over Beijing, a control centre in the Western Hills, and supply arteries big enough for trucks to drive down. Fortunately it was never put to use; it was too close to the surface to offer protection against any but the smallest conventional bombs.

Today the tunnels are falling into disrepair and most of the entrances are sealed, but it's worth visiting to get a sense of the old days of communist paranoia. You can get in using an **entrance** sunk deep in the *hutongs* southeast of Qianmen (daily 8.30am–5pm; ¥20): maps of the *hutongs* aren't reliable, but one foolproof approach

is to head east from Qianmen along the north side of Qianmen Dong Dajie. When you reach Zhengyi Lu, which leads north off the road, cross to the south side of Qianmen Dong Dajie and head down the narrow *hutong* here, then take the first left past a sign in English for the *Liyun Duck* restaurant. Head left at the end of this *hutong*, and the entrance is 300m down here on the right. From the entrance, stairs lead down to a claustrophobic, dimly lit, arched tunnel that echoes with your footsteps. The walls are covered with camouflage netting and posters of soldiers, there's an arbitrary showroom selling quilts for no good reason, and rusty metal doors, labelled with landmarks, lead off to the rest of the network. If it's your sort of thing, make sure to check out the *Red Capital Residence* (see p.192), whose bar is located in an old bomb shelter.

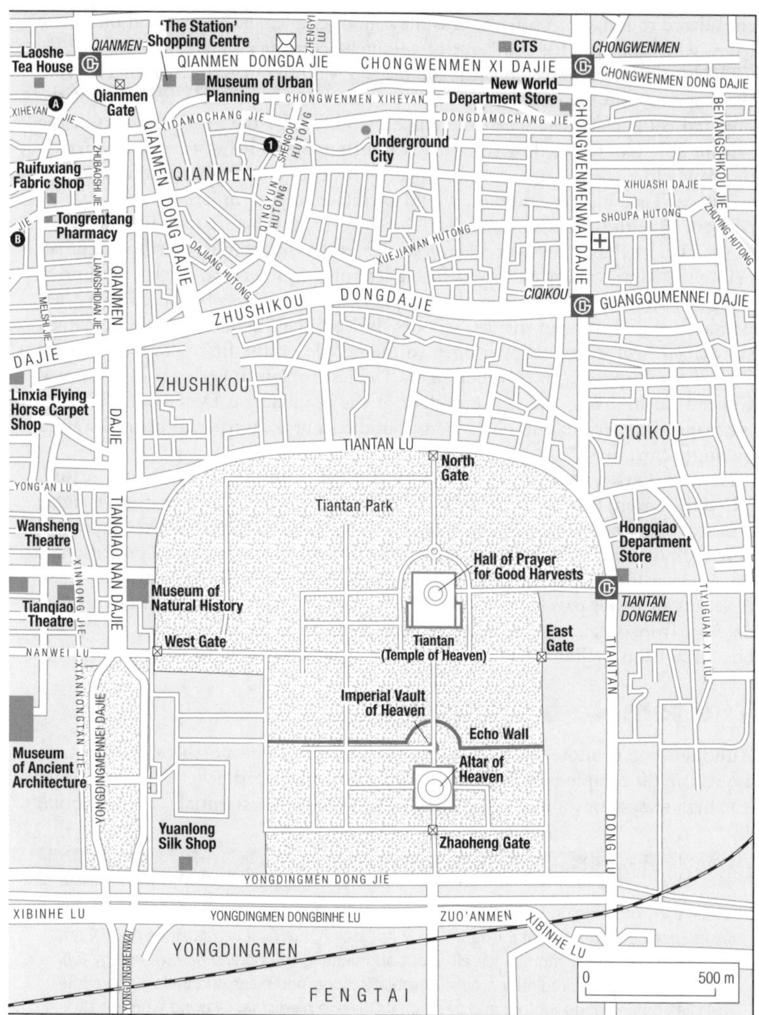

Tiantan and around

Set in its own large, tranquil park about 2km south of Tian'anmen, **Tiantan** (天坛, *tiāntán*), the **Temple of Heaven**, is widely regarded as the pinnacle of Ming design. For five centuries it was at the very heart of imperial ceremony and symbolism, and for many modern visitors its architectural unity and beauty remain more appealing – and on a much more accessible scale – than the Forbidden City.

Construction of the sumptuous temple was begun during the reign of Emperor Yongle and completed in 1420. It was conceived as the prime meeting point of earth and heaven, and symbols of the two are integral to its design. Heaven was considered round, earth square; thus the round temples and altars stand on square bases, while the park has the shape of a semicircle beside a square.

The intermediary between earth and heaven was of course the **Son of Heaven**, the emperor, and the temple was the site of the most important ceremony of the imperial court calendar, when the emperor prayed for the year's harvests at the **winter solstice**. Purified by three days of fasting, he made his way to the park on the day before the solstice, accompanied by his court in all its magnificence. On arrival at Tiantan, the emperor would meditate in the Imperial Vault, ritually conversing with the gods on the details of government, before spending the night in the Hall of Prayer for Good Harvests. The following day he sacrificed animals before the Altar of Heaven. It was forbidden for commoners to catch a glimpse of the great annual procession to the temple, and they were obliged to bolt their windows and remain, in silence, indoors. Indeed, the Tiantan complex remained sacrosanct until it was thrown open to the people on the first Chinese National Day of the Republic, in October 1912. The last person to perform the rites was General Yuan Shikai, the first president of the republic, on December 23, 1914. He planned to declare himself emperor but died a broken man, his plans thwarted by opponents, in 1916.

Tiantan Park (天坛公园, *tiāntán gōngyuán*; daily 6am–8pm; ¥10 low season, ¥15 high season) is possibly the best in the city, and worth a visit in its own right; it's easy to find peaceful seclusion away from the temple buildings. Old men gather here with their pet birds and crickets, while from dawn onwards, *tai ji* practitioners can be seen lost in concentration among the groves of 500-year-old *thuja* trees. A variety of **buses** pass by: #106 from Dongzhimen (for the north gate); bus #17 or #54 from Qianmen (west gate); bus #41 from Qianmen (east gate); and bus #120 from Beijing Zhan or #803 from Qianmen (south gate).

The temple buildings

Although you're more likely to enter the park from the north or the west, to appreciate the temple buildings (daily 8am–5pm; combined ticket ¥30 low season, ¥35 high season, or individual building tickets ¥20), it's best initially to skirt round

Tai ji

In the early morning, in Beijing's every park, you'll see folk going through the mesmerizing, precise moves of **tai ji quan**. It may not look it, but *tai ji* is actually a martial art, developed by Taoist monks. It's all about augmenting the body's natural energy (*qi*), which supposedly circulates around the body along particular channels – the same idea lies behind acupuncture and traditional Chinese medicine. *Qi gong* – breath skills – are used to build up an awareness of *qi* and the ability to move it around, eventually replacing excess muscular movements and rendering all actions fluid and powerful.

Forms – pre-arranged movement sets – are used to develop speed and power. Acute sensitivity is cultivated, allowing the martial artist to anticipate attacks and strike first; counter-attacks are made with the body in a state of minimal tension, creating *tai ji's* characteristic **soft appearance**. Students are taught not to directly resist but to redirect the attackers' energy, applying a principle from the Taoist Tao de Qing, "the soft and the pliable will defeat the hard and the strong".

The original Chen form is closely related to kung fu, but the form that you'll most often see is a slowed down and simplified version, stripped of explicit martial content and used to promote health. *Tai ji* was codified in 1949 to make it easier to teach, and so bring it to the masses: to see the best *tai ji*, visit Tiantan Park (see above), and Beijing's gymnasiums (see p.168).

onto the ceremonial route up from the **Zhaoheng Gate**, the park's south entrance. This main pathway leads straight to the circular **Altar of Heaven**, consisting of three marble tiers representing (from the top down) heaven, earth and man. The tiers are comprised of blocks in various multiples of nine, cosmologically the most powerful number, symbolizing both heaven and emperor. The centre of the altar's bare, roofless top tier, where the Throne of Heaven was placed during ceremonies, was considered to be the middle of the Middle Kingdom – the very centre of the earth. Various acoustic properties are claimed for the altar; from this point, it is said, all sounds are channelled straight upwards to heaven. To the east of the nearby fountain, which was reconstructed after fire damage in 1740, are the ruins of a group of buildings used for the preparation of sacrifices.

Directly ahead, the **Imperial Vault of Heaven** is an octagonal tower made entirely of wood, with a dramatic roof of dark blue glazed tiles, supported by eight pillars. This is where the emperor would change his robes and meditate. The shrine and stone platforms inside held stone tablets representing the emperor and his ancestors, and the two chambers either side held tablets representing the elements. The tower is encircled by the **Echo Wall**, said to be a perfect whispering gallery, although the unceasing cacophony of tourists trying it out makes it impossible to tell.

The principal temple building – the **Hall of Prayer for Good Harvests**, at the north end of the park – amply justifies all this build-up. Made entirely of wood, without the aid of a single nail, the circular structure rises from another tiered marble terrace and has three blue-tiled roofs. Four compass-point pillars, representing the seasons, support the vault, enclosed in turn by twelve outer pillars (one for each month of the year and the hour of the day). The dazzling colours of the interior, surrounding the central dragon motif on the coffered ceiling, give the hall an ultramodern look; it was in fact rebuilt, faithful to the Ming design, after the original was destroyed by lightning in 1889. The official explanation for this appalling omen was that it was divine punishment meted out on a sacrilegious caterpillar, which was on the point of crawling to the golden ball on the hall's apex when the lightning struck. Thirty-two court dignitaries were executed for allowing this to happen.

The museums

Two museums are worth combining with a visit to Tiantan. Just north of Tiantan Park's western gate, the **Museum of Natural History** (自然博物馆, *zìrán bówùguǎn*; daily 8.30am–4.30pm; ¥15) includes a terrific room full of dinosaur skeletons – the rest of the dusty place can be safely skipped. A short walk to the southwest is the former **Xiannong Temple**, reconverted from a school into a rather fine little **Museum of Ancient Architecture** (古代建筑博物馆, *gǔdài jiànzhù bówùguǎn*; daily 9am–5pm; ¥15). Look for the red arch south off Beiwei Lu; the ticket office is just beyond here and the museum itself is further down the road on the right. The temple, twin of the nearby Temple of Heaven, was dedicated to the god of earth, and every year the emperor ritually ploughed a furrow to ensure a good harvest. The buildings and the flat altar are refined, though not spectacular. The **Hall of Worship** holds oddments such as the gold-plated plough used by the emperor, as well as a display explaining the building's history. More diverting is the main **Hall of Jupiter**, with its beautifully ornate ceiling and an enlightening collection of architectural exhibits showing how China's traditional buildings were put together. There are wooden models, many with cutaways, of famous and distinctive buildings, including Yingxian's pagoda (west of Beijing in Shanxi province), and a stilt house of Yunnan province's Dong people. Also on hand are samples of

dougongs, interlocking, stacked brackets, as complex as puzzle boxes. The giant floor model (1:1000 scale) of how Beijing looked in 1949 – before the communists demolished most of it – is informative, revealing how all the surviving imperial remnants are fragments of a grand design, with a precise north–south imperial axis and sites of symbolic significance at each of the cardinal points. For those who prefer spectacle, there's a great sinuous wooden dragon on show, once part of a temple ceiling.

Niu Jie and the Fayuan Temple

Some 3km southwest of Qianmen, **Niu Jie** (牛街, *niújiē*; Ox Street) is a congested thoroughfare in the city's **Muslim quarter**, in a rather shabby section of the city. It's a 1km walk south along Changchun Jie from Changchun Jie subway stop, or you could get here on bus #6 from the north gate of Tiantan Park. Head under the arch at the north end of Niu Jie and you enter a chaotic street lined with offal stalls, steamy little restaurants and hawkers selling fried dough rings, rice cakes and *shaobing*, Chinese-style muffins with a meat filling. The white caps and the beards sported by the men distinguish these people of the Muslim **Hui minority** – of which there are nearly 200,000 in the capital – from the Han Chinese.

The street's focus is the bright green **mosque** at its southern end (牛街清真寺, *niújiē qīngzhēnsì*; daily 8am–5pm; ¥10, free for Muslims), an attractive, colourful marriage of Chinese and Islamic design, with abstract and flowery decorations and text in Chinese and Arabic over the doorways. You won't get to see the handwritten copy of the Koran, dating back to the Yuan dynasty, without special permission, or be allowed into the main prayer hall if you're not a Muslim, but you can inspect the courtyard, where a copper cauldron, used to cook food for the devotees, sits near the graves of two Persian imams who came here to preach in the thirteenth century. Also in the courtyard is the "tower for viewing the moon", which allows imams to ascertain the beginning and end of Ramadan, the Muslim period of fasting and prayer.

Take the last *hutong* on the left at the south end of the street, and after a few hundred metres you'll come to the **Fayuan Temple** (法源寺, *fǎyuán sì*; daily 8.30am–5pm; ¥5). This is one of Beijing's oldest temples, though the present structures are in fact Qing and thus relatively recent. A long way from tourist Beijing, it's appealingly ramshackle and authentic, with the well-worn prayer mats and shabby fittings of a working temple. Monks sit outside on broken armchairs counting prayer beads or bend over books in halls that stink of butter – burned in lamps – and incense. There are two great Ming bronze lions in the first courtyard, resembling armoured were-puppies, and more fine bronzes of the four Heavenly Guardians and a chubby Maitreya in the hall beyond. The halls behind are home to a miscellany of Buddhist sculpture, the finest of which is a 5m-long wooden reclining Buddha in the back hall.

West of the centre

Heading west from Tian'anmen Square along **Chang'an Jie** (长安街, *cháng'ān jiē*), the giant freeway that runs dead straight east–west across the city, you pass a string of grandiose buildings, the headquarters of official and corporate power. Architectural styles are jumbled together here, with International style, postmodern whimsy and brute Stalinism side by side. Though most of the sites and amenities are elsewhere, and the area has not modernized as fast as the rest of the city, western Beijing has enough of interest tucked away to entertain the curious for a few days. Along Chang'an Jie itself, there's a hectic shopping district, **Xidan**, where you can rub shoulders with locals, and visit the impressive **Capital** and **Military Museums**. Just off Chang'an Jie is the pleasant **Baiyun Guan**, a Taoist temple that seems worlds away from its surroundings.

Zhongnanhai to Xidan

As you head west from Tian'anmen Square along Xichang'an Jie, the first major building you pass is, on the left, the **National Centre for the Performing Arts** (中国国家大剧院, *zhōngguó guójiā dàjùyuàn*). Designed by French architect Paul Andreu and nicknamed, for obvious reasons, the "Egg", the glass and titanium dome houses a concert hall, two theatres and a 2500-seat opera house. Visitors enter through a tunnel under the lake outside. Critics already call it a white elephant but it makes an undeniably striking contrast to the surrounding, somewhat po-faced, monumentalism.

On the north side of the road you'll see the Communist Party headquarters, the **Zhongnanhai** (中南海, *zhōngnánhǎi*), a walled complex guarded by armed sentries to ensure that only invited guests get inside. Once home to the Empress Dowager Cixi (see p.100), since 1949 it's been the base of the party's Central Committee and the Central People's Government; Mao Zedong and Zhou Enlai both worked here. In 1989, pro-democracy protesters camped outside hoping to petition their leaders, just as commoners with grievances waited outside the Forbidden City in imperial times. In 1999, a similar, large protest was held by **Falun Gong**, a quasi-religious sect followed mostly by the aged in search of health and longevity. Ten thousand devotees sat down cross-legged on the pavement for the afternoon. Religious groups and secret societies have always flourished in China – the Boxers (see p.100) are a particularly prominent example – and governments have tended to treat them warily, as potential sources of organized dissent. Falun Gong have been ruthlessly suppressed ever since.

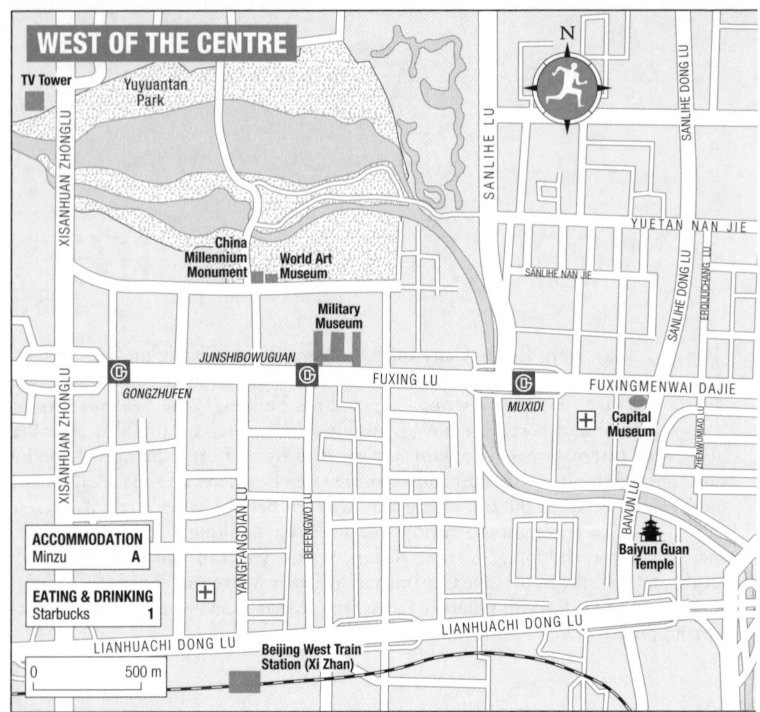

After the next junction, you'll see the **Aviation Office** (中国民用航空局, *zhōngguó mínyòng hángkōng jú*), the place to buy tickets for domestic flights and catch the airport bus. It stands on the site of Democracy Wall, which received its name in 1978, when, as part of the so-called "Beijing Spring", posters questioning Mao and his political legacy, and calling for political freedoms, were pasted up here. The movement was suppressed the following year.

The next major junction is **Xidan** (西单, *xīdān*), site of some ambitious modern buildings, the most eye catching of which is I.M. Pei's Bank of China at the northwest corner. Inside, the giant atrium leads the eye up to his signature glass pyramids in the ceiling. The shopping district of **Xidan Bei Dajie** (西单北大街, *xīdān běi dàjiē*), the street running north of here, is worth exploring, at least along its initial few blocks (though avoid it on weekends, when it's heaving). The dense concentration of **department stores and malls** sell everything the burgeoning middle class requires. The sixth and seventh floors of the **Xidan Shopping Centre** (the ugly brown glass building) are the places to go to check out pop fashions; the taste – at least at the time of writing – was for a Japanese-influenced sartorial excess. When you've had enough of feeling trapped in a pop video, head upstairs to the giant **food court** and **games arcade**. A more upmarket (but just as claustrophobic) shopping experience is on offer at the **Xidan CVIK Store**, a couple of hundred metres further north of here on the west side of the street. It mostly sells clothes and household goods.

Xichang'an Jie continues west into Fuxingmennei Dajie. On the north side of the street, 400m west of Xidan intersection, the **Cultural Palace of National Minorities** (民族文化宫, *mínzú wénhùa gōng*) is used for trade fairs, which is a shame,

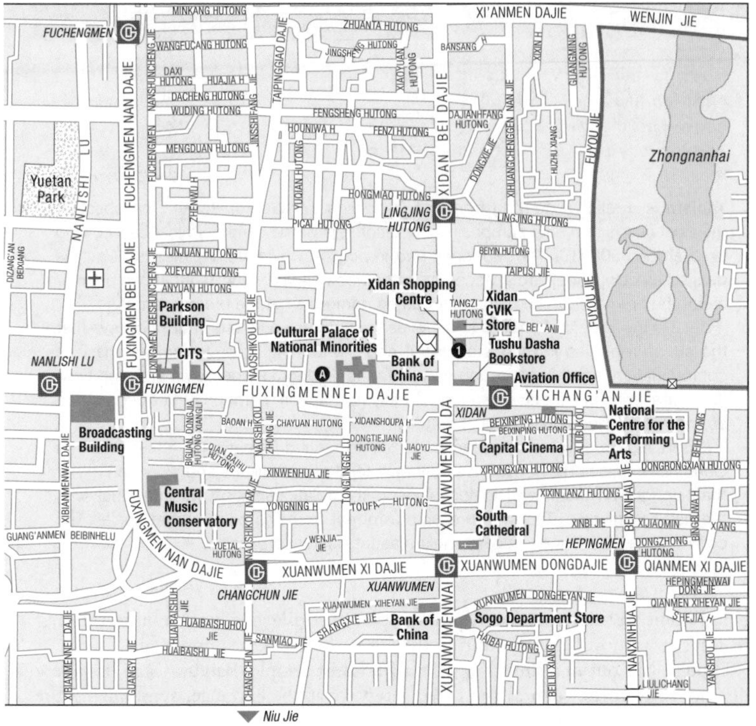

as it is quite striking architecturally, with some grand Socialist-Realist wall reliefs of minority peoples and Tibetan and Islamic elements incorporated into the decoration. Plans are afoot to convert it back to its original function, as a centre for minority culture.

The **Parkson Building** (百盛购物中心, *bǎishèng gòuwùzhōngxīn*) at the next large intersection, is an upmarket **mall**. Skip the overpriced clothes and head for the sixth floor, which holds an **arts and crafts exhibition** – most showpieces are in jade but there are ceramics and ivory too – by contemporary masters. Look out for the four renowned jade works, each over 1m high: a dragon relief, a mountain, a vase with chains on the handles and a two-eared cup. Begun in 1985, each piece took forty or so craftsmen four years to make.

Baiyun Guan and around

Five hundred metres south of Fuxingmenwai Dajie, **Baiyun Guan** or **White Cloud Temple** (白云观, *báiyún gùan*; daily 8am–5.30pm; ¥10) is well worth hunting out; it's signposted in English from Baiyun Lu whose northern end is not far from Muxidi subway stop, and can also be reached on bus #212 from Qianmen or #40 from Nansanhuan Zhong Lu. Once the most influential Taoist centre in the country, the temple was renovated after a long spell as a barracks during communist times, and now houses China's national Taoist association, as well as

Taoism

Humans model themselves on earth
earth on heaven
heaven on the way
and the way on that which is naturally so

Lao Zi, *Daodejing*

Taoism is a religion deriving from the *Daodejing* or "Way of Power", an obscure, mystical text (see p.180) comprising the teachings of the semi-mythical Lao Zi, who lived around 500 BC. The Tao (spelt *dao* in *pinyin*), which literally means "Way", is defined as being indefinable; accordingly the book begins: "The Tao that can be told/ is not the eternal Tao/The name that can be named/is not the eternal name".

But it is the force that creates and moves the natural world, and Taoists believe that the art of living lies in understanding it and conforming to it. Taoism emphasizes contemplation, meditation, a non-committance to dogma, and going with the flow. Its central principle is that of *wu wei*, literally non-action, perhaps better understood as "no action which goes against nature".

In part Taoism developed in reaction to the rigour and formality of state-sponsored Confucianism (see p.91). Taoism's holy men tend to be artisans and workmen rather than upright advisers, and in focusing on the relationship of the individual with the natural universe, Taoism represents a retreat from the political and social. The communists, accordingly, regard Taoism as fatalistic and passive.

being home to thirty monks. A popular place for pilgrims, with a busy, thriving feel, it's at its most colourful during the Chinese New Year temple fair.

Though laid out in a similar way to a Buddhist temple, Baiyun Guan has a few distinctive features, such as the three gateways at the entrance, symbolizing the three states of Taoism – desire, substance and emptiness. Each hall is dedicated to a different deity, whose respective domains of influence are explained in English outside; the thickest plumes of incense emerge from the hall to the gods of wealth. The eastern and western halls hold a great collection of Taoist relics, including some horrific paintings of hell showing people being sawn in half. An attached bookshop has plenty of CDs of devotional music and lucky charms, though only one text in English, the *I-Ching*. In the western courtyard, a shrine houses twelve deities, each linked with a different animal in the Chinese version of the zodiac; here, visitors light incense and kowtow to the deity that corresponds to their birth year. Also in the courtyard is a shrine to **Wen Cheng**, the deity of scholars, with a 3m-high bronze statue of him outside. Rubbing his belly is supposed to bring success in academic examinations.

Worship in China can be a lively affair, and there are a number of on-site amusements. Three **monkeys** depicted in relief sculptures around the temple are believed to bring you good luck if you can find, and stroke, them all. One is on the gate, easy to spot as it's been rubbed black, while the other two are in the first courtyard. Another playful diversion is trying to ding the bell under the courtyard bridge by throwing a coin at it. In the back courtyard, devotees close their eyes and try to walk from a wall to an incense burner.

Capital Museum

On the south side of Fuxingmenwai Dajie and not far from Muxidi subway stop, the **Capital Museum** (首都博物馆, *shǒudū bówùguǎn*; Tues–Sun 9am–5pm; ¥30; Ⓦwww.capitalmuseum.org.cn/en) is easy to miss, despite its size – from the outside it rather resembles the bank headquarters that precede it. Inside, the architecture is much more interesting; a bronze cylinder shoots down through the roof as if from heaven. Despite this, and though a lot of money has obviously been spent, the museum doesn't quite reach its full potential: considering the size of the building the exhibition spaces are measly, there's a lot of walking to get from one to another and the exhibits have few English captions. The layout is simple: Beijing exhibition halls are in the **cube**, cultural relics in the **cylinder**. If you're short on time or energy skip the cube and head for the rarer pieces instead.

The cylinder's ground-floor gallery holds Ming and Qing paintings, mostly landscapes – well presented, but not as comprehensive as the display in the Forbidden City (see p.58). The calligraphy upstairs can be safely missed unless you have a special interest, but the bronzes on level three are pretty interesting: a sinister third-century BC owl-headed dagger, for example, or the strangely modern-looking three-legged cooking vessels decorated with geometric patterns – which are more than three thousand years old. The display of jade on the fourth floor is definitely worth lingering over; the qualities that combine to create the best jade is an esoteric subject (it's all about colour, lustre and clarity) but anyone can appreciate the workmanship that has gone into the buckles, boxes and knick-knacks here; the white quail-shaped vessels are particularly lovely.

The cube of exhibition halls on the building's west side can be navigated rather more quickly. The bottom level hosts a confusing and disappointing show on the history of Beijing: exhibits are jumbled together – a modern lathe is displayed next to a stele, for example – without enough English captions to make any sense of the showcase at all. The next level up displays models of historical buildings, which can be skipped in favour of the show-stealing Buddhist figurines on the top floor. As well as depictions of serene long-eared gentlemen, there are some very esoteric lamaist figures from Tibet; the goddess Marici, for example, comes with her own pig-drawn chariot and other fierce deities have lion heads or many arms.

Yuyuantan Park and around

Yuyuantan Park (玉渊潭公园, *yùyuāntán gōngyuán*; daily 6am–9.30pm; ¥10) offers respite from the traffic: it's low on trees and grass, but there's a large, pleasant lake; you can take out a pedal boat for ¥30 per hour. In the southwest corner stands the dome-shaped China Millennium Monument, a sterile public work and "Centre for Patriotic Education". The Communist Party's version of Chinese history is inscribed on bronze plates that form a walkway leading up to a flat altar.

Now that all the communists have been to marketing school, it's almost refreshing to be confronted with the old-fashioned Soviet-style brutalism of the stern building in front of the park – the **Military Museum** (军事博物馆, *jūnshì bówùguǎn*; daily 8am–4.30pm; ¥15; Military Museum subway stop) – which is as subtle as a cattleprod. The entrance hall is full of big, bad art, photo-collages of Mao inspecting his army and soldiers performing an amphibious landing (a hint at Taiwan's fate perhaps) and the like. The last Chinese public image of Marx hung here until 1999. The hall beyond has a wealth of Russian and Chinese weaponry on show, including tanks and rockets, with – in case martial feelings have been stirred – an air-rifle shooting gallery at the back. In the rear courtyard a group of miscellaneous old aircraft includes the shells of two American spy planes (with Nationalist Chinese markings) shot down in the 1950s. Upstairs, you'll find plaster casts of statues of military and political leaders.

Head back to the lobby, turn west and climb the unsignposted, dim staircase to the much more engaging **upper halls**. The exhibition on the third floor commemorates the Korean War, whose chief interest for foreign visitors lies in the fact that it's one of those places that isn't meant for them – captions are only in Chinese and there is much crowing over what is presented as the defeat of American power. There are also more paintings of lantern-jawed soldiers charging machine-gun posts and the like. The fourth floor holds a large exhibition on historical warfare, this time with English captions. Arranged in chronological order, it presents Chinese history as a series of bloody conflicts between rival warlords – which is, actually, not far from the truth. The suits of armour worn by Qing soldiers and Japanese pirates are intimidating even when empty. Also on display are mock-ups of ingenious Chinese siege weapons, Ming dynasty gunpowder-driven devices for firing eighty arrows at a time, and the world's earliest handgun, from the fifteenth century. Opposite this hall lies another treat for connoisseurs of kitsch – the "Friendship Hall", containing gifts given to representatives of the Chinese military abroad. Competition for the most tasteless item is fierce, but the gold sub-machine gun from Lebanon and the silver model tractor from Romania certainly deserve a mention.

A short walk from here, the grandiose Millenium Monument (中华世纪坛, *zhōnghuá shìjì tán*) is of most interest as the home of the new **World Art Museum** (世界艺术馆, *shìjiè yìshùguǎn*; daily 8am–6pm; ¥30; Ⓦwww.worldartmuseum.cn); it's intended to foster cultural understanding by displaying visiting exhibitions from abroad. There's no permanent collection, but its long shows – on the great ancient civilizations, for example – are very impressive.

The TV tower

Northwest of the Military Museum, a 3km walk away through Yuyuantan Park, Beijing's **TV tower** (电视塔, *diànshì tǎ*; daily 8am–5pm; ¥50) is the capital's tallest building. A giant, needle-like structure on the Third Ring Road, the tower stands on the foundation of the Altar of the Moon, a Ming-dynasty sacrificial site. You ride up to the top in a lift – and though the Coke and piece of cake you're given once you get there don't justify the steep admission fee, the outdoor viewing platform 400m above ground does offer stunning views of the city on a clear day. Telescopes are dotted around for closer examination – unfortunately the view into Zhongnanhai is blocked by some judiciously placed buildings.

4

East of the centre

If you head east from Tian'anmen, the first thing you encounter, setting the tone for the rest of this cosmopolitan sector of the city, is the incongruously European architecture of the **legations quarter**, once home to foreign diplomats and recently redeveloped as a high-end dining zone. Just to the north, the eastern section of **Chang'an Jie** is glamorous and commercial, with lashings of shopping – the best in China outside Shanghai and Hong Kong – plus flashy hotels and plenty of restaurants and amenities. It's Beijing's most fashionable area; for anyone who's been in China for a while it's the place to come to stock up on luxuries, and for newcomers it offers the chance to experience the new realities of life for privileged locals. The most obvious landmark here is the **Beijing Hotel**, on the corner where **Wangfujing Dajie**, Beijing's most famous shopping street, leads north off Dongchang'an Jie.

Beyond the intersection with Dongdan Bei Dajie and Chongwenmennei Dajie, about 1500m east of Tian'anmen Square, Dongchang'an Jie becomes **Jianguomen Dajie**. The strip around here is a ritzy area with an international flavour and a casual, affluent atmosphere thanks to its large contingent of foreigners, many of them staff from the Jianguomen embassy compound. Eating and staying here will soon sap many tourists' budgets (first-time visitors can be heard expressing disappointment that China is as expensive as New York), but the wide variety of shopping on offer – cheap clothes markets, and plazas that wouldn't look out of place in Hong Kong – will suit all pockets. Jianguomen Dajie is about as far away from traditional China as you can get, but the **Ancient Observatory** halfway along, and the unusual Dongyue Temple to the north, offer respite from rampant modernity. Finally, it's a long way out, well beyond the Second Ring Road, but the **798 Art District** is the one of the best of the new Beijing sights, a trendy complex of galleries showcasing the best of contemporary Chinese art.

The foreign legations and the Police Museum

Head east down Dongjiaomin Xiang, the first alley opposite the Mao Memorial Hall, and, still within sight of the Soviet-inspired symbols of Chinese power, you'll come to an odd stretch of street that shows very different influences. This was the **legation quarter**, created at the insistence of foreign officials in 1861, and run as an autonomous district with its own postal system, taxes and defences; initially, Chinese were not permitted entry without a pass. By the 1920s more than twenty countries had legations here, most built in the style of their home

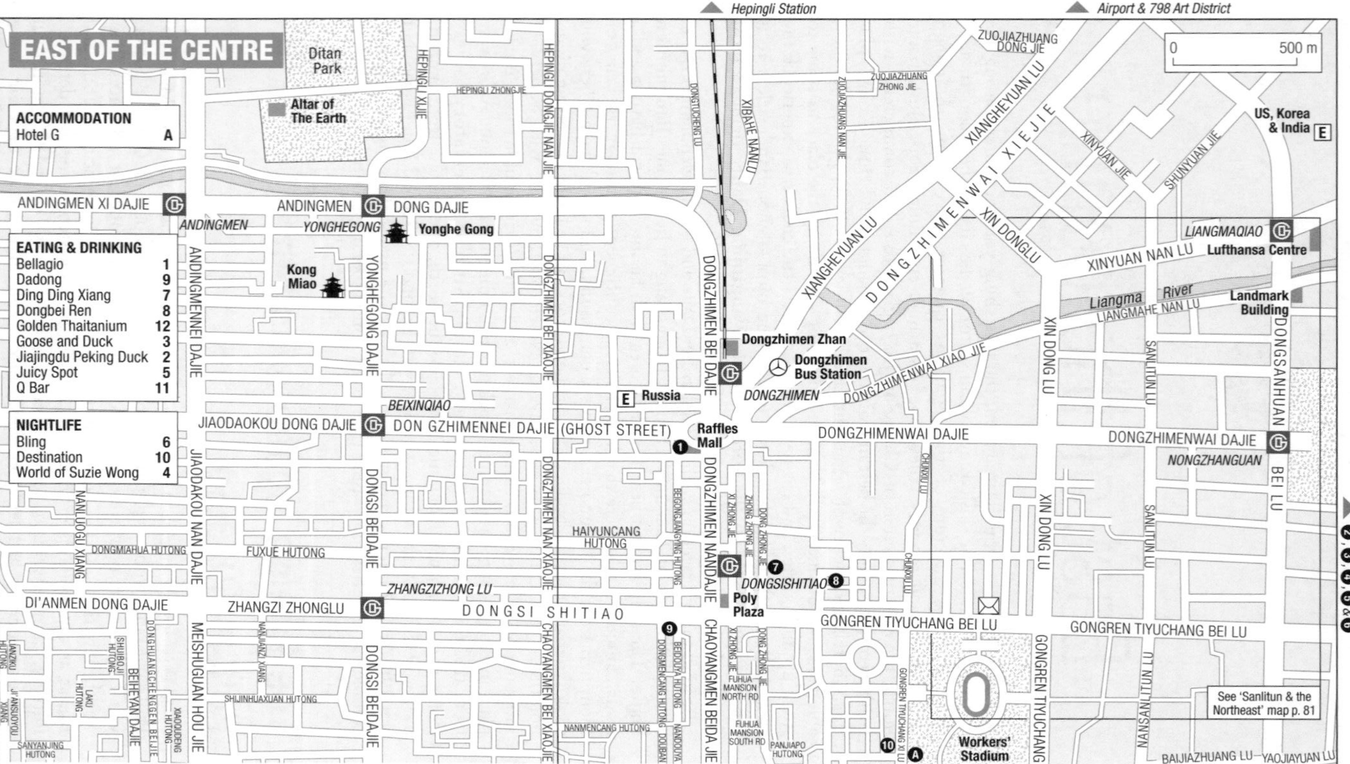
EAST OF THE CENTRE
ACCOMMODATION
Hotel G A
EATING & DRINKING
Bellagio 1
Dadong 9
Ding Ding Xiang 7
Dongbei Ren 8
Golden Thaitanium 12
Goose and Duck 3
Jiajingdu Peking Duck 2
Juicy Spot 5
Q Bar 11
NIGHTLIFE
Bling 6
Destination 10
World of Suzie Wong 4
0 500 m
Hepingli Station
Airport & 798 Art District
2, 3, 4, 5 & 6
Ditan Park
Altar of The Earth
US, Korea & India
Russia
Yonghe Gong
Kong Miao
Dongzhimen Zhan
Dongzhimen Bus Station
Raffles Mall
Poly Plaza
Lufthansa Centre
Landmark Building
Liangma River
Workers' Stadium
See 'Sanlitun & the Northeast' map p. 81
ANDINGMEN XI DAJIE
ANDINGMEN
DONG DAJIE
YONGHEGONG
ANDINGMENNEI DAJIE
YONGHEGONG DAJIE
HEPINGLI XIJIE
HEPINGLI ZHONGJIE
HEPINGLI DONGJIE NAN JIE
DONGZHIMEN BEI XIAOJIE
BEIXINQIAO
JIAODAOKOU DONG DAJIE
DON GZHIMENNEI DAJIE (GHOST STREET)
JIAODAKOU NAN DAJIE
DONGSI BEIDAJIE
DONGZHIMEN NAN XIAOJIE
NANLUOGU XIANG
DONGMIAHUA HUTONG
FUXUE HUTONG
ZHANGZIZHONG LU
DI'ANMEN DONG DAJIE
ZHANGZI ZHONGLU
DONGSI SHITIAO
MEISHUGUAN HOU JIE
NANJIANZI XIANG
SHIJINHUAXUAN HUTONG
CHAOYANGMEN BEI XIAOJIE
LIANZIKU HUTONG
JI'ANSUOYOU XIANG
LAKU HUTONG
SHUIBOJI HUTONG
DONGHUANGCHENGGEN BEIJIE
BEIHEYAN DAJIE
XIAOQUDENG HUTONG
SANYANJING HUTONG
HAIYUNCANG HUTONG
BEIGONGJIANGYING HUTONG
NANMENCANG HUTONG
DONGMENCANG HUTONG
BEIDOUYA HUTONG
DOUBAN
NANDOUYA
DONGTUCHENG LU
XIBAHE NANLU
ZUOJIAZHUANG NAN JIE
ZUOJIAZHUANG ZHONG JIE
ZUOJIAZHUANG DONG JIE
XIANGHEYUAN LU
DONGZHIMENWAI XIEJIE
XINYUAN JIE
SHUNYUAN JIE
XIN DONGLU
LIANGMAQIAO
XINYUAN NAN LU
LIANGMAHE NAN LU
DONGZHIMEN BEI DAJIE
DONGZHIMEN
DONGZHIMENWAI XIAO JIE
DONGZHIMENWAI DAJIE
NONGZHANGUAN
DONGSANHUAN BEI LU
XIN DONG LU
SANLITUN LU
CHUNXIU LU
DONGZHIMEN NANDAJIE
XI ZHONG JIE
ZHONG ZHONG JIE
DONG ZHONG JIE
DONGSISHITIAO
GONGREN TIYUCHANG BEI LU
CHAOYANGMEN BEIDA JIE
FUHUA MANSION NORTH RD
FUHUA MANSION SOUTH RD
PANJIAPO HUTONG
GONGREN TIYUCHANG XI LU
GONGREN TIYUCHANG
NANSANLITUN LU
BAIJIAZHUANG LU
YAOJIAYUAN LU

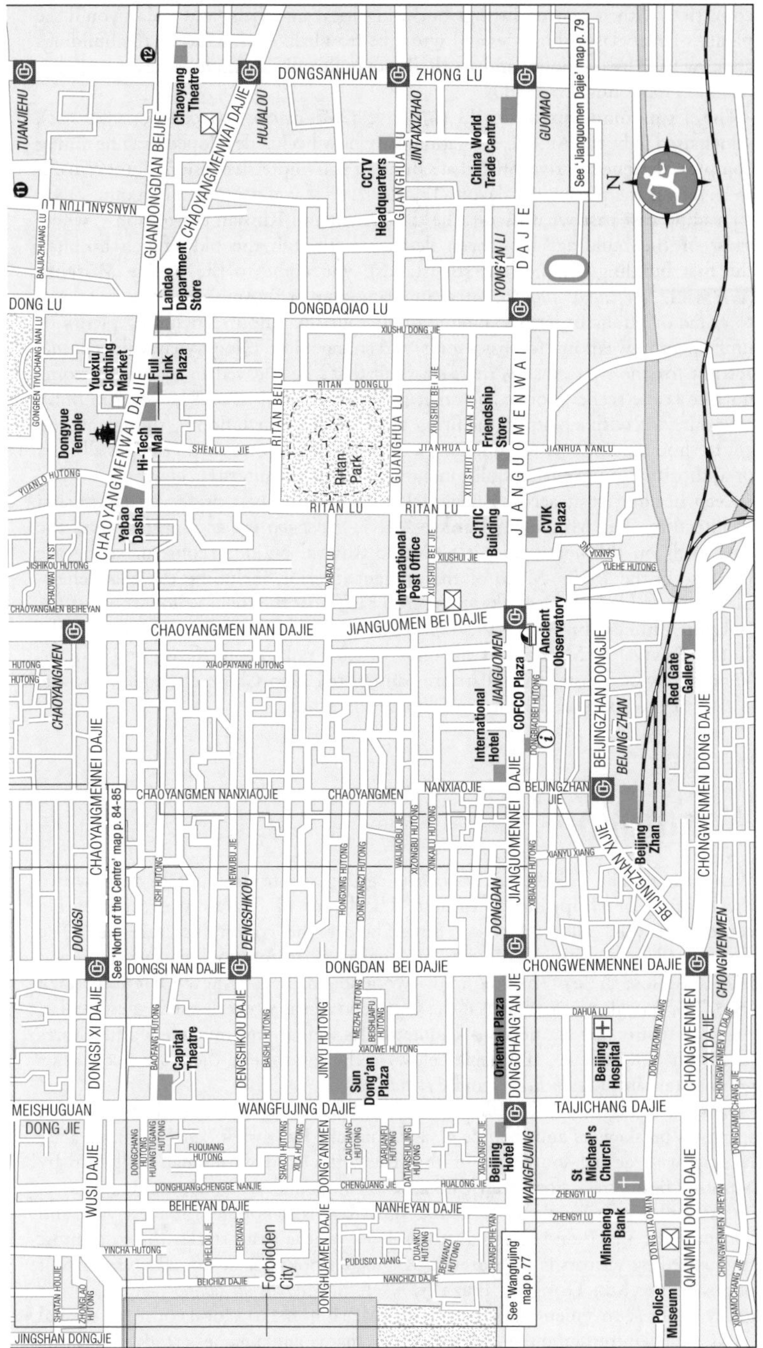

TUANJIEHU
DONGSANHUAN
ZHONG LU
Chaoyang Theatre
GUANDONGDIAN BEIJIE
CHAOYANGMENWAI DAJIE
HUJIALOU
NANSANLITUN LU
BAIJIAZHUANG LU
JINTAIXIZHAO
GUANGHUA LU
CCTV Headquarters
China World Trade Centre
GUOMAO
See 'Jianguomen Dajie' map p. 79
N
DONG LU
GONGREN TIYUCHANG NAN LU
Landao Department Store
DONGDAQIAO LU
YONG'AN LI
DAJIE
XIUSHUI DONG JIE
Yuexiu Clothing Market
Full Link Plaza
RITAN BEILU
RITAN DONGLU
XIUSHUI BEI JIE
XIUSHUI NAN JIE
Dongyue Temple
Hi-Tech Mall
SHENLU JIE
Ritan Park
GUANGHUA LU
JIANHUA LU
Friendship Store
JIANGUOMENWAI
JIANHUA NANLU
YUANLO HUTONG
Yabao Dasha
RITAN LU
RITAN LU
CITIC Building
CVIK Plaza
CHAOYANGMENWAI DAJIE
JISHIKOU HUTONG
CHAOWAI N ST
YABAO LU
International Post Office
XIUSHUI JIE
SANXIANG
YUEHE HUTONG
CHAOYANGMEN BEIHEYAN
CHAOYANGMEN NAN DAJIE
JIANGUOMEN BEI DAJIE
Ancient Observatory
XIAOPAIYANG HUTONG
HUTONG
HUTONG
CHAOYANGMEN
JIANGUOMEN
International Hotel
COFCO Plaza
DONGBIAOBEI HUTONG
BEIJINGZHAN DONGJIE
BEIJING ZHAN
Red Gate Gallery
CHAOYANGMENNEI DAJIE
See 'North of the Centre' map p. 84-85
CHAOYANGMEN NANXIAOJIE
CHAOYANGMEN
NANXIAOJIE
JIANGUOMENNEI DAJIE
BEIJINGZHAN JIE
Beijing Zhan
CHONGWENMEN DONG DAJIE
LISHI HUTONG
NEIWUBU JIE
HONGXING HUTONG
DONGTANGZI HUTONG
WAIJIAOBU JIE
XIZONGBU HUTONG
XINKAILU HUTONG
XIBIAOBEI HUTONG
XIANYU XIANG
BEIJINGZHAN XIJIE
DONGSI
DENGSHIKOU
DONGDAN
DONGSI NAN DAJIE
DONGDAN BEI DAJIE
CHONGWENMENNEI DAJIE
CHONGWENMEN
DONGSI XI DAJIE
Capital Theatre
BAOFANG HUTONG
DENGSHIKOU DAJIE
BAISHU HUTONG
JINYU HUTONG
MEIZHA HUTONG
BEISHUAIFU HUTONG
XIAOWEI HUTONG
Sun Dong'an Plaza
Oriental Plaza
DONGOHANG'AN JIE
DAHUA LU
Beijing Hospital
DONGJIAOMIN XIANG
CHONGWENMEN XI DAJIE
CHONGWENMEN XI DAJIE
MEISHUGUAN DONG JIE
WANGFUJING DAJIE
TAIJICHANG DAJIE
DONGDAMOCHANG JIE
WUSI DAJIE
DONGCHANG HUTONG
HUANGTUGANG HUTONG
FUQIANG HUTONG
SHAOJI HUTONG
XILA HUTONG
DONG'ANMEN
CAICHANG HUTONG
DAFUANFU HUTONG
DATIANSHULING HUTONG
XIAGONGFU JIE
Beijing Hotel
WANGFUJING
St Michael's Church
DONGHUANGCHENGGE NANJIE
CHENGUANG JIE
HUALONG JIE
ZHENGYI LU
BEIHEYAN DAJIE
NANHEYAN DAJIE
ZHENGYI LU
Minsheng Bank
QIANMEN DONG DAJIE
CHONGWENMEN XIHEYAN
OHELOU JIE
BEIXIANG
DONGHUAMEN DAJIE
DUANKU HUTONG
BEIWANZI HUTONG
CHANGPUHEYAN
DONGJIAOMIN
YINCHA HUTONG
Forbidden City
PUDUSIXI XIANG
See 'Wangfujing' map p. 77
BEICHIZI DAJIE
NANCHIZI DAJIE
Police Museum
SHATAN HOUJIE
ZHONGLAO HUTONG
XIDAMOCHANG JIE
JINGSHAN DONGJIE

countries, with imported fittings but using local materials, and today you'll see plenty of Neoclassical facades and wrought-iron balconies. Most of the buildings are now used by the police and are therefore politically sensitive – the area was left blank on maps until the 1980s.

The elegant **mansions at no. 23** (前门东大街23号, *qiánmén dōngdàjiē èrshísān hào*), which used to be the American legation, have now been redeveloped as a fine dining complex, designed to rival Shanghai's Bund; it's an impressive vision, but it remains to be seen if the place will take off. Try *Zen 1903* if you want to splash out.

Heading east past what used to be the French and Russian concession – where most of the buildings have been destroyed (though the old French hospital, the first building on the left, still stands), you come to the **Police Museum** (警察博物馆, *jǐngchá bówùguǎn*; Tues–Sun 9am–4pm; ¥5). Anything vaguely related to crime or public order is exhibited on its four small floors, including plenty of uniforms and weapons, forensics tools, and an ingenious Qing dynasty fire engine. It's not for the squeamish – there's a skull that's been caved in by an axe, some horrific crime scene photos, and ancient execution tools. For ¥15 you can finish off your visit with a blast on the firing range on the fourth floor – though all you get to shoot, alas, is a laser gun. Check out the gift shop tat – you can get all sorts of authority figure keyring dolls, including one of the internet censor.

Keep heading east, across Zhengyi Lu, to find the best-preserved concession architecture. The **Minsheng Bank**(民生银行, *mínshēng yínháng*), just beyond the crossroads on the north side, is a Gothic Revival building constructed by the Japanese in the 1930s. Much of the opulent interior, including the chandeliers, tiled floor and balustrades, is original. You can't miss the steep yellow roofs of the **Belgian Concession** – now the *Zijin Hotel* – a little further on. Opposite it, the Gothic Revival **St Michael's Church** is worth a poke about if you find it open. Yielding to local taste, the pillars are painted red as in Chinese temples, and the statues of the saints are labelled in Chinese characters.

Wangfujing

Wangfujing Dajie (王府井大街, *wángfǔjǐng dàjiē*) is where the capital gets down to the business of **shopping** in earnest. The haunt of quality stores for over a century, it was called Morrison Street before the communist takeover. The western side of the street has plenty of department stores, small clothes shops and photo studios; the eastern side holds two giant malls. The new **Oriental Plaza** (东方广场, *dōngfāng guǎngchǎng*) at the south end of the street, is the biggest mall in Asia, stretching east for nearly a kilometre. As well as interminable clothes stores (fancy on ground level, affordable below) at the eastern end there are a couple of good restaurants (*South Beauty* and *Crystal Jade*).

Back on Wangfujing, for "shock the folks back home" food – silk worms and sparrows on skewers and the like – visit **Xiaochi Jie** (小吃街, *xiǎochī jiē*), an alley leading west at the south end of the street. It's lined with small stalls run by Muslim Uigurs from northwest China, who compete fiercely, haranguing passers-by. As well as exotica, plenty of stalls do tasty bowls of noodles for a few yuan and coconuts for ¥10 (you stick in a straw). Back on the main street, the store most frequented by visitors is the Foreign Language Bookstore at no. 235 (see p.162); opposite, the **Sun Dong'an Plaza** (新东安广场, *xīndōng'ān guǎngchǎng*), another glitzy mall, is convenient for a snack – the place is home to a food court and several fast-food chain restaurants – and also has a cinema and a games arcade. Continue

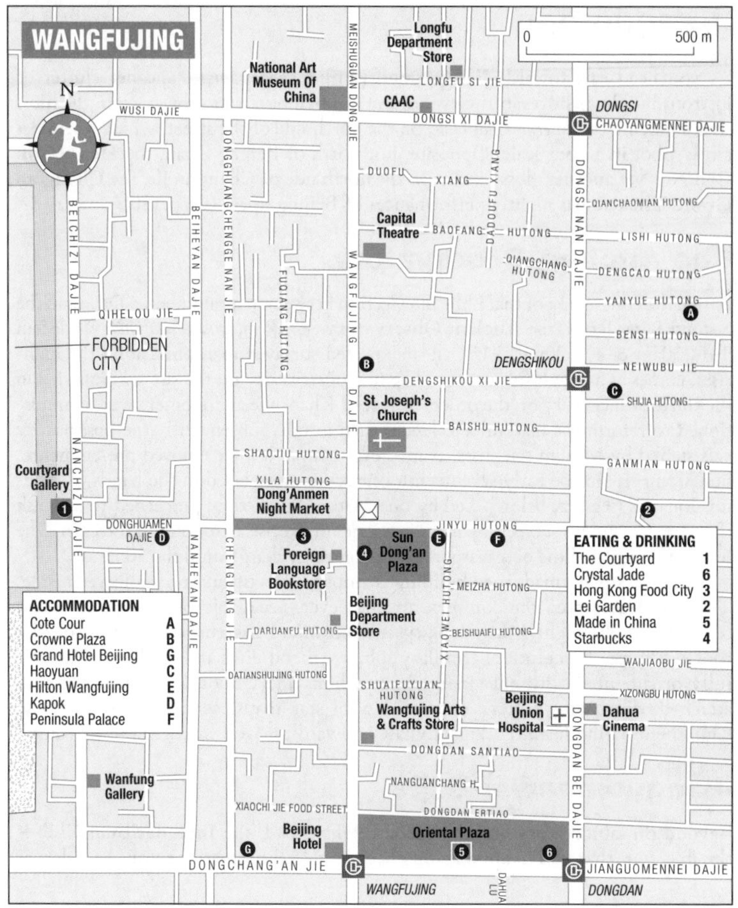

heading north up Wangfujing for 1km and you'll come to the **National Art Museum of China** (中国美术馆, *zhōngguó měishùguǎn*), a huge exhibition hall showcasing state-approved artworks (see p.158).

A number of *hutongs* lead off from Wangfujing Dajie into a quiet area well away from the bustle of the main street. If you're here in the evening, don't miss the **Donghuamen Yeshi night market** (东华門夜市, *dōnghuámēn yèshì*) at the intersection of Wangfujing Dajie and Jinyu Hutong, where all sorts of food, from regional delicacies, scorpions and starfish to simple street snacks, are sold at the rows of red stalls: nothing costs more than ¥15. At the end of **Shuaifuyuan Hutong** (帅府园胡同, *shuàifŭyuán hútōng*), the graceful medical college building is a former palace where the ten brothers of a Ming-dynasty emperor were once persuaded to live, so that he could keep a wary eye on them. Today, it's been so rebuilt that only the ornate flying eaves hint at its former function. Continuing east for about 300m through the *hutongs*, you'll reach Dongdan Bei Dajie, parallel to Wangfujing, a shopping area full of boutiques, mostly selling Western imports.

Jianguomen

As you head east towards **Jianguomen** (建国门, *Jiànguómén*), another cluster of lustrous buildings hoves into view around the Beijing Zhan subway stop, the most striking being the *International Hotel* on the north side of the street, which resembles a toy robot in all but scale. Opposite, just north of Beijing Zhan, the **Henderson Centre** is yet another glossy mall. On the north side of Chang'an Jie, the **Chang'an Grand Theatre** has nightly performances of Beijing opera (see p.150).

The Ancient Observatory

Beside the concrete knot that is the intersection between Jianguomennei Dajie and the Second Ring Road, the **Ancient Observatory** (古观象台, *gŭguānxiàngtái*; Wed–Sun 9–11.30am & 1–4.30pm; ¥15), an unexpected survivor marooned amid the high-rises, comes as a delightful surprise. The first observatory on the site was founded in the thirteenth century on the orders of Kublai Khan; the astronomers were commissioned to reform the inaccurate calendar then in use. Subsequently the observatory was staffed by Muslim scientists, as medieval Islamic science enjoyed pre-eminence, but, strangely, in the early seventeenth century it was placed in the hands of Jesuit missionaries (see box below). Led by one Matteo Ricci, they proceeded to astonish the emperor and his subjects by making a series of precise astronomical forecasts. The Jesuits re-equipped the observatory and remained in charge until the 1830s.

Today the squat, unadorned building is empty, and visitors aren't allowed inside. The best features of the complex are, however, accessible: its garden, a placid retreat; and the eight Ming-dynasty **astronomical instruments** sitting on the roof – stunningly sculptural armillary spheres, theodolites and the like, all beautifully ornamented with entwined dragons, lions and clouds. The small museum attached, displaying pottery decorated with star maps, as well as navigational equipment dating from the Yuan dynasty onwards, is well worth a wander round.

Jianguomenwai Dajie

Beyond the observatory and the Second Ring Road, the **International Club** is the first sign that you're approaching the capital's diplomatic sector. Turn left at

The Jesuits in China

Jesuit missionaries began to arrive in China in the seventeenth century. Though they weren't allowed to preach freely at first, they were tolerated for their scientific and astronomical skills, and were invited to stay at court: precise astronomical calculations were invaluable to the emperor who, as master of the calendar, was charged with determining the cycle of the seasons in order to ensure good harvests, and observing the movement of celestial bodies to harmonize the divine and human order. Some Jesuits rose to high positions in the imperial court, and in 1692 they finally won the right to preach in China. The missionaries made little headway in spreading Catholicism, however, as a Vatican edict forced them to condemn all Chinese rites and rituals, such as sacrifices to ancestors, as anti-Christian.

Matteo Ricci (1552–1610) was the most illustrious of the early Jesuit missionaries to China. A keen Chinese scholar, he translated the Confucian analects into Portuguese and created the first system for romanizing Chinese characters. He began studying the Chinese language in 1582, when he arrived in Macau. In 1603 he moved to Beijing and won the respect of the local literati with his extensive knowledge of cartography, astronomy, mathematics and the physical sciences.

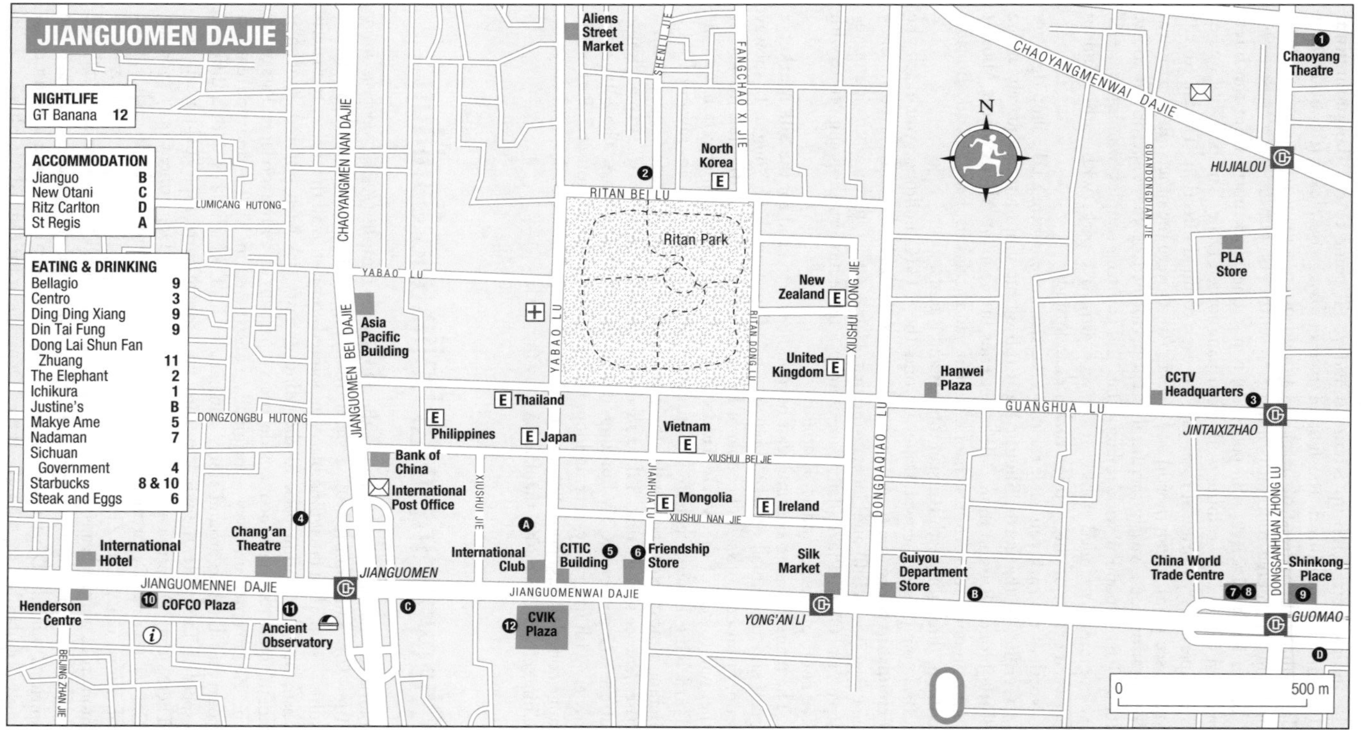

JIANGUOMEN DAJIE
NIGHTLIFE
GT Banana 12
ACCOMMODATION
Jianguo B
New Otani C
Ritz Carlton D
St Regis A
EATING & DRINKING
Bellagio 9
Centro 3
Ding Ding Xiang 9
Din Tai Fung 9
Dong Lai Shun Fan Zhuang 11
The Elephant 2
Ichikura 1
Justine's B
Makye Ame 5
Nadaman 7
Sichuan Government 4
Starbucks 8 & 10
Steak and Eggs 6
Aliens Street Market
Chaoyang Theatre
CHAOYANGMENWAI DAJIE
HUJIALOU
GUANDONGDIAN JIE
PLA Store
SHENLU JIE
FANGCHAO XI JIE
North Korea
RITAN BEI LU
Ritan Park
LUMICANG HUTONG
CHAOYANGMEN NAN DAJIE
YABAO LU
New Zealand
XIUSHUI DONG JIE
RITAN DONG LU
United Kingdom
Asia Pacific Building
JIANGUOMEN BEI DAJIE
Hanwei Plaza
CCTV Headquarters
GUANGHUA LU
JINTAIXIZHAO
Thailand
Philippines
Japan
Vietnam
DONGZONGBU HUTONG
Bank of China
XIUSHUI BEI JIE
DONGDAQIAO LU
International Post Office
XIUSHUI JIE
JIANHUA LU
Mongolia
Ireland
XIUSHUI NAN JIE
DONGSANHUAN ZHONG LU
International Hotel
Chang'an Theatre
International Club
CITIC Building
Friendship Store
Silk Market
Guiyou Department Store
China World Trade Centre
Shinkong Place
JIANGUOMEN
JIANGUOMENNEI DAJIE
JIANGUOMENWAI DAJIE
Henderson Centre
COFCO Plaza
Ancient Observatory
CVIK Plaza
YONG'AN LI
GUOMAO
BEIJING ZHAN JIE
0
500 m
Train Station

the International Club up Ritan Lu and you'll come to the **Jianguomenwai diplomatic compound**, the first of two embassy complexes (the other is at Sanlitun, well northeast of here). It's an odd place, a giant toy-town with neat buildings in ordered courtyards and frozen sentries on plinths.

Ritan Park (日坛公园, *rìtán gōngyuán*) is just one block north from the International Club, a five-minute walk from Jianguomen Dajie. The park was one of the imperial city's original four, one for each cardinal direction; Tiantan (to the south; see p.63), Ditan (north) and Yuetan (west) were the others. Each park was the location for a yearly sacrificial ritual performed by the emperor but today, Ritan Park is popular with embassy staff and courting couples, who make use of its numerous secluded nooks. It's a very attractive park, with paths winding between groves of cherry trees, rockeries and ponds.

North of the park you enter the city's Russian zone, where all the shop signs are in Cyrillic: to the north, **Shenlu Jie** is full of fur shops aimed squarely at the bottle-blonde Russian moll. The street ends in the giant **Aliens Street Market** (9.30am–6pm; see p.163), a chaotic mall of gaudy trinkets, fakes and questionable fashion, thronging with Russian tourists and traders.

Back on Jianguomenwai Dajie, beyond the CITIC building, you reach the **Friendship Store** (see p.144), which hosts, at the back, the expat favourite *Steak and Eggs* (see p.140) and Tibetan-themed *Makye Ame*. On the south side of the street, the **CVIK Plaza** (daily 9am–9pm) is a more modern shopping centre with five floors of clothes and accessories.

The main reason to continue east beyond here is to head for the **Silk Market**, a giant six-storey mall of fake goods (see p.164) just north of Yong'an Li subway stop. From here, it's a dull couple of kilometres to the new CBD area, marked by the twin towers of the **World Trade Centre** just before the intersection with the Third Ring Road. Dedicated consumers who make it here are rewarded with Beijing's most exclusive **malls**; the one under the World Trade Centre holds a basement ice skating rink. Take a small diversion north of here to catch a glimpse of the strange new CCTV building, designed by Rem Koolhaas. The 230m-high tower, with its gravity-defying loop, is nicknamed "twisted trousers". Part of the huge complex next door, home of the *Mandarin Hotel*, notoriously burnt down on Chinese New Year 2009 thanks to a stray firework.

Chaoyangmenwai Dajie and Sanlitun

North of Jianguomenwai Dajie, the **Dongyue Temple** (东岳庙, *dōngyuè miào*; Tues–Sun 8am–5pm; ¥10), a short walk from Ritan Park or Chaoyangmen subway stop, is an intriguing place, in pointed contrast to all the shrines to materialism outside. Dating back to the Ming dynasty, it's been restored, though it doesn't seem to attract too many devotees – perhaps it's a little too large. Pass under the Zhandaimen archway – originally constructed in 1322 – and you enter a courtyard holding around thirty annexes, each of which deals with a different aspect of Taoist life, the whole making up a sort of surreal spiritual bureaucracy. There's the "Department of Suppressing Schemes", "Department of Wandering Ghosts", even a "Department for Fifteen Kinds of Violent Death". In each, a statue of Taoist deity Lao Zi holds court over brightly painted figures, many with monstrous animal heads, too many limbs and the like. The temple shop sells red tablets for worshippers to sign and leave outside the annexes as petitions to the spiritual officials. Departments dealing with longevity and wealth are unsurprisingly popular, but so, tellingly, is the "Department for Official Morality".

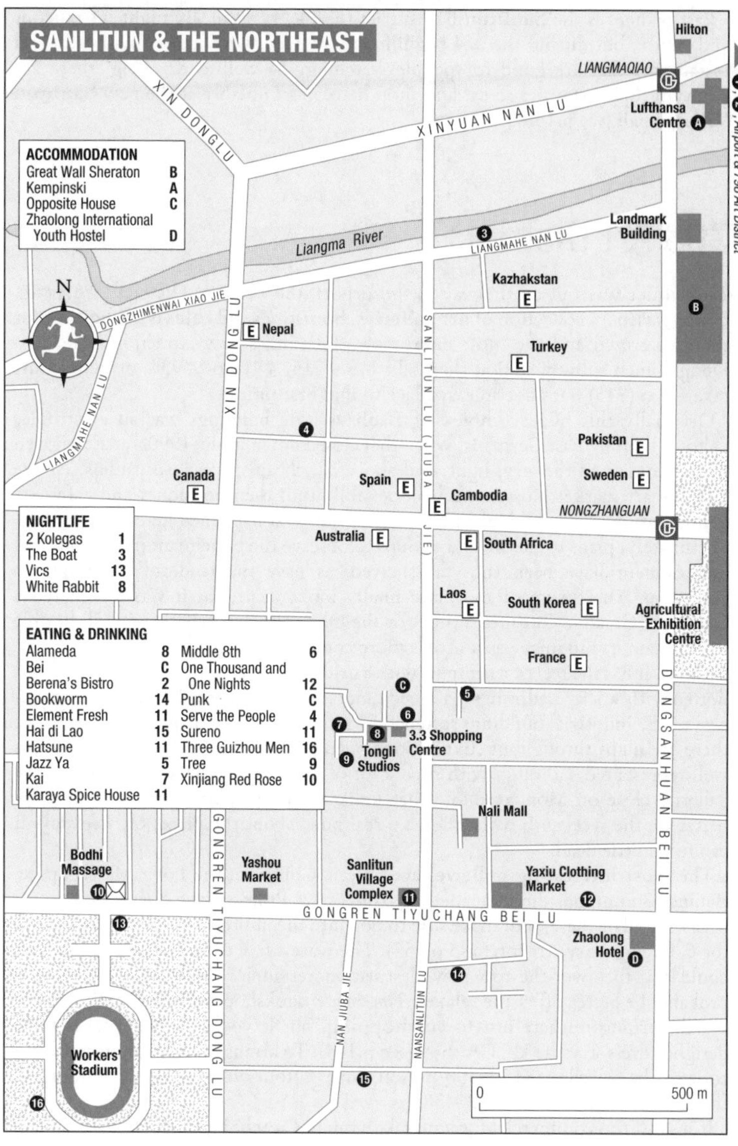

Not far northwest of here is the **Poly Plaza**, at Dongsishitiao subway stop. It's mostly offices, but on the second floor lies a small **museum** (保利博物馆, *bǎolì bówùguǎn*; Mon–Sat 9.30am–4.30pm; ¥50) that has one of the most select collections of antiquities in the capital. In the hall of ancient bronzes you'll find four of the twelve bronze animals that were looted from the Old Summer Palace (see p.99); all were bought in the west by patriotic businessmen, and their return was much heralded. The second hall displays ancient Buddha statues.

East of here is the **Sanlitun** bar district (三里屯, *sānlǐtún*). By night it's raucous and gaudy, but during the day beguilingly civilized, with many small cafés and restaurants that are good for people-watching. As well as drinking, there are plenty of opportunities to eat and shop here, most notably at the new **Sanlitun Village** mall (see p.159).

798 Art District

Though it's way out on the way to the airport, the **798 Art District** (798艺术区, *qījiǔbā yìshùqū*) a collection of **art galleries**, **boutiques** and **cafés** is the hotspot for the arty crowd and the most interesting of Beijing's new attractions. Head to Dongzhimen subway station then take bus #915, #918 or #934, or better, just take a taxi (¥15) – it's not an easy place to find first time.

Originally this huge complex of Bauhaus-style buildings was an electronics factory, built by East Germans; when that closed down in the 1990s, artists moved in and converted the airy, light, and above all, cheap spaces into studios. As the Chinese art market blossomed, galleries followed, then boutiques and cafés – a gentrification that would take fifty years in the West happened here in about five. Fortunately, plans to bus in tour groups to observe the bohemians in their natural environment have been thus far shelved, as have the landlord's attempts to redevelop. The future of the place finally looks secure, as it was designated a Centre of Creative Culture in time for the Olympics, but whether it will be able to maintain its hip image as it grows more commercial is less certain.

Today, it has the feel of a campus, with a grid of pedestrianized, tree-lined streets dotted with wacky sculptures – a caged dinosaur, a forlorn gorilla – and the gnarliness of the industrial buildings softened by artsy graffiti. It's surprisingly large, but there are maps throughout. Exhibitions open every week, and every art form is well represented – though with such a lot of it about, it varies in quality. Many galleries close on Monday. Note that unlike all other Beijing sites, it's actually better on the weekend, when there's a real buzz about the place; on weekdays it can feel a little dead.

The **most interesting galleries** are Galeria Continua, the Long March Space, Beijing Commune, the huge Beijing Tokyo Art Projects, and White Space (see p.157 for all of these); but make sure to pop into the impressive new Ullens Centre for Contemporary Art too (also p.157). There are a few decent places to **eat**; you could try the over-the-top new destination restaurant *Superganbei*, but you'll probably be better off at the relaxed *Timezone 8* bookshop café (see p.137). It's not worth turning up here just to go **shopping**, but if you're in the market for a designer dress, try the UCCA shop (see p.164). To arrange a three-hour **walking tour** of the complex (¥100–300/person) email Ⓔtour798@yahoo.com.cn, or call the mobile number Ⓣ13811224385.

If it's just too commercial for you, take a cab to **Caochangdi** (草场地, *cǎochǎngdì*) a couple of kilometres towards the airport and just off the expressway, near the Fifth Ring Road. This overspill gallery area, away from the tourists and boutiques, is where the hardcore avant-gardeists escaped to when 798 became too mainstream for them – though it's increasingly becoming the place for parties and hype. Many of the spaces here were designed by artsy provocateur Ai Weiwei. See p.157 for more on Caochangdi.

5

North of the centre

The area north of the Forbidden City has a good collection of sights you could happily spend days exploring. Just outside the Forbidden City are **Jingshan** and **Beihai parks**, two of the finest in China; north of here, the area around the Shicha Lakes – **Qianhai** and **Houhai** – is filling up with lakeside bars, restaurants and cafés. Around the lakes you'll find Beijing's last big **hutong** district, once the home of princes, dukes and monks. The alleys are a labyrinth, with something of interest around every corner; some regard them as the final outpost of a genuinely Chinese Beijing. Buried deep within them is **Prince Gong's Palace**, with the **Bell and Drum towers**, once used to mark dawn and dusk, standing on the eastern edge of the district.

A kilometre east of here, the appealing **Nanluogu Xiang**, a pedestrianized alley where the artsy set hang out, is a good place for people-watching over a coffee; the area is also great for accommodation. Another 2km farther, right next to the Yonghe Gong subway stop, the **Yonghe Gong** Tibetan lamasery is one of Beijing's most colourful (and popular) attractions. While you're in the vicinity, don't miss the peaceful, and unjustly ignored, **Confucius Temple** (Kong Miao) and **Ditan Park**, within easy walking distance of one another.

Heading west from the drum tower, you'll find a number of little **museums** – the homes of two twentieth-century cultural icons, **Lu Xun** and **Xu Beihong** now hold exhibitions of their works, while the Baita Temple functions as a museum of religious relics as well as a place of pilgrimage.

In the northwest of the city, around the transport hub of Xizhimen and easy to reach on the subway, are a couple of architectural oddities – the new **Exhibition Centre** and the old **Wuta Temple** – plus the zoo and an enjoyable museum, the **Wanshou Temple**, housed in a grand temple complex.

Jingshan and Beihai parks

A visit to **Jingshan Park** (景山公园, *jǐngshān gōngyuán*; daily 6am–9pm; ¥3) is a natural way to round off a trip to the Forbidden City, which most visitors exit from the north gate, just across the road from the park. Otherwise you can get here on bus #101 from Fuchengmen or Chaoyangmen subway stops. An artificial mound, the park was the byproduct of the digging of the palace moat, and served as both a windbreak and a barrier to keep malevolent spirits (believed to emanate from the north) from entering the imperial quarter of the city. Its history, most momentously, includes the suicide in 1644 of the last Ming emperor, **Chong Zhen**, who hanged himself here from a tree after rebel troops broke into the imperial palace.

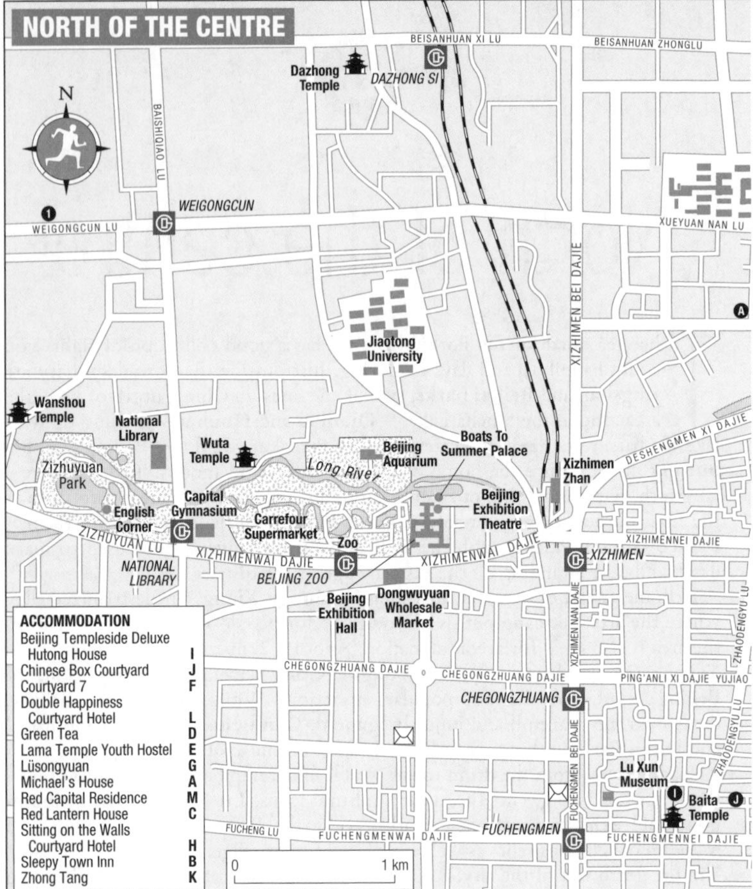

The site, on the eastern side of the park, is easy to find – English-language signs for it appear everywhere (beneath those pointing the way to a children's playground) – but the tree that stands here is not the original. Though he was a dissolute opium fiend, the suicide note pinned to his lapel was surprisingly noble:

> **My own insufficient virtue and wretched nature has caused me to sin against heaven above. I die knowing I am wholly unworthy to stand before my sacred ancestors... let the rebels tear my miserable body to pieces but let them touch not a single hair on the head of the least of my subjects.**

Afterwards, the tree was judged an accessory to the emperor's death and as punishment was manacled with an iron chain.

The **views** from the top of the hill make this park a compelling target: they take in the whole extent of the Forbidden City and a fair swathe of the city outside, a great deal more attractive than seen from ground level. To the west is a lake, Beihai; to the north the Bell and Drum towers; and to the northeast the Yonghe Gong.

Beihai Park

Just a few hundred metres west of Jingshan Park, **Beihai Park** (北海公园, *běihǎi gōngyuán*; daily 6.30am–10pm, park buildings till 4pm; ¥5 for the park, ¥20 for the park and entry to all buildings), most of which is taken up by a lake, is a favourite spot for many locals. Supposedly created by Kublai Khan, long before any of the Forbidden City structures were conceived, the park is of an ambitious scale: the lake was man-made, the island in its midst created with the excavated earth. Qing Emperor Qianlong oversaw its landscaping into a classical Chinese garden in the eighteenth century. Featuring willows and red-columned galleries, it's still a grand place to retreat from the city and recharge. Bus #101 passes Beihai Park's south gate en route between Fuchengmen and Chaoyangmen subway stops, while you can get to the park's north gate on bus #13 from Yonghe Gong subway stop.

Just inside the main gate, which lies on the park's southern side, the **Round**, an enclosure of buildings behind a circular wall, has at its centre a courtyard, where there's a large jade bowl said to have belonged to Kublai Khan. The white-jade Buddha in the hall behind was a present from Burmese Buddhists. From here, a walkway provides access to the island, which is dotted with buildings – including the **Yuegu Lou**, a hall full of steles (stone slabs carved with Chinese characters); and the giant **dagoba** sitting on the crown of the hill, built in the mid-seventeenth century to celebrate a visit by the Dalai Lama. It's a suitable emblem for a park that contains a curious mixture of religious constructions, storehouses for cultural relics and imperial garden furniture. Nestling inside the dagoba is a shrine to the demon-headed, multi-armed Lamaist deity, Yamantaka.

On the north side of the lake stands the impressive **Nine Dragon Screen**, its purpose to ward off evil spirits. An ornate wall of glazed tiles, depicting nine stylized, sinuous dragons in relief, it's one of China's largest, at 27m in length, and remains in good condition. Nearby are the **Five Dragon Pavilions**, supposedly in the shape of a dragon's spine. Even when the park is crowded at the weekend, the gardens and rockeries over the other side of the lake remain tranquil and soothing – it's easy to see why the area was so favoured by Qianlong. It's popular with courting couples today, some of whom like to dress up for photos in period costume – there's a stall outside the Nine Dragon Screen (¥25) – or take boats out on the lake. Piers on either side rent out pedaloes and rowboats for ¥40/¥50 an hour. The park's north exit brings you out at the south end of the Shicha lakes.

Around the Shicha lakes

The area north of Beihai Park is the only district where the city's traditional street plan, a tangle of **hutongs**, has been preserved on any scale. These cluttered, grey alleyways show Beijing's other, private, face: here you'll see poky courtyards and converted palaces, and come across small open spaces where old men sit with caged pet birds. The network of *hutongs* centres on the two artificial **Shicha lakes**, Qianhai and Houhai. Created during the Yuan dynasty, they were once the terminus for a canal network that served the capital. Two giant old buildings, the Bell and Drum towers, are half hidden away to the east of the area.

Much of the district has been recast as a heritage area and is full of restaurants, bars and cafés. All the public toilets have been spruced up and there's even a government-sponsored rickshaw-driver who gives free rides to the nearest convenience to any tourist who's caught short. Still, stray away from the lakeside and the showcasing vanishes quickly.

The best way to get around is by **bike**. Traffic within the *hutongs* is light, and you're free to dive into any alley you fancy, though you're almost certain to get lost – in which case cycle around until you come to a lake. You could walk here from Jishuitian or Gulou subway stop, though the best entry is opposite the northern entrance to Beihai Park – to get here by **bus**, take trolleybus #111 from Dongdan Bei Dajie, or bus #13 from the Yonghe Gong.

Regular **hutong tours** leave from the courtyard between the Bell and Drum towers. More imaginative than most tours (visitors are biked about in rickshaws), they are very popular with tour groups. Private drivers are hard to avoid – they'll pressurize you to go with them. If you do go for this option, be sure to barter; you should pay around ¥60 for an hour, and expect to be taken to a few

Courtyard houses

Beijing's *hutongs* are lined with **siheyuan** (四合院, *sìhéyuàn*), single-storey **courtyard houses** that are home to about a fifth of the city's population. These traditional Chinese dwellings follow a plan that has hardly changed since the Han dynasty, in essence identical to that of the Forbidden City.

A typical courtyard house has its entrance in the south wall. Just outside the front door stand two flat stone blocks – sometimes carved into lions – for mounting horses and to demonstrate the family's wealth and status. Step over the threshold and you are confronted with a freestanding wall; this is to keep out evil spirits, which can only travel in straight lines. Behind it is the outer courtyard, with the servants' quarters to the right and left. The entrance to the inner courtyard, where the family lived, would be in the north wall. The most important rooms, used by the elders, are those at the back, facing south.

With the government anxious to turn Beijing into a showcase for Chinese modernity, however, it seems unlikely that many of these houses will survive, and there are barely 100,000 courtyard houses left, the majority in Qianmen. A wander around the *hutongs* here shows the houses in their worst light; the dwellings are cramped and poorly maintained, the streets dirty, the plumbing and sanitation inadequate; it's only a matter of time before their inhabitants are rehoused in the new suburbs. But in the *hutongs* you'll also see how the system creates a neighbourliness absent from the new high-rises – here, you can't help knowing everyone else's business.

Responding to increasingly vocal complaints about the destruction of Beijing's architectural heritage, city planners point out that *hutongs* full of courtyard houses are unsuitable for contemporary living: besides the difficulty of providing them with proper plumbing, the houses are very cold in winter, and with only one storey they're an inefficient use of land. Anyway, they argue, the population of a modern city ought to live outside the centre. Ironically, the area around the Shicha lakes, where most of the city's other remaining courtyard houses are to be found, has become a fashionable district for high-ranking cadres to live, and some properties here have sold for more than a million dollars. The majority of the houses are in much better condition than in Qianmen, and many are earmarked for protection. A number of new luxury housing estates have been built in courtyard-house style – the best examples are around Deshengmen in the north of the city. They're very popular with foreigners.

shops where the driver gets commission. You'd be better off, however, booking a tour from the booking office on the west side of the Drum Tower; these cost ¥80 an hour. Best of all, take one of the three-hour tours run by the China Culture Club (see p.28).

Qianhai and Houhai

Just north of Beihai Park and across Di'anmen Xi Dajie is the pretty lake, **Qianhai** (前海, *qiánhǎi*). It's an appealing place, removed from the traffic and with an easygoing feel. Having been dredged and cleaned up, the area around it has become a drinking and dining hotspot. Be warned that the lakeside bars and restaurants are over-designed and tacky, and the staff, annoyingly, hector passers by; for the really pleasant places, you'll have to head in from the shore – see p.143 for recommendations.

As you head north along Qianhai, look out for the hardy folk who swim here every day, year-round, cutting a hole in the ice in winter. You can hire pedaloes and row boats from two jetties on the east bank (¥40/¥50 per hour). From the top of the cute humpback **Yinding Bridge** (银锭桥, *yíndìng qiáo*), spanning the lake's

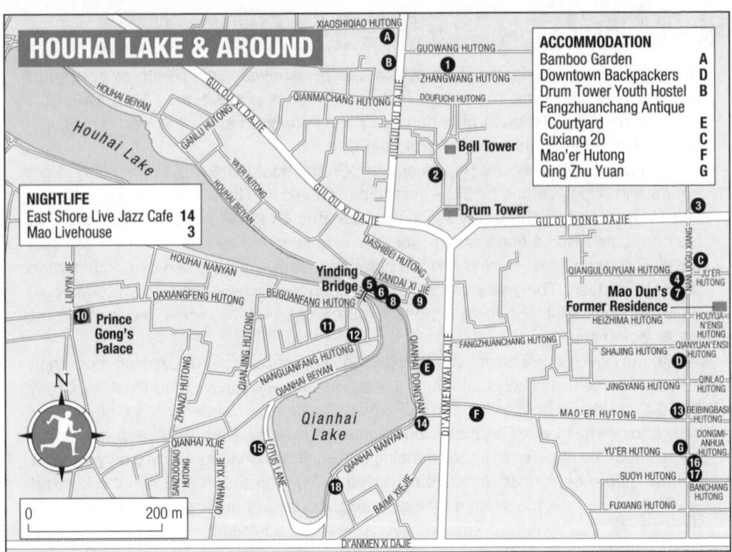

EATING & DRINKING

						Old Character Hakka	18
Bed Bar	1	Fish Nation	7	Kaorouji	5	Pass By Bar	17
Drum and Bell	2	Gong Wang Fu Restaurant	10	No Name Bar	8	Sauveurs de Coree	4
Drum and Gong	16	Hutong Pizza	12	No Name Restaurant	11	Sex and da City	15
East Shore Live Jazz Cafe	14	Huxleys	9	Nuage	6	Xiaoxin's	13

narrowest point and marking the divide between Qianhai and **Houhai** (后海, *hòuhǎi*), you can see the western hills on (very rare) clear days. Here you can sit over a coffee at the *No Name Bar* (see p.147) and enjoy the scenery, something that can't be said for too many public places in Beijing. There's a famous restaurant just by the *No Name*, the *Kaorouji* (see p.143), that's been here for centuries. Turn right, and you're on Yandai Xie Jie (烟袋斜街, *yāndài xiéjiē*), an alley of little jewellery and trinket shops that's one of the best places in Beijing to buy contemporary souvenirs (see p.160).

Prince Gong's Palace and the courtyard museums

Situated on Liuyun Jie, the charming **Prince Gong's Palace** (恭王府, *gōngwáng fǔ*; daily 8.30am–4.30pm; ¥30) was once the residence of Prince Gong, the brother of Emperor Xianfeng and father of the last Qing emperor, Pu Yi. Its nine courtyards, joined by covered walkways, have been restored to something like their former elegance, and the landscaped gardens are attractively leafy. The largest hall now hosts **Beijing opera** performances, at around 11am and 4pm (for tour groups). Just north of the exit lies the excellent *Gong Wang Fu Sichuan Restaurant* (see p.143).

You can get to Prince Gong's palace from Beihai Park by following the curving alley north that starts opposite the park's north entrance – Qianhai will be on the right as you walk along – then taking the first left onto Qianhai Xi Jie. Follow this as it bends round, until you reach an intersection with the music conservatory on your right; here you turn right into Liuyun Jie. There are plenty of other old palaces in the area, for this was once something of an imperial pleasure ground, and home to a number of high officials and distinguished eunuchs. Head north up Liuyin Jie and you pass the former **Palace of Tao Beile**, now a school, after about 200m. It's one of a number of converted buildings in the area, some of which are identified by plaques.

Just behind Prince Gong's Palace you'll find a couple of old courtyard houses-turned-museums, perfect for a *hutong* stroll. The small **Mei Lanfang Museum** (梅兰芳博物馆, *méilánfāng bówùguǎn*; Tues–Sun 9am–4pm; ¥10; Ⓦwww.meilanfang.com) was once the home of the greatest opera singer of the twentieth century, Mei Lanfang, whose tragic life was the basis for Chen Kaige's opulent movie *Farewell My Concubine* (see p.155). There are plenty of pictures of Mei Lanfang famously dressed as a woman, playing female roles. Head back towards the lake and on Qianhai Xi Jie, behind Lotus Lane, you'll find **Guo Morou's Residence** (郭沫若故居, *guōmòruò gǔjū*; Tues–Sun 9am–4.30pm; ¥20). Guo (1892–1978) was a revered writer in his day, though now he's considered a little stuffy. His elegantly furnished and spacious house is worth a peek around – less for the exhibits of dusty books and bric-a-brac than for an insight into how snug courtyard houses could be.

Song Qingling's residence

On the northern shore of Houhai, **Song Qingling's** former **residence** at 46 Houhai Beiyan (宋庆龄故居, *sòngqìnglíng gùjū*; daily 9am–4pm; ¥20) is another Qing mansion, with an agreeable, spacious garden. The wife of Sun Yatsen, who was leader of the short-lived republic that followed the collapse of imperial China (see p.175), Song commands great respect in China, and the exhibition inside details her busy life. It's all pretty dry, but check out the revolver Sun Yatsen – obviously not a great romantic – gave his wife as a wedding gift.

More interesting is the interior, which gives a glimpse of a typical Chinese mansion from the beginning of the twentieth century – all the furnishings are pretty much as they were when she died, and her personal effects, including letters and cutlery, are on display. It's not much of a diversion from here to head west to the Xu Beihong Museum (see below), about 1km from Deshengmennei Dajie.

The Drum and Bell towers

The formidable two-storey **Drum Tower** (鼓楼, *gǔlóu*; daily 9am–5.30pm; ¥20), a squat, fifteenth-century Ming creation, sits at the eastern end of Gulou Xi Dajie, about 1km southeast of the Song Qingling residence. In every city in China, drums like these were banged to mark the hours of the day, and to call imperial officials to meetings. Nowadays, every half-hour between 9.30am and 11.30am and from 1.30pm to 5pm a troupe of drummers in traditional costume whack cheerfully away at the giant drums inside. They're not, to be blunt, terribly artful, but it's still an impressive sight; as is the working replica of an ancient Chinese water clock, a *kelou*.

The building's twin, the **Bell Tower** (钟楼, *zhōnglóu*; same times and prices), at the other end of the small plaza, was originally Ming. Destroyed by fire and rebuilt in the eighteenth century, it still has its original iron bell, which, until 1924, was rung every evening at 7pm to give an indication of the time. It's easy to reach the lakes from the towers: take the first *hutong* you see on the right as you walk south along Di'anmenwai Dajie from the Drum Tower, then turn left for Yinding Bridge.

Xu Beihong Museum

Just outside the quarter of *hutongs*, but easily combined with a visit to the Shicha lakes, the **Xu Beihong Museum** at 53 Xinjiekou Bei Dajie (徐悲鸿纪念馆, *xúbēihóng jìniànguǎn*; Tues–Sun 9–11am & 1.30–4.30pm; ¥5) is 500m south of the Jishuitian subway stop. The son of a wandering portraitist, Xu Beihong (1895–1953) did for Chinese art what his contemporary Lu Xun did for literature – modernize an atrophied tradition. Xu had to look after his entire family from the age of 17 after his father died, and spent much of his early life labouring in semi-destitution and obscurity before receiving the acclaim he deserved. His extraordinary talent is well in evidence here in seven halls, which display a huge collection of his works. These include many ink paintings of horses, for which he was most famous, and Western-style oil paintings, which he produced while studying in France (and that are now regarded as his weakest works); the large-scale allegorical images also on display allude to tumultuous events in modern Chinese history. However, the pictures it's easiest to respond to are his delightful sketches and studies, in ink and pencil, often of his infant son.

Nanluogu Xiang

There aren't, to be frank, too many streets in Beijing that could be called appealing, so the pedestrianized north–south *hutong* of **Nanluogu Xiang** (南锣鼓巷, *nánluó gǔxiàng*) is a little oasis. Dotted with cafés, boutiques and restaurants, it has become a playground for the city's bo-bos (bourgeois-bohemians). Still, in the alleys around there are enough open-air mahjong games, rickety mom-and-pop stores, and old men sitting out with their caged birds to maintain that ramshackle, backstreet Beijing charm. If there seems to be a surfeit of bright and beautiful young things, that's because of the drama school just around the corner. All in all, it's a great place to idle over a cappuccino; *Xiaoxin's* (see p.37) is a recommended café. For a meal, try *Fish Nation* for English grub, *Sauveurs de Coree* for Korean or the *Drum and Gong* for Sichuan (see p.143). At the north end of the street the grungy rock venue *Mao Livehouse* (see p.154) is a good place to sample the live music scene. If you want to stay in the area, head for the *Downtown Backpackers*, or the more upmarket *Lusongyuan* (see p.132).

The only sight in the area is **Mao Dun's Former Residence** (茅盾故居, *máodùn gùjū*; Tues, Thurs & Sat 9am–4pm; ¥5) a charming little courtyard house at 13 Yuanenesi Hutong. Mao Dun was the pen name of Shen Dehong, writer, communist and ex-minister of culture, whose best work is *Midnight*, a tale of cosmopolitan Shanghai. His house today has been preserved since he died in 1981, and is full of manuscripts and knick-knacks, with some elegant period furniture.

Yonghe Gong and around

Though it is a little touristy, **Yonghe Gong** (雍和宫, *yōngghé gōng*; daily 9am–5pm; ¥25) is well worth a visit – you won't see many bolder or brasher temples than this, built towards the end of the seventeenth century to be the residence of Prince Yin Zhen. In 1723, when the prince became Emperor Yong Zheng and moved into the Forbidden City, the temple was re-tiled in imperial yellow and restricted thereafter to religious use. It became a lamasery in 1744, housing monks from Tibet and Inner Mongolia. The temple has supervised the election of the Mongolian Living Buddha (the spiritual head of Mongolian Lamaism), who was chosen by drawing lots out of a gold urn. After the civil war in 1949, Yonghe Gong was declared a national monument and closed for the following thirty years. Remarkably, it escaped the ravages of the Cultural Revolution (see p.176), when most of the city's religious structures were destroyed or turned into factories and warehouses.

The temple couldn't be easier to reach; it's right next to the Yonghe Gong subway stop. There are five main **prayer halls**, arranged in a line from south to north, and numerous side buildings housing Bodhisattva statues and paintings, where monks study scripture, astronomy and medicine. Visitors are free to wander through the prayer halls and pretty, ornamental gardens, the experience largely an aesthetic rather than a spiritual one nowadays. As well as the amazingly intricate mandalas hanging in side halls, the temple contains some notable statuary. The statues in the third hall, the **Pavilion of Eternal Happiness**, are *nandikesvras*, representations of Buddha having sex. Once used to educate emperors' sons, the statues are now completely covered by drapes. The chamber behind, the **Hall of the Wheel of Law**, has a gilded bronze statue of Gelugpa, the founder of the Yellow Hats (the largest sect within Tibetan Buddhism) and paintings that depict his life, while the thrones at its side are for the Dalai Lama (each holder of the post used to come here to teach). In the last, grandest hall, the **Wanfu Pavilion**, stands an 18m-high statue of the Maitreya Buddha, the world's largest carving made from a single piece of wood – in this case, the trunk of a Tibetan sandalwood tree. Gazing serenely out, the giant reddish-orange figure looms over you; details, such as his jewellery and the foliage fringing his shoulders, are beautifully carved. It took three years for the statue, a gift to Emperor Qianlong from the seventh Dalai Lama, to complete its passage to Beijing.

The lamasery also functions as an active Tibetan Buddhist centre. It's used basically for propaganda purposes, to show that China is guaranteeing and

Confucius

Confucius was born in 552 BC into a declining aristocratic family in an age of petty kingdoms where life was blighted by constant war and feuding. An itinerant scholar, he observed that life would be much improved if people behaved decently, and he wandered from court to court teaching adherence to a set of moral and social values designed to bring the citizens and the government together in harmony. Ritual and propriety were the system's central values, and great emphasis was placed on the five "**Confucian virtues**": benevolence, righteousness, propriety, wisdom and trustworthiness. An arch-traditionalist, he believed that society required strict hierarchies and total obedience: a son should obey his father, a wife her husband, and a subject his ruler.

Nobody paid Confucius much attention during his lifetime, and he died in obscurity. But during the Han dynasty, six hundred years later, **Confucianism** became institutionalized, underscoring a hierarchical system of administration that prevailed for the next two thousand years. Seeing that its precepts sat well with a feudal society, rulers turned Confucianism into the state religion, and Confucius became worshipped as a deity. Subsequently, officials were appointed on the basis of their knowledge of the Confucian texts, which they studied for half their lives.

The great sage only fell from official favour in the twentieth century with the rise of the egalitarian communists, and today there are no functioning Confucian temples left in China. Ironically, those temples that have become museums or libraries have returned to a vision of the importance of **learning**, which is perhaps closer to the heart of the Confucian system than ritual and worship.

respecting the religious freedom of minorities. Nonetheless, it's questionable how genuine the state-approved monks you see wandering around are. After all, this was where the Chinese state's choice for Panchen Lama – the Tibetan spiritual leader, second only to the Dalai Lama in rank – was officially sworn in, in 1995. Just prior to that, the Dalai Lama's own choice for the post, the then 6-year-old Gedhum Choekyi Nyima, had "disappeared" – becoming the youngest political prisoner in the world – neither he nor his family have been heard of since.

If the temple leaves you hungry for more things Tibetan, visit the *Makye Ame* restaurant (see p.139) off Jianguomen Dajie.

Kong Miao

On the west side of Yonghegong Dajie, opposite the alley by which you enter Yonghe Gong, is a quiet *hutong* lined with shops selling incense, images and tapes of religious music. Down the alley and on the right, on Guozijian Dajie, the Kong Miao, or **Confucius Temple** (孔庙, *kǒngmiào*; daily 8.30am–5pm; ¥10) is as restrained as the Yonghe Gong is gaudy. One of the best things to do here is sit on a bench in the peaceful courtyard among the ancient, twisted trees, and enjoy the silence, though there's plenty to look at inside, too.

The dark main hall is the **museum**, holding incense burners and musical instruments. Museums in the side halls hold a diverse range of objects, something from every dynasty – the Tang pottery, which includes images of pointy-faced foreigners, is the most diverting.

Ditan Park

Just 100m north of Yonghe Gong is **Ditan Park** (地坛公园, *dìtán gōngyuán*; daily 6am–9pm; ¥2), the northern member in the imperial city's original quartet of four parks (see p.64). As befits the park's name (*dì* means "ground" or "earth"), this was where the emperor once performed sacrifices to the earth god using the huge, tiered stone platform in the park's northwest corner as an altar. A small museum (¥5) next to it holds the emperor's sedan chair – covered, of course, so that no commoner could glimpse the divine presence on his journey here. Wandering among the trees is probably the most diverting way to spend time here; at weekends the place is busy with old folk playing croquet, kids playing fishing games and *tai ji* practitioners hugging trees and the like. The park is at its liveliest during Chinese New Year, when it hosts a temple fair.

The Olympic Park

Good infrastructure means that it doesn't take long to travel a few kilometres north to the site of the 2008 Olympic triumphs; just take the little-used **subway line 5** to the Olympic Park. China used the 2008 Olympics to make an impact on the world stage; facilities built for the occasion were accordingly lavish. The **Olympic Park** (奥林匹克公园, *àolínpǐkè gōngyuán*) was placed on the city's north–south axis, laid down during the Yuan dynasty – so it's bang in line with the Forbidden City. Centrepiece here is the 90,000-seater **National Stadium** (奥林匹克体育馆, *àolínpǐkè tǐyùguǎn*), nicknamed the "Bird's Nest" because of its exterior steel lattice. It was built for nearly half a billion dollars by Heurzog and de Meuron, with input from Ai Weiwei, China's greatest living self-publicist (see p.157). It made a grand stage for such memorable events as the spectacular opening display, Ussain Bolt's amazing runs, and a titanic medal haul for China. Since the Olympics though, it hasn't seen much use, hosting a couple of concerts and football games and a misguided, and mercifully shortlived, winter themepark. A few hundred people visit every day, mostly out-of-towners; you can join them in wandering round the empty shell for an extortionate fee (daily 8am–5pm, ¥50). For ¥120 you can mount the winner's podium and be handed a fake medal.

Just next door, the **National Aquatics Centre** (国家游泳中心, *guójiā yóuyǒng zhōngxīn*) called the Water Cube after its exterior bubble-like membrane, has fared much better, its public pool having become a popular place to swim since the games. At the time of writing it was being redeveloped as a waterpark, and will be open by the time you read this; it should hold several pools, with wave machines, slides, diving and an Olympic sized competition pool, and entry is slated to cost a steep ¥200. A souvenir shop outside sells themed swimwear, jewellery and even perfume.

Around Fuchengmennei Dajie

East of Fuchengmen subway stop, **Fuchengmennei Dajie** (复兴门内大街, *fùxīngménnèi dàjīe*) is rather a pleasant street, lined with trees and equipped with a diverse range of shops, and a few sights all within walking distance of each other. Accessed through an alley off Fuchengmennei Dajie, the massive white dagoba of the **Baita Temple** (白塔寺, *bátǎ sì*; daily 9am–5pm; ¥20) is visible from afar, rising over the rooftops of the labyrinth of *hutongs* that surround it. Shaped like an upturned bowl with an inverted ice cream cone on top, the 35m-high dagoba, designed by a Nepalese architect, was built in the Yuan dynasty. It's a popular spot with Buddhist pilgrims, who ritually circle it clockwise. The temple is worth visiting simply for the collection of thousands of small statues of Buddha – mostly Tibetan – housed in one of its halls, very impressive en masse. Another hall holds bronze *luohans* (Buddha's original group of disciples), including one with a beak; small bronze Buddhas; and other, outlandish Lamaist figures. The silk and velvet priestly garments on display here were unearthed from under the dagoba in 1978. A shop beside it sells religious curios, such as Buddha images printed on dried leaves.

Nearly 1km east along Fuchengmennei Dajie is the **Guangji Temple** (广济寺, *guǎngjì sì*; daily; free), headquarters of China's Buddhist Association and a working Buddhist temple with an important collection of painting and sculpture. Visitors can look around, though only academics with a specialist interest in the art are normally allowed to see the collection.

Lu Xun Museum

Just east of the giant Fuchengmen Bei Dajie intersection, Xisantiao Hutong leads north off Fuchengmennei Dajie to the **Lu Xun Museum** (鲁迅博物馆, *lǔxùn bówùguǎn*; Tues–Sun 9am–4pm; ¥10). A large and extensively renovated courtyard house, this was where Lu Xun (1881–1936), widely accepted as the greatest Chinese writer of the modern era, once lived. He gave up a promising career in medicine to write books, with the aim, so he declared, of curing social ills with his pithy, satirical stories. One of the most appealing and accessible of his tales is *The True Story of Ah Q*, a lively tragicomedy written in the plain style he favoured as an alternative to the complex classical language of the era. Set in 1911, during the inception of the ill-fated republic, it tells the life story of a worthless peasant, Ah Q, who stumbles from disaster to disaster, believing each outcome to be a triumph. He epitomized every character flaw of the Chinese race, as seen by his creator; Ah Q dreams of revolution and ends up being executed, having understood nothing.

As someone who abhorred pomp, Lu Xun might feel a little uneasy in his house nowadays. His possessions have been preserved like treasured relics, giving a good idea of what Chinese interiors looked like at the beginning of the twentieth century, and there's a photo exhibition lauding his achievements. Unfortunately there are no English captions, though a bookshop on the west side of the compound sells English translations of his work.

Xizhimen, the zoo and beyond

The area around **Xizhimen** (西直门, *xīzhímén*) is one of the city's transport hubs, and you're likely to pass through it on your way to the Summer Palaces or Haidian. If you head west from Xizhimen subway stop (buses #107 and #904, among others, pass by en route to Zizhuyuan Park), over the gargantuan traffic intersection, the first place of interest you come to on Xizhimenwai Dajie is the **Beijing Exhibition Hall** (北京展览馆, *běijīng zhǎnlǎn guǎn*), easily distinguishable by its slim, star-topped spire. It's certainly worth inspection, and will stir anyone with a sense of historical irony. Built by the Russians in 1954, it's by far the city's best overtly communist construction, a work of grandiose Socialist Realism with great details, including heroic workers atop columns carved with acorns. Now it's badly maintained – the electric chandeliers are unlit and the escalators flanking the grand staircases lie still – and is used, in thoughtless affront, for the most banal forms of capitalism: the arches of the colonnade outside are hung with billboards and its twelve magnificent, cavernous halls host tacky clothes markets. The road on the east side leads to the dock for boats to the Summer Palace (see p.99). Head up the alley on the west side and you'll come to the city's oldest Western restaurant, the *Moscow* – the food is mediocre, but check out the grand decor if you're passing.

The zoo and the aquarium

Next along Xizhimenwai Dajie, the **zoo** (动物园, *dòngwùyuán*; daily 7.30am–5.30pm; ¥20), is worth visiting for the panda house. Here you can join the queues to have your photo taken sitting astride a plastic replica of the creature, then push your way through to glimpse the living variety – kept in relatively palatial quarters and familiar through the much-publicized export of the animals to overseas zoos for mating purposes. While the pandas lie on their backs in their luxury pad, waving their legs in the air, other animals, less cute or less endangered, slink, pace or flap around their miserable cells. The children's zoo, with plenty of farmyard animals and ponies to pet, is rather better (¥10) and the new **Beijing Aquarium** (adults ¥100, children ¥50, children under 1.2m free; Ⓦwww.bj-sea.com) in the northwest corner of the compound, is surprisingly good. As well as thousands of varieties of fish, including sharks, it has a **dolphin show** every day at 10am and 2.30pm.

Wuta Temple

Beyond the zoo, head north up Baishiqiao Lu, take the first right and follow the canal, and ten minutes' walk will bring you to the **Wuta Temple** (五塔寺, *wǔtǎ sì*;

trying to throw a coin into the small hole in the top. The method of its construction and the history of Chinese bell-making are explained by displays, with English captions, in side halls. The shape of Chinese bells dampens vibrations, so they only sound for a short time and can be effectively used as instruments: you can buy CDs of the bells in action.

Haidian

It's not an obvious tourist attraction – the only foreigners you're likely to see here are students, and the area looks much like other parts of the city – but the **Haidian district** (海淀, *hǎidiàn*) northwest of the Third Ring Road has a distinctive, laid-back atmosphere, courtesy of the local universities and the students, artists and intellectuals who have taken advantage of the area's low rents. You'll find plenty of internet cafés, and, in the **Zhongguancun** area (中关村, *zhōngguāncūn*), a hi-tech zone of **computer shops** (see p.165). You can get here using Wudaokou or Zhongguancun subway stops, on bus #320 from Xi Zhan, or bus #332 from the zoo.

In the north of the area, on the way to the Summer Palace, you'll pass **Beijing Daxue** (北京大学, *běijīng dàxúe*). Beida, as it's referred to colloquially, is the most prestigious **university** in China, with a pleasant campus – the old buildings and quiet, well-maintained grounds make it nicer than most of the city's parks. Bring your passport if you want to poke around, as you may be required to fill out a visitor's form by the guard at the gate. Originally established and administered by Americans at the beginning of the twentieth century, the university stood on the hill in Jingshan Park before moving to its present site in 1953. Now busy with new contingents of students from the West, it was half-deserted during the Cultural Revolution (see p.176), when students and teachers alike, regarded as suspiciously liberal, were dispersed for "re-education". Later, in 1975–76, Beida was the power base of the radical left in their campaign against Deng Xiaoping, the pragmatist who was in control of the day-to-day running of the Communist Party's Central Committee during Mao's twilight years. The university's intake suffered when new students were required to spend a year learning Party dogma after 1989; now it's once again a centre for challenging political thought. The **lake** is a popular place to skate in the winter – you can rent skates for ¥10 an hour.

Just inside the university west gate you'll find the diverting Arthur M. Sackler **Museum of Art and Anthropology** (赛克勒考古与艺术博物馆, *sàikèlè kǎogǔyúyìshù bówùguǎn*; daily 9.30am–4pm; ¥20; Ⓦwww.sackler.org/china/amschina.htm). Used as a teaching museum, it holds a well-presented permanent collection of ceramics and tools from prehistory to the present, with English captions throughout; check the website for details of frequent temporary exhibitions.

You can meet China's new **intellectuals** by hanging out in the bars clustered around the university's gates. The **Wudaokou** district nearby is regarded as the home of Beijing's alternative culture; it's a good place to catch the local rock bands, for example. See "Entertainment and art", p.149, for more on Haidian.

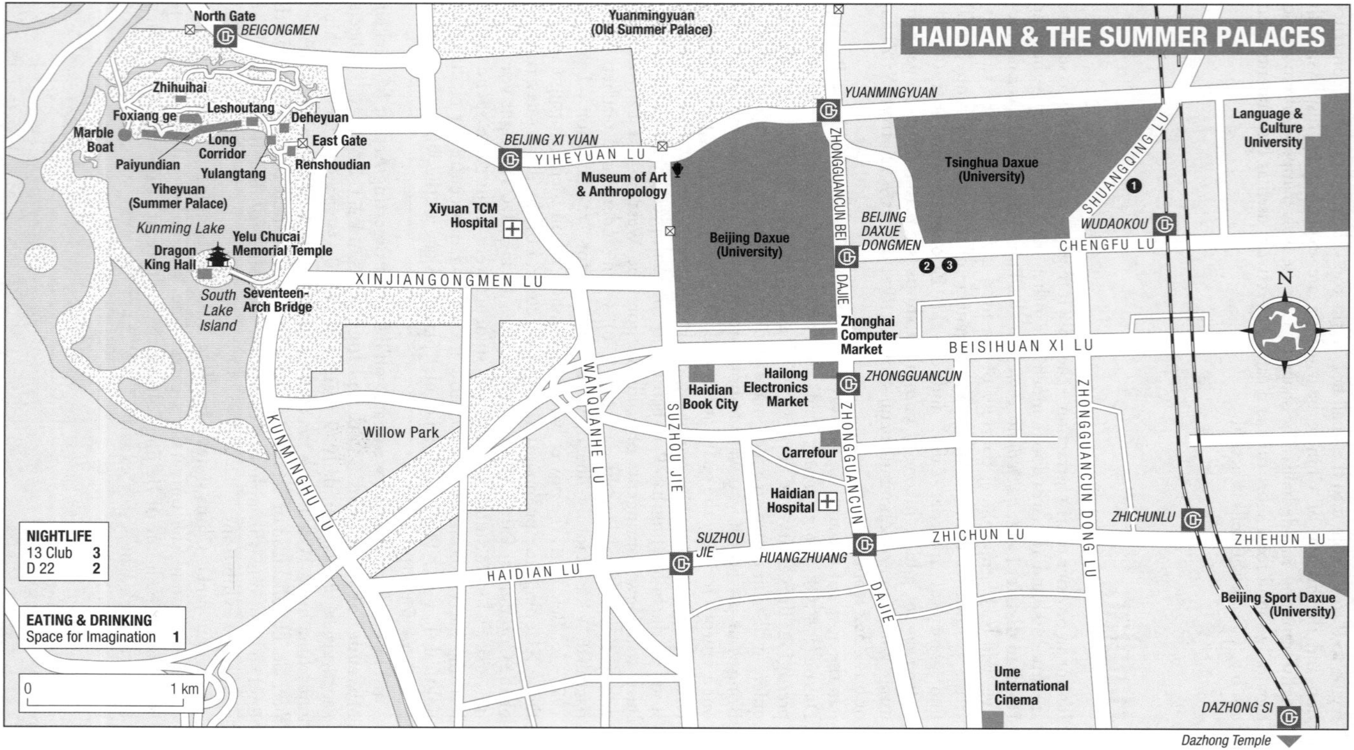

HAIDIAN & THE SUMMER PALACES

North Gate
BEIGONGMEN
Yuanmingyuan
(Old Summer Palace)
Zhihuihai
Foxiang ge
Leshoutang
Deheyuan
Marble Boat
Long Corridor
East Gate
Paiyundian
Yulangtang
Renshoudian
Yiheyuan
(Summer Palace)
Kunming Lake
Dragon King Hall
Yelu Chucai Memorial Temple
South Lake Island
Seventeen-Arch Bridge
BEIJING XI YUAN
YIHEYUAN LU
Museum of Art & Anthropology
Xiyuan TCM Hospital
XINJIANGONGMEN LU
Willow Park
KUNMINGHU LU
WANQUANHE LU
SUZHOU JIE
HAIDIAN LU
Beijing Daxue (University)
Haidian Book City
Hailong Electronics Market
Carrefour
Haidian Hospital
SUZHOU JIE
HUANGZHUANG
YUANMINGYUAN
ZHONGGUANCUN BEI DAJIE
BEIJING DAXUE DONGMEN
Zhonghai Computer Market
ZHONGGUANCUN
ZHONGGUANCUN DAJIE
Tsinghua Daxue (University)
SHUANGQING LU
WUDAOKOU
CHENGFU LU
BEISIHUAN XI LU
ZHONGGUANCUN DONG LU
ZHICHUN LU
ZHICHUNLU
ZHIEHUN LU
Language & Culture University
Beijing Sport Daxue (University)
Ume International Cinema
DAZHONG SI
Dazhong Temple
N

NIGHTLIFE
13 Club 3
D 22 2

EATING & DRINKING
Space for Imagination 1

0 1 km

Yuanmingyuan

Beijing's original summer palace, the **Yuanmingyuan** (圆明园, *yuánmíng yuán*; daily 9am–6pm; ¥15; Yuanmingyuan subway stop) was built by the Qing Emperor Kangxi in the early eighteenth century. Once nicknamed China's Versailles for its elegant, European-influenced design, the palace boasted the largest royal gardens in the world, containing some two hundred pavilions and temples set around a series of lakes and natural springs. Today there is precious little left; in 1860, the entire complex was burnt and destroyed by British and French troops, who were ordered by the Earl of Elgin to make the imperial court "see reason" during the Opium Wars (see p.174). The troops had previously spent twelve days looting the imperial treasures, many of which found their way to the Louvre and British Museum. This unedifying history is described in inflammatory terms on signs all over the park and it's a favoured site for brooding nationalists. Still, don't let that put you off, as the overgrown ruins are rather appealing and unusual.

There are actually three parks here, the Yuanmingyuan (Park of Perfection and Brightness), Wanchunyuan (Park of Ten Thousand Springs; ¥10) and Changchunyuan (Park of Everlasting Spring; ¥10), all centred around the lake, Fuhai (Sea of Happiness). The best-preserved structures are the fountain and the **Hall of Tranquillity** in the northeastern section. The stone and marble fragments hint at how fascinating the original must once have been, with its marriage of European Rococo decoration and Chinese motifs.

Yiheyuan (Summer Palace)

There have been imperial summer pavilions at **Yiheyuan** (颐和园, *yíhé yuán*; daily 8am–7pm, buildings close at 4pm; ¥40, plus additional charges of ¥5–10 to enter some buildings) since the eleventh century, although the present park layout is essentially eighteenth-century, created by the Manchu Emperor Qianlong. However, the key character associated with the palace is the **Dowager Empress Cixi** (see p.100), who ruled over the fast-disintegrating Chinese empire from 1861 until her death in 1908. Yiheyuan was very much her pleasure ground; it was she who built the palaces here in 1888 after Yuanmingyuan was destroyed, and determinedly restored them after another bout of European aggression in 1900.

The palace buildings, many connected by a suitably majestic gallery, are built on and around **Wanshou Shan** (Longevity Hill), north of the lake and west of the main gate. Many of these edifices are intimately linked with Cixi – anecdotes about whom are the stock output of the numerous tour guides – but to enjoy the site, you need know very little of its history: like Beihai (see p.85), the park, its lake and pavilions form a startling visual array, akin to a traditional Chinese landscape painting brought to life.

The fastest route to Yiheyuan is to take the subway to Yiheyuan stop. There's also a **boat service** (daily 10am–4pm, leaving on the hour; 1hr; ¥40 one-way, ¥70 return) to Yiheyuan, taking the old imperial approach along the now dredged and prettified Long River; the trip embarks from a new dock at the back of the Exhibition Hall (see p.94). Your vessel is either one of the large, dragon-shaped cruisers or a smaller speedboat holding four people, passing the Wuta Si, Zizhuyuan Park, and a number of attractive bridges and willow groves en route.

The Dowager Empress Cixi

The notorious Cixi entered the imperial palace at 15 as the **Emperor Xianfeng's concubine**, quickly becoming his favourite and bearing him a son. When the emperor died in 1861 she became regent, ruling in place of her infant boy. For the next 35 years she, in effect, ruled China, displaying a mastery of intrigue and court politics. When her son died of syphilis, she installed another puppet infant, her nephew, and retained her authority. Her fondness for extravagant gestures (every year she had ten thousand caged birds released on her birthday) drained the state's coffers, and her deeply conservative policies were inappropriate for a time when the nation was calling for reform.

With foreign powers taking great chunks out of China's borders on and off during the nineteenth century, Cixi was moved to respond in a typically misguided fashion. Impressed by the claims of the xenophobic **Boxer Movement** (whose Chinese title translated as "Righteous and Harmonious Fists") that their members were invulnerable to bullets, in 1899 Cixi let them loose on all the foreigners in China. The Boxers laid siege to the foreign legation's compound in Beijing for nearly two months before a European expeditionary force arrived and, predictably, slaughtered the agitators. Cixi and her nephew, the emperor, only escaped the subsequent rout of the capital by disguising themselves as peasants and fleeing the city. On her return, Cixi clung on to power, attempting to delay the inevitable fall of the dynasty. One of her last acts, the day before she died in 1908, was to oversee the murder of her puppet emperor.

The palace compound

The East Gate, by which most visitors enter, and where buses stop, is overlooked by the main palace compound. A path leads from the gate, past several halls (all signposted in English), to the lakeside. The strange bronze animal in the first courtyard is a *xuanni* or *kylin*, with the head of a dragon, deer antlers, a lion's tail and ox hooves. It was said to be able to detect disloyal subjects. The building behind is the **Renshoudian** (Hall of Benevolence and Longevity), a majestic, multi-eaved hall where the empress and her predecessors gave audience; it retains much of its original nineteenth-century furniture, including an imposing red sandalwood throne carved with nine dragons and flanked by peacock feather fans. The inscription on the tablet above reads "Benevolence in rule leads to long life". Look out, too, for the superbly well-made basket of flowers studded with precious stones.

A little way further along the main path, to the right, the **Deheyuan** (Palace of Virtue and Harmony) is dominated by a three-storey theatre, complete with trap doors in the stage for surprise appearances and disappearances by the actors. Theatre was one of Cixi's main passions – she even took part in performances sometimes, playing the role of Guanyin, the goddess of mercy. Today some of the halls function as a museum of theatre, with displays of costumes, props and waxworks of Cixi and attendants. The most unusual exhibit is a vintage Mercedes-Benz, a gift to the warlord Yuan Shikai (see p.64) in the early twentieth century and the first car to appear in China.

The next major building along the path is the lakeside **Yulangtang** (Jade Waves Palace). This is where the Emperor Guangxu, then still a minor, was kept in captivity for ten years while Cixi exercised his powers. A pair of decorative rocks in the front courtyard, supposed to resemble a mother and her son, were put there by Cixi to chastise Guangxu for insufficient filiality. The main hall contains a tablet of Cixi's calligraphy reading "The magnificent palace inspires everlasting moral integrity". One character has a stroke missing; apparently no one dared tell her.

North of here, behind Renshoudian, are Cixi's private quarters, three large courtyards connected by a winding gallery. The largest, the **Leshoutang** (Hall of Joy and Longevity), houses Cixi's hardwood throne. The large table in the centre of the main hall was where she took her infamous meals of 128 courses. The chandeliers were China's first electric lights, installed in 1903 and powered by the palace's own generator.

The north shore of Kunming Lake

From Leshoutang, the **Long Corridor** runs to the northwest **corner** of **Kunming Lake**. Flanked by various temples and pavilions, the corridor is actually a 700m covered way, its inside walls painted with more than eight thousand restored images of birds, flowers, landscapes and scenes from history and mythology. Near the west end of the corridor is Cixi's ultimate flight of fancy, a magnificent lakeside pavilion in the form of a 36m-long **marble boat**, boasting two decks. Completed by Cixi using funds intended for the Chinese navy, it was regarded by her acolytes as a characteristically witty and defiant snub to her detractors. Her misappropriations helped speed the empire's decline, with China suffering heavy naval defeats during the 1895 war with Japan. Close to the marble boat is a jetty – the tourist focus of this part of the site – with rowing boats for hire (see box below).

Wanshou Shan

About halfway down the Long Corridor you'll see an archway and a path that leads uphill away from the lake. Head up the path and through two gates to the **Paiyundian** (Cloud Dispelling Hall), which was used by Cixi as a venue for her infamously extravagant birthday parties. The elegant objects on display here are twentieth-birthday presents to her from high officials (the rather flattering oil painting of her was a present from the American artist Hubert Vos). The largest building here, near the top of the hill, is the **Foxiang ge** (Tower of Buddhist Incense), a charming three-storey octagonal pagoda built in 1750. It commands a panoramic view of the whole park and, deservedly, the area around it is a popular picnic spot.

The **Zhihuihai** (Sea of Wisdom Hall), on top of the hill, is strikingly different in style from the other buildings: there's not a single beam or column, and it's tiled in green and yellow ceramic tiles and dotted with niches holding Buddha statues. At the foot of the hill on the far (north) side lies a souvenir market and the little-visited but very attractive back lake. Walk along the side of this lake for half a kilometre and you arrive at the **Garden of Harmonious Interests**, a pretty collection of lotus-filled ponds and pavilions connected by bridges. Cixi used to fish from the large central pavilion; to keep her sweet, eunuchs dived in and attached fish to her hook. The bridge up to the pavilion is called "Know the Fish

Boating and skating on Kunming Lake

Boating on Kunming Lake is a popular pursuit and well worth the money (boats can be hired at any of the jetties for ¥40/hr). In addition to the jetty by the marble boat, you can dock over below Longevity Hill, on the north side of the lake by the gallery. You can row out to the two bridges spanning narrow stretches of water – the gracefully bowed Jade Belt on the western side and the long, elegant seventeen-arch bridge on the east. In winter, the Chinese **skate** on the lake here – a spectacular sight, as some of the participants are really proficient. Skates are available for rent at the main entrance (¥10/hr).

Bridge" after an argument that took place here between two Ming dynasty philosophers: one declared that the fish he could see were happy; the other snorted, "How could you know? You're not a fish", whereupon the first countered, "You're not me, so how do you know I don't know?"

The south of the park

It's a pleasant fifteen-minute walk to the southern part of Kunming Lake, where the scenery is wilder and the crowds thinner. Should you need a destination, the main attraction to head for is the white **Seventeen-Arch Bridge**, 150m long and topped with 544 cute, vaguely canine lions, each with a slightly different posture. The bridge leads to **South Lake Island**, where Qianlong used to review his navy, and which holds a brace of fine halls, most striking of which is the **Yelu Chucai Memorial Temple**. Yelu, an adviser to Genghis Khan during the Yuan dynasty, is entombed next to the temple, in the company of his wives and concubines, slaughtered for the occasion. The small, colourful **Dragon King Hall** nearby was used to pray for rain.

7

Around Beijing

Some great destinations, offering both countryside and culture, lie within a few hours of the capital. Most compelling is the **Great Wall**, whose remains, either crumbling or spruced up, can be seen in a number of places in the hills a few hours north and east of the city. The hilly, wooded landscape to the **west of Beijing**, called the **Western Hills**, is the most attractive countryside in the city's vicinity, and easily accessible from the centre. The **Botanical Gardens**, **Xiangshan Park** and **Badachu** – the last of these a collection of eight temples – make for an excellent day retreat; a little further out, the striking **Fahai**, **Tanzhe** and **Jietai temples** stand in superb rural isolation. All are at their quietest and best on weekdays.

Though less scenic than the Western Hills, the area **north of the city** contains a couple of sights of particular natural beauty, as well as the vast **Aviation Museum** and the much-visited **Ming Tombs**. Unfortunately though, these places are so spread out that it's impractical to visit more than one in a day. The town of **Chengde** is within easy travelling distance, and boasts some of the finest imperial architecture in the country. There are fewer places of interest south of the city, but the wilderness valley of **Shidu** is worth exploring.

Much of the area covered in this chapter is shown on the "Beijing & around" colour map at the end of this book.

The Great Wall

This is a Great Wall and only a great people with a great past could have a great wall and such a great people with such a great wall will surely have a great future.

Richard M. Nixon

The practice of building walls along China's northern frontier began in the fifth century BC and continued until the sixteenth century. Over time, the discontinuous array of fortifications and ramparts came to be known as **Wan Li Changcheng** (literally, "Long Wall of Ten Thousand Li" – *li* being a Chinese measure of distance roughly equal to 500m), or, more pithily, the **Great Wall** (长城, *chángchéng*). Stretching from Shanhaiguan, where the wall meets the sea, to Jiayuguan Pass in the Gobi Desert, it's an astonishing civil engineering project.

Even the most-visited section at **Badaling**, constantly overrun by Chinese and foreign tourists, is still easily one of China's most spectacular sights. The section at **Mutianyu** is somewhat less crowded; distant **Simatai** much less so, and far more beautiful. To see the wall in its crumbly glory, head out to **Jingshanling, Jiankou** or **Huanghua**, as yet largely untouched by development. For other trips to unreconstructed sections, check out ⓦwww.wildwall.com or contact China Culture Club (see p.28).

Some history

Since the earliest times, the Chinese walled their cities and, during the Warring States period (around the fifth century BC), simply extended the concept by using walls to separate rival territories. The **Great Wall's origins** lie in these fractured lines of fortifications and in the vision of the first Emperor Qin Shi Huang, who, having unified the empire in the third century BC, joined and extended the sections to form one fairly continuous defence against barbarians. Under subsequent dynasties, whenever insularity rather than engagement drove foreign policy, the wall continued to be maintained and, in response to shifting regional threats, grew and changed course. It lost importance under the Tang, when borders were extended north, well beyond it. The Tang was in any case an outward-looking dynasty that kept the barbarians in check far more cheaply, by fostering trade and internal divisions. With the emergence of the insular Ming, however, the wall's upkeep again became a priority, and from the fourteenth to the sixteenth century, military technicians worked on its reconstruction.

The 7m-high, 7m-thick wall, with its 25,000 battlements, served to bolster Ming sovereignty, as it restricted the movement of the nomadic peoples of the distant, non-Han minority regions, preventing plundering raids. Signals made by gunpowder blasts, flags and smoke swiftly sent news of enemy movements to the capital: in the late sixteenth century, a couple of huge Mongol invasions were repelled, at Jinshanling and Badaling.

But a wall is only as strong as its guards, and by the seventeenth century the Ming royal house was corrupt and its armies weak; the wall was little hindrance to the invading Manchus, who, after they had established their own dynasty (the Qing), let the wall fall into disrepair. Slowly it crumbled away, useful only as a source of building material – recent demolitions of old *hutongs* in Beijing have turned up bricks from the wall, marked with the imperial seal.

Country retreats around Beijing

For the ultimate in **luxury breaks**, visit **Commune** (ⓣ010/81181888, ⓦwww.communebythegreatwall.com; ¥1830), a "lifestyle retreat" at Shuiguan, at the base of the Great Wall and just east off the Badaling Expressway. Each of the eleven striking buildings was designed by a different architect (the complex won an architectural award at the 2002 Venice Biennale) and is run as a small boutique hotel. If you can't afford their rates – it's expensive – you can take a tour of the complex for ¥120, or pop in for lunch (around ¥400).

The **Goose and Duck Ranch** (ⓣ010/65381691, ⓦwww.gdclub.net.cn), in Qiaozi near Hauirou, and run by the bar of the same name, is rather more sensibly priced, with cabins starting at ¥300 and rising to over ¥900. It's a chirpy family holiday camp, with plenty of outdoor purusits on offer, including archery, go-karting and horseback riding. Their all-inclusive weekend getaways (¥500 per person per day) are popular and convenient – turn up at the bar and they'll look after you from there. You'll have to book three days in advance.

For something much more restful, stay at the **Red Capital Ranch** (ⓣ010/84018886, ⓦwww.redcapitalclub.com.cn/ranch; ¥1860), run by the Red Capital Club (see p.143). It's an idyllic boutique eco-lodge set in attractive countryside, a short walk from the Great Wall and two hours north of the city. Each of the ten traditional courtyard buildings was constructed from local materials.

Today, this great monument to state paranoia is big business – the restored sections are besieged daily by rampaging hordes of tourists – and is touted by the government as a source of national pride. Its image adorns all manner of products, from wine to cigarettes, and is even used – surely rather inappropriately – on visa stickers.

Badaling and Juyong Pass

The best-known section of the wall is at **Badaling** (八达岭, *bādá lǐng*), 70km northwest of Beijing (daily 8am–4.30pm; ¥45). It was the first section to be restored (in 1957) and opened up to tourists. Here the wall is 6m wide, with regularly spaced watchtowers dating from the Ming dynasty. It follows the highest contours of a steep range of hills, forming a formidable defence, such that this section was never attacked directly but instead taken by sweeping around from the side after a breach was made in the weaker, low-lying sections.

Badaling may be the easiest part of the wall to get to from Beijing, but it's also the most packaged. At the entrance, a giant tourist circus – a plethora of restaurants and souvenir stalls – greets you. As you ascend to the wall, you pass a train museum (¥5), a cable car (¥30) and the **Great Wall Museum** (included in the main ticket). The wall museum, with plenty of aerial photos, models and construction tools, is worth a browse, though it's more useful visited on the way down.

Once you're up on the wall, flanked by guardrails, it's hard to feel that there's anything genuine about the experience. Indeed, the wall itself is hardly original here, as the "restorers" basically rebuilt it wholesale on the ancient foundations. To get the best out of this part of the wall you need to walk – you'll quickly lose the crowds and, generally, things get better the further you go. You come to unreconstructed sections after heading 1km north (left) or 2km south (right). That's as far as you are allowed to go; guards posted here will turn you back.

Practicalities

As well as CITS (see p.25), all the more expensive Beijing hotels (and a few of the cheaper ones) run **tours** to Badaling, usually with a trip to the Ming Tombs thrown in. If you come with a tour you'll arrive in the early afternoon, when the place is at its busiest, spend an hour or two at the wall, then return, which really gives you little time for anything except the most cursory of jaunts and the purchase of an "I climbed the Great Wall" T-shirt. It's just as easy, and cheaper, to travel under your own steam. The easiest way to get here is on **bus** #919 from Deshengmen (a 2min walk east from Jishuitan subway stop) – there's an ordinary service (2hr; ¥7) and a much quicker air-conditioned luxury bus (1hr; ¥12). Note that private minibuses also call themselves #919 and that you might get scalped on these; the real buses are larger and have "Deshengmen–Badaling" written in the window.

Or there are plenty of **tourist buses** (outward journeys daily 6–10am; every 20min; ¥110–130 for a return ticket): route #1 leaves from Qianmen, route #2 from the train station, #4 from outside the zoo. The journey to Badaling on one of these takes about ninety minutes, and the buses visit the Ming Tombs (see p.112) on the way back. Returning to Beijing shouldn't be a problem, as tourist buses run until about 6pm.

Juyong Pass

The closest section to Beijing, the wall at **Juyong Pass** (居庸关, *jūyōng guān*; daily 8am–5pm; ¥45), only fifteen minutes' bus ride south of the Badaling section, has been rather over-restored by enthusiastic builders. That said, it's not too popular (and thus not crowded), and is easily reached on the ordinary bus #919 (not the luxury version) from Deshengmen bus station, or on tourist bus #1 from

Qianmen. Strategically, this was an important stretch, guarding the way to the capital, just 50km away. From the two-storey gate, the wall climbs steeply in both directions, passing through modern copies of the mostly Ming fortifications. The most interesting structure, and one of the few genuinely old ones, is the intricately carved stone base of a long-vanished stupa just beyond here. Access to unreconstructed sections is blocked, but you can walk for about an hour in either direction.

Mutianyu

A 2km-long section, the **Mutianyu Great Wall**, 90km northeast of the city (慕田峪, *mùtiányù*; daily 8am–5pm; ¥40), is more appealing to most foreign visitors than Badaling, as it has rather fewer tourist trappings. Passing along a ridge through some lush, undulating hills, this part of the wall is well endowed with guard towers, built in 1368 and renovated in 1983.

From the entrance, steep steps lead up to the wall; you can get a cable car up (¥35) though it's not far to walk. The stretch of wall you can walk here is about 3km long (barriers in both directions stop you continuing any further).

To get here, take **bus #916** from Dongzhimen and get off at Mingzhu Square in Huairou, where you can catch a minibus to the wall (¥20 or so), or take bus #936 from Dongzhimen (hourly 7am–3pm; 2hr; there are a few different routes for this bus, so confirm with the driver that yours goes to Mutianyu Great Wall).

You could also get tourist bus #6 (mid-April to mid-Oct, outward journeys daily 6.30am–8am; ¥45) from the #42 bus station, just south of Dongsi Shitiao subway stop; they'll wait around at the site for an hour or two before heading back to Beijing. Returning by other means shouldn't be a hassle, provided you do so before 6pm; plenty of minibuses wait in the car park to take people back to the city. If you can't find a minibus back to Beijing, get one to the town of **Huairou** (怀柔, *huáiróu*), from where you can get regular bus #916 back to the capital – the last bus leaves at 6.30pm.

Simatai

Peaceful and semi-ruined, **Simatai** (司马台, *sīmătái*; daily 8am–4pm; ¥40), 110km northeast of the city, is the most unspoilt section of the Great Wall around Beijing. The wall snakes across purple hills resembling crumpled velvet from afar, and blue mountains in the distance, fulfilling the expectations of most visitors more than the other sections – though it does get a little crowded at weekends. Most of this section is unrenovated, dating back to the Ming dynasty, and sports a few late innovations, such as slits for cannons, as well as inner walls at right angles to the outer wall to thwart invaders who breached the first defence.

At the time of writing though, the whole area was closed for a two-year renovation, and there are reports of civil unrest in the area, with farmers warring with the local government over land requisitions (such battles are increasingly common across rural China). It is due to re-open in 2012, and will no doubt have been spruced up considerably.

At all the less visited places, each tourist, or group of tourists, will be followed along the wall, for at least an hour, by a villager selling drinks and postcards; if you don't want to be pestered make it very clear from the outset that you are not interested in anything they are selling – though after a few kilometres you might find that ¥5 can of Coke very welcome.

Turning left when you first reach the wall, you can do the popular hike to Jinshanling in three hours (see below). Most people though, do the walk in the other direction, as it's more convenient to finish up in Simatai.

Practicalities

The journey out from the capital to Simatai takes about three hours by private transport. **Tours** run from the backpacker hotels and hostels for around ¥150, generally once or twice a week in low season or daily in the summer, and sometimes offer overnight stays. Most other hotels can arrange transport, too (usually a minibus), though you should expect to pay a little more for these.

You can travel here independently, but considering the logistical hassles and expense, this is only worth doing if you want to stay for a night or two. To get here under your own steam, catch a direct Simatai bus from Dongzhimen bus station (buses leave 7–9am; ¥40) or take bus #980, #970 or #987 to **Miyun** (密云县, *mìyún xiàn*; ¥10) and negotiate for a minibus or taxi to take you the rest of the way (you shouldn't have to pay more than ¥100). Between mid-April and mid-October tourist bus #12 heads to Simatai (6am–8am; ¥95 including entrance ticket) from the #42 bus station south of Dongsi Shitiao subway stop, and from opposite Xuanwumen subway stop; buses return between 4pm and 6pm. A rented **taxi** will cost about ¥500 return, including a wait.

To get from Simatai back to Beijing, you can either take a taxi from Simatai to Miyun (¥70 or so, after some negotiaton), from where the last public bus back to Beijing is at 4pm, or wait at the Simatiai car park for a tourist bus; they start to head back to the city at 4pm.

The *Simatai Youth Hostel* (Ⓣ010/69035311), by the entrance, has rooms (¥160) and hard beds in an eight-bed **dorm** (¥70); there's hot water for two hours a day. You'll get rather better value if you head off with one of the locals who hang around the car park; they will charge ¥70 or so for a spare room in their house, though facilities will be simple, with only cold water on tap; ask, and your host will bring a bucket of hot water to the bathroom for you. As for **eating**, avoid the youth hostel's overpriced restaurant and head to one of the nameless places at the side of the car park, where the owners can whip up some very creditable dishes; if you're lucky, they'll have some locally caught wild game in stock.

Jinshanling

Jinshanling (金山岭长城, *jīnshānlǐng chángchéng*; ¥50), 10km west of Simatai, is one of the least visited and best preserved parts of the wall, with jutting obstacle walls and oval watchtowers, some with octagonal or sloping roofs. It's not easy to reach without your own transport, but there are plenty of tours out here from the hostels (¥180); they'll drop you off in the morning and pick you up at Simatai in the afternoon. Otherwise, a taxi from Miyun (see above for routes) will cost around ¥100. Or take a bus to Chengde from Liuliqiao Long Distance Bus Station (buses leave hourly between 8am and 6pm) and get off at the Jinshanling intersection; minibuses run from there to the wall for ¥10–15 or so.

Turn left when you hit the wall and it's a three-hour walk to Simatai along an unreconstructed section. You won't meet many other tourists, and will experience something of the wall's magnitude; a long and lonely road that unfailingly picks the toughest line between peaks. Take the hike seriously, as you are scrambling up and down steep, crumbly inclines, and you need to be sure of foot. Watch, too, for loose rocks dislodged by your companions. When you reach Simatai there's a ¥30 toll at the suspension bridge. Note that this walk is still possible while Simatai is being renovated – you just can't go any further after the bridge.

Finally, if you head right when you get onto the wall at Jinshanling, you quickly reach an utterly abandoned and overgrown section. After about four hours walk along here, you'll reach a road that cuts through the wall, and from here you can flag down a passing bus back to Beijing. This route is only recommended for the intrepid.

Huanghua

The section of the wall at **Huanghua** (黄花长城, *huánghuā chángchéng*; ¥25), 60km north of Beijing, is completely unreconstructed. It's a telling example of Ming defences, complete with wide ramparts, intact parapets and beacon towers. You can hike along the wall for as long as you like, though some sections are a bit of a scramble. It's not too hard to get here: backpacker hotels have started offering **tours**, or you can take **bus** #916 from Dongzhimen bus station to Huairou (¥11), and catch a minibus taxi from there (around ¥10; agree the fare before setting off, as the driver may try to overcharge foreigners). You'll be dropped off on a road that cuts through the wall. The section to the left is too hard to climb, but the section on the right, beyond a little reservoir, shouldn't present too many difficulties for the agile; indeed, the climb gets easier as you go, with the wall levelling off along a ridge.

The wall here is attractively ruined – so watch your step – and its course makes for a pleasant walk through some lovely countryside. Walk the wall for about 2km, to the seventh tower, and you'll come to steps that lead south down the wall and onto a stony path. Follow this path down past an ancient barracks to a pumping station, and you'll come to a track that takes you south back to the main road, through a graveyard and orchards. When you hit the road you're about 500m south of where you started. Head north and after 150m you'll come to a bridge where taxis (¥10) and buses to Huairou congregate. The last bus from Huairou to Beijing leaves at 6.30pm.

Jiankou

Every few years a new section of the Great Wall is discovered by travellers, somewhere that's not too tricky to get to but has yet to be commercialized, where you can hike along the wall alone, experiencing this winding mountain road in all its ruined glory. Once it was Simatai, then Huanghua, but now that these have become entrenched on the tourist trail the new intrepid destination is **Jiankou** (箭扣, *jiànkòu*) about 30km north of Huairou.

The wall here is white, as it's made of dolomite, and there is a hikeable and very picturesque section, about 20km long, that winds through thickly forested mountain. Whichever part you decide to walk, don't take the trip without a local guide, however, as the wall is a little tricky to find in the first place. Much of the stone is loose, so you really need to watch your step, and some nerve-wracking sections are so steep that they have to be climbed on all fours.

Only the most determined choose to travel the full 20km hike from west to east; most people do the first 12km or so, or choose to walk the **spectacular middle section**, which is easier to get to and has no tricky parts (though a guide is still recommended). The far western end of the hike starts at **Nine Eye Tower**, one of the biggest watchtowers on the wall, and named after its nine peepholes. It's a tough 12km from here to the Beijing Knot, a watchtower where three walls come together. Around here the views are spectacular, and for the next kilometre or so the hiking is easier, at least until you reach a steep section called "Eagle Flies Vertically". Though theoretically you can scale this, then carry on for another 10km to Mutianyu, it is not recommended; the hike gets increasingly dangerous and includes some almost vertical climbs, such as the notorious "sky stairs". When you've had enough you'll need to head back to Xizhazi village (see below), where you can get a ride back to Huairou.

Practicalities

It's possible to get to Jiankou and back in a day, if you leave very early, but you'd be better off planning to stay a night. To get here, take **bus** #916 to Huairou, then charter a minibus for about ¥50 to **Xizhazi** village (西栅子, *xīzhàzi*), which will take another ninety minutes or so; villagers will charge you an entry fee of ¥20. Xizhazi should be considered base camp for the hike – plenty of local farmers rent out rooms, but it's recommended that you call in at the spartan but clean *Jiankou Zhao's* **hostel** (dorms ¥15, rooms ¥70). Mr Zhao is full of information on the hike, and will either guide you himself or sort out someone else to do it. The homecooked **food**, incidentally, is excellent. From Xizhazi it takes an hour or so just to reach the wall – but without a local to guide you it's easy to get lost.

The Western Hills

Like the Summer Palace (see p.99), the **Western Hills** (西山, *xīshān*) are somewhere to escape urban life for a while, though they're more of a rugged experience. Thanks to their coolness at the height of summer, the hills have long been favoured as a restful retreat by religious men and intellectuals, as well as politicians – Mao lived here briefly, and the Politburo (Political Bureau) assembles here in times of crisis.

The hills are divided into three parks. Nearest the centre, the **Botanical Gardens** are 3.5km west of the Summer Palace. Two kilometres farther west, **Xiangshan** is the largest and most impressive of the parks, but just as pretty is **Badachu**, its eight temples strung out along a hillside 2.5km south of Xiangshan.

About 20km from the centre, the hills take roughly an hour to reach on public transport. You can explore two of the parks in one day, but each deserves a day to itself. For a weekend escape and some in-depth exploration of the area, the *Xiangshan Hotel*, close to the main entrance of Xiangshan Park, is a good base (Ⓣ010/62591155; ¥688). A startlingly incongruous sight, the light, airy hotel looks like something between a temple and an airport lounge. It was designed by Bei Yuming (more usually known as I.M. Pei in the West), who also designed the pyramid at the Louvre in Paris and the Bank of China building at Xidan (see p.68).

The Botanical Gardens

Beijing's **Botanical Gardens** (植物园, *zhíwù yuán*; daily 8am–6pm; ¥5) boast two thousand varieties of trees and plants, arranged in formal gardens that are particularly attractive in spring, when most of the flowers are in bloom. Plants are labelled in English; some varieties have whole gardens dedicated to them – the peony and cherry-tree gardens are worth seeking out. There's also a huge hothouse which boasts tropical and desert environments (¥50), and has a lot of fleshy flora from Yunnan province in southwest China.

The path from the main gate, where the buses drop visitors (you can get here on bus #333 from outside the Yuanmingyuan or #360 from the zoo), leads after 1km to the **Wofo Temple** (卧佛寺, *wòfó sì*; daily 8am–4.30pm; ¥5), housing a huge reclining Buddha, over 5m in length and cast in copper. Calm in repose, with two giant feet protruding from the end of his painted robe, and a pudgy baby-face, he looks rather cute, although he isn't actually sleeping, but dying – about to enter nirvana. Suitably huge shoes, presented as offerings, are on display around the hall. Behind the temple is a bamboo garden, from which paths, signposted in English, wind off into the hills. One heads northwest to a pretty cherry valley, just under 1km away, where Cao Xueqiao is supposed to have written *The Dream of Red Mansions* (see p.181).

Xiangshan Park

Two kilometres west of the gardens lies **Xiangshan Park** (香山公园, *xiāngshān gōngyuán*; Fragrant Hills; daily 7am–6pm; ¥5; same buses as for the Botanical Gardens, stopping at the main entrance), a range of hills dominated by Incense Burner Peak in the western corner. It's at its best in the autumn (before the sharp November frosts), when the leaves turn red in a massive profusion of colour. Though busy at weekends, the park is too large to appear swamped, and is always a good place for a hike and a picnic.

Just northeast of the main entrance, on the eastern side of the park, is the **Zhao Miao** (Temple of Clarity), one of the few temples in the area to escape being vandalized by Western troops in 1860 and 1900. Built in 1780 by Qing Emperor Qianlong in Tibetan style, it was designed to make visiting lamas feel at home. From here, it's worth following the path west up to the peak (an easy 1hr walk) from where, on clear days, there are magnificent views down towards the Summer Palace and as far as distant Beijing. You can hire a horse to ride down (¥20), though you're not free to go where you please; the horse will be led by a lackey to the park's north entrance, which is also where the cable car (¥20) from the summit sets you down.

Just outside the park gate here is the superb **Biyun Temple** (daily 7.30am–4.30pm; ¥10). A striking building, it's dominated by a bulbous dagoba and topped by extraordinary conical stupas. The giant main hall is now a maze of corridors lined with statues of *arhats* – five hundred of these Buddhist saints in all. The benignly smiling golden figures are all different – some have two heads or sit on animals (one is even pulling his own face off); you might see monks moving among them and bowing to each. The temple also contains a tomb containing the hat and clothes of Sun Yatsen (president of the short-lived republic founded in 1911); his body was stored here for a while before being moved to Nanjing in 1924. Unfortunately, the tomb isn't open to public view.

Badachu

A forested hill 10km south of Xiangshan Park, **Badachu** (八大处, *bādàchù*; Eight Great Sites; daily 8am–5pm; ¥10) derives its name from the presence of eight temples here. Fairly small affairs, lying along the path that curls around the hill, the temples and their surroundings are nonetheless quite attractive, at least on weekdays; don't visit at weekends when the place is swamped. Bus #347 comes here from the zoo, or you can take the east–west subway line to the westernmost stop, Pingguoyuan, and get a taxi the rest of the way (¥10).

At the base of the path is a pagoda holding what's said to be one of Buddha's teeth, which once sat in the fourth temple, about halfway up the hill. The third temple is a nunnery, and is the most pleasant, with a relaxing teahouse in the courtyard. There's a statue of the rarely depicted, boggle-eyed thunder deity inside the main hall. The other temples make good resting points as you climb up the hill.

Inevitably, there's a cable car that you can ride to the top of the hill (¥20); you'll see it as you enter the park's main (north) gate. To descend, there's also a metal sled that you can use to slide down the hill (¥40). You'll whizz to the bottom in a minute.

Fahai Temple

Though its exterior is unremarkable, **Fahai Temple** (法海寺, *fǎhǎi sì*; daily 9am–5pm; ¥20) is worth a visit for its beautiful, richly detailed Buddhist frescoes. It lies west of the capital, and the easiest way to get here is to take subway line 1 to the last stop, Pingguoyuan, then take a cab (¥10). The halls where the frescoes are painted are rather dark; you're issued with a small torch at the entrance, but if you've got a decent one of your own, take it along. The lively, expressive images, painted in the 1440s, depict the pantheon of Buddhist deities travelling for a meeting. Look out for the elegant God of Music, Sarasvati, whose swaying form seems appropriately melodic, and the maternal-looking God of children, Haritidem, with her attendant babies. There are plenty of animals, too; as well as the rather dog-like lions, look out for the six-tusked elephant – each tusk represents a quality required for the attainment of enlightenment.

Tanzhe Temple and Jietai Temple

Due west of Beijing, two splendid temples sit in the wooded country outside the industrial zone that rings the city. Though the **Tanzhe** and **Jietai temples** are relatively little-visited by tourists, foreign residents rate them as among the best places to escape the city smoke. Take a picnic and make a day of it, as getting there and back can be time-consuming.

Tourist bus #7 from Fuchengmen visits both temples (mid-April to mid-Oct outward journeys 7–8.30am; ¥38 return), giving you ninety minutes at each, before returning to Qianmen. Otherwise, you could ride the east–west subway line all the way to its western terminus at Pingguoyuan, then catch bus #931 (¥3; this bus has two routes, so make sure the driver knows where you're going) to Tanzhe Temple. From here you'll be able to find a taxi on to Jietai Temple (¥20) – get one back to the city from here as well. Or you can save yourself some hassle by hiring a taxi to visit both temples, which should cost around ¥250 if you start from the city centre.

Tanzhe Temple

Forty kilometres west of Beijing, **Tanzhe Temple** (潭柘寺, *tánzhé sì*; daily 8am–6pm; ¥35) has the most beautiful and serene location of any temple near the city. The site is the largest of Beijing's temples, too, and one of the oldest, first recorded in the third century as housing a thriving community of monks. Wandering through the complex, past terraces of stupas, you reach an enormous central courtyard, with an ancient, towering gingko tree that's over a thousand years old (christened the "King of Trees" by Emperor Qianlong) at its heart.

Across the courtyard, a second, smaller gingko, known as "The Emperor's Wife", was once supposed to produce a new branch every time a new emperor was born. From here you can take in the other buildings, arrayed on different levels up the hillside, or look around the lush gardens, whose bamboo is supposed to cure all manner of ailments. Back at the entrance, the spiky *zhe* trees nearby (*Cudrania tricuspidata*, sometimes called the Chinese mulberry), after which the temple is named, "reinforce the essence of the kidney and control spontaneous seminal emission", so a sign here says.

Jietai Temple

In complete contrast, **Jietai Temple** (戒台寺, *jiètái sì*; daily 8am–6pm; ¥35), sitting on a hillside 12km east, looks more like a fortress than a temple, surrounded by forbiddingly tall, red walls. It's an extremely atmospheric, quiet place, made slightly spooky by its dramatically shaped pines, eccentric-looking venerable trees growing in odd directions. Indeed, one, leaning out at an angle of about thirty degrees, is pushing over a pagoda on the terrace beneath it.

In the main hall is an enormous tenth-century platform of white marble at which novice monks were ordained. At 3m high, it's intricately carved with figures – monks, monsters (beaked and winged) and saints. The chairs on top are for the three masters and seven witnesses who oversaw ordinations. Another, smaller side hall holds a beautiful wooden altar that swarms with dragon reliefs.

The Ming Tombs (Shisan Ling)

After their deaths, all but three of the sixteen Ming-dynasty emperors were entombed in giant underground vaults, the **Shisan Ling** (十三陵, *shísān líng*; literally, Thirteen Tombs), usually referred to in English as the **Ming Tombs**. Two of the tombs, Chang Ling and Ding Ling, were restored in the 1950s; the latter was also excavated.

The tombs are located in and around a valley 40km northwest of Beijing. The location, chosen by the third Ming emperor, Yongle, for its landscape of gentle hills and woods is undeniably one of the loveliest around the capital, the site marked above ground by grand halls and platforms. That said, the fame of the tombs is overstated in relation to the actual interest of their site, and unless you've a strong archeological bent, a trip here isn't worth making for its own sake. The tombs are, however, very much on the tour circuit, being conveniently placed on the way to Badaling Great Wall (see p.105). The site also makes a nice place to picnic, especially if you just feel like taking a break from the city. To get the most out of the place, it's better not to stick to the tourist route between the car park and Ding Ling, but to spend a day here and hike around the smaller tombs further into the hills. You'll need a map to do this – you'll find one on the back of some Beijing city maps, or you can buy one at the site (¥2).

The easiest way to get to the Ming Tombs is to take any of the **tourist buses** that go to Badaling (see p.105), which visit the tombs on the way to and from Beijing. You can get off here, then rejoin another tourist bus later, either to continue to Badaling or to return to the city. To get there on ordinary public transport, take bus #845 from Xizhimen to the terminus at Changping, then get bus #345 the rest of the way. All buses drop you at a car park in front of one of the tombs, Ding Ling, where you buy your ticket (¥35).

The Spirit Way and Chang Ling

The approach to the Ming Tombs, the 7km **Spirit Way**, is Shisan Ling's most exciting feature, well worth backtracking along from the ticket office. The road commences with the **Dahongmen** (Great Red Gate), a triple-entranced triumphal arch, through the central opening of which only the emperor's dead body was allowed to be carried. Beyond, the road is lined with colossal stone statues of animals and men. Alarmingly larger than life, they all date from the fifteenth

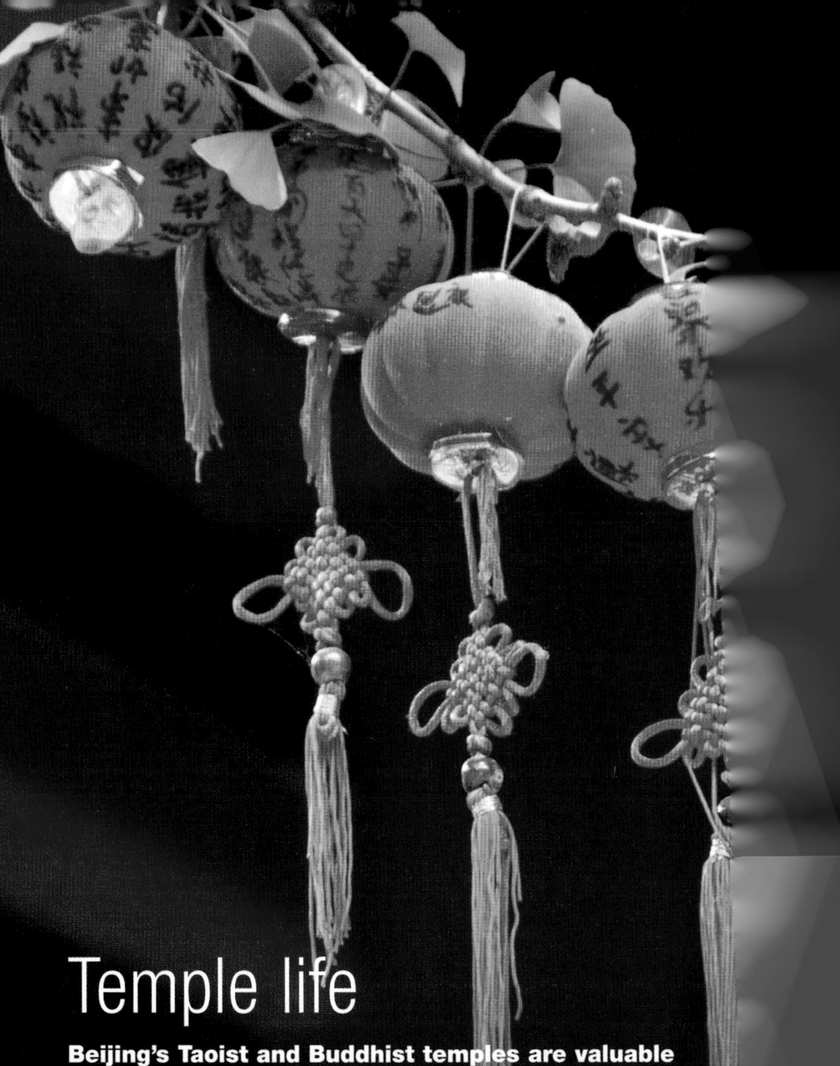

Temple life

Beijing's Taoist and Buddhist temples are valuable repositories of heritage: as well as being often the only recognizably Chinese buildings around, they are rich wi artefacts and long-preserved traditions. Outside, you'll s a glorious array of tat for sale – from flashing Buddhas t credit card-sized images of gods to be kept in your walle luck. Inside, smoke billows from burners – as well as inc you'll see worshippers burning fake money, ingots or eve paper cars to enrich ancestors in heaven. The atmosphe lively and devout; devotees kowtow before fantastic imag and robed monks genuflect.

Temple gate ▲

Maitreya Buddha, Yonghe Gong ▼

Design

In Beijing, as in China as a whole, temples are not as old as they look; most were trashed during the Cultural Revolution and have been rebuilt from scratch. But the layout and design elements are genuinely ancient, and based on principles set down thousands of years ago.

Like private houses, all Chinese temples face **south** (barbarians and evil spirits come from the north), and are surrounded by **walls**. Gates are sealed by heavy doors and guarded by **statues** – Buddhists use the four Heavenly Kings, while Taoists have a dragon and a lion. Further protection is afforded by a **spirit wall** in the first courtyard – easy enough for the living to walk around but a block to evil, which can supposedly only travel in straight lines.

Following this, there'll be a succession of **halls** and **courtyards**, arranged symmetrically – it's all about maintaining harmony. The courtyards will be enclosed by walls – creating so-called "sky wells" – and will usually feature ornate incense burners full of ash, venerable trees, and perhaps a pond. The buildings are placed according to a strict hierachy, with those facing front and at the rear being the most important.

The halls are supported by lacquered **pillars** – Buddhists colour them bright red, Taoists use black. Some of the most elegant details are in the roof, where interlocking beams create a characteristic curved roofline and elegantly made and beautifully painted brackets (*dougongs*) allow the jauntily curving eaves to extend well beyond the main pillars. Look out for the procession of figures, including a dragon and a man riding a phoenix among various mythological beasties, that run along the edges of the roof. They're put there for luck and protection.

Symbols

The main hall of a **Buddhist temple** is dominated by three large **statues** – the Buddhas of the past, the present and the future – while the walls are lined by rather outlandish **arhats**, or saints. Around the back of the Buddhist trinity will probably be a statue of Guanyin, the multi-armed Goddess of Mercy. Believed to help with childbirth, she's very popular, and you'll see the same figure in Taoist temples.

Taoist temples are much more diverse in iconography. The Taoist holy trinity is made up of the three **immortals**, who each ride different animals (a crane, tiger and deer) and represent the three levels of the Taoist afterlife. You'll see dragons and phoenixes depicted in all Chinese temples, but **animal carvings** are more popular with the animist Taoists, too: look out for bats and cranes – symbols, respectively, of good luck and longevity. Other figures in Taoist temples include the red-faced God of War, Guan Yu, and the general Zhuge Liang – characters in the ancient story the *Three Kingdoms* (see Contexts, p.181), and based on real-life figures. Around the edges of the halls you'll see often fantastical depictions of other immortals and saints, usually shown with a magical talisman and evidence of some kind of special power. All are presided over by the stern looking Jade Emperor.

Confucian temples are rather formal, with little imagery, though you will see plenty of tombstone-like steles supported by stone tortoises – perhaps a nod towards the Indian story that a tortoise carries the world on its back. Recently, new statues of the great sage have been erected in the recently approved official likeness.

▲ Dongyue Temple

▼ Yonghe Gong

▼ Temple drummers

Taoist temple during Chinese New Year ▲

Temple fairs

Every Beijing temple holds a **fair** at Chinese New Year, integrating worship, entertainment and commerce. At these boisterous carnivals, the air is thick with incense, and locals queue to kneel to altars and play games that bring good fortune – lobbing coins at the temple bell, for example. Priests are on hand to perform rituals and write prayers.

Beijing's biggest fairs are at the Tibetan **Yonghe Gong** (see p.90) and the Taoist **Baiyun Guan** (see p.69): pick one or the other, as it's considered inauspicious to visit both during the same festival. To help you decide, Taoist festivals concentrate on renewal, Tibetan Lamaist ones on enlightenment.

Buddhist monk ▼

A monk's life

Buddhist monks wear orange robes and keep their heads shaved, while **Taoist monks** wear blue and keep their long hair tied up. Both sets of monks are celibate and vegetarian, and avoid garlic or onion, which are said to enflame the passions.

Under the strict rule of an abbot, the monks and nuns live a regimented and quiet life, taken up with study, prayer and observance and celebration of significant dates. There are also plenty of practical tasks concerning the day-to-day running of the institution. Meals are communal and there is at least three hours of prayer and meditation every day.

The need to defend the temple, and to balance meditation with activity, led to the development of **martial arts**: Taoist monks generally practice *tai ji quan* (see p.64) while Buddhists are famous for having developed kung fu – though you're not likely to see it being practised.

century and are among the best surviving examples of Ming sculpture. Their precise significance is unclear, although it is assumed they were intended to serve the emperors in their next life. The animals depicted include the mythological *qilin* – a reptilian beast with deer's horns and a cow's tail – and the horned, feline *xiechi*; the human figures are stern, military mandarins. Animal statuary reappears at the entrances to several of the tombs, though the structures themselves are something of an anticlimax.

At the end of the Spirit Way stands **Chang Ling** (daily 8.30am–5pm; ¥35), which was the tomb of Yongle himself, the earliest at the site. There are plans to excavate the underground chamber – an exciting prospect since the tomb is contemporary with some of the finest buildings of the Forbidden City in the capital. At present, the enduring impression above ground is mainly one of scale – vast courtyards and halls, approached by terraced white marble. Its main feature is the Hall of Eminent Flowers, supported by huge columns consisting of individual tree trunks which, it is said, were imported all the way from Yunnan in the south of the country.

Ding Ling

The main focus of the area is **Ding Ling** (定陵, *dìnglíng*; daily 8.30am–5pm; ¥35), the underground tomb-palace of the Emperor Wanli, who ascended the throne in 1573 at the age of 10. Reigning for almost half a century, he began building his tomb when he was 22, in line with common Ming practice, and hosted a grand party within on its completion. The mausoleum, a short distance east of Chang Ling, was opened up in 1956 and found to be substantially intact, revealing the emperor's coffin, flanked by those of two of his empresses, and floors covered with scores of trunks containing imperial robes, gold and silver, and even the imperial cookbooks. Some of the treasures are displayed in the tomb, a huge musty stone vault, undecorated but impressive for its scale; others have been replaced by replicas. It's a cautionary picture of useless wealth accumulation, as the tour guides are bound to point out.

Other sights north of Beijing

Heading north out of the city, you'll see vast swathes of new tree growth – the **Great Green Wall**. There are some areas of great natural beauty in the rugged landscape beyond, notably **Longqing Gorge** and, oddly, the rather good **Aviation Museum**. There's public transport to all these areas, but having a car and driver makes it easier.

Aviation Museum

Out in the sticks 60km north of the city, the **Aviation Museum** is a fascinating place (航空博物馆, *hángkōng bówùguàn*; daily 8.30am–5.30pm; ¥40; bus #912 from Andingmen subway stop). This enormous museum contains over three hundred aircraft, displayed in a giant hangar inside a hollow mountain and on a concourse. These range from the copy of the Wright brothers' plane flown by Feng Ru, a pioneering Chinese aviator, in 1909, to Gulf War helicopter gunships. As well as plenty of fighter planes, many of which saw action in the Korean War, the bomber that flew in China's first atom-bomb test is here, as is Mao's personal jet (with his teacup and frilly cushions still inside) and the plane that scattered the ashes of the deceased Zhou Enlai, which is covered with wreaths and tributes. But unless you have a special interest in aircraft, it's the sight of archaic downed machines en masse – like the setting for a J.G. Ballard story – that makes the place memorable.

Longqing Gorge

Longqing Gorge (龙庆峡, *lóngqìng xiá*; ¥40) is a local recreation spot at the edge of a reservoir some 90km northwest of the capital, known as the place to come for outdoor pursuits such as canoeing, horseriding and rock climbing, all of which can be arranged when you arrive, for between ¥60 and ¥120. The main attraction, though, is the **Ice Festival** held on the shore of the reservoir (late Jan & Feb, sometimes into March), at which groups of sculptors compete to create the most impressive ice sculpture. The enormous resulting carvings depict cartoon characters, dragons, storks and figures from Chinese popular culture; with coloured lights inside for a gloriously tacky psychedelic effect, they look great at night.

There are two ways to reach the gorge by public **transport**: either tourist bus #8 (mid-April to mid-Oct, and during the Ice Festival; 2hr 30min) from the #328 bus terminus near Andingmen subway stop, or train #575 from Xizhimen Zhan (daily at 8.30am; 2hr 30min). Unfortunately, the **hotels** around the reservoir are expensive and a bit dirty, and their rooms are especially pricey during the festival – though you needn't feel compelled to stay, as there are buses back to Beijing until at least 10pm. The nearest decent hotel in this area is the *Yanqing Guesthouse* in **Yanqing**, a few kilometres south (Ⓣ010/69142363; ¥300).

South of Beijing: Shidu

The "wilderness area" of **Shidu** (十渡, *shídù*; literally, Ten Bends), around 90km southwest of the city, is Beijing's equivalent to Guilin; the Juma river twists between steep karst peaks to create a landscape that resembles a classical Chinese painting. The trip here on bus #917 from Tianqiao will take about two hours. As at Longqing Gorge, you can go horseriding, boating, fishing and rock climbing – all of which cost ¥120 or so, can be organized on your arrival, and are aimed at novices. There's even a bungee jump (¥150). But perhaps it's most rewarding simply as a place to **hike** – pick up a map at the entrance and set off. Though it can get crowded, few visitors seem to get much further than the restaurants that line the only road, so the experience rather improves the further into the resort you go.

Chengde

CHENGDE (承德, *chéngdé*), a country town 250km northeast of Beijing, is a quiet, unimportant place, but on its outskirts are some of the most magnificent examples of imperial architecture in China, remnants from its glory days as the **summer retreat** of the Manchu emperors. Gorgeous temples punctuate the cabbage fields around town, and a palace-and-park hill complex, **Bishu Shanzhuang**, covers an area nearly as large as the town itself.

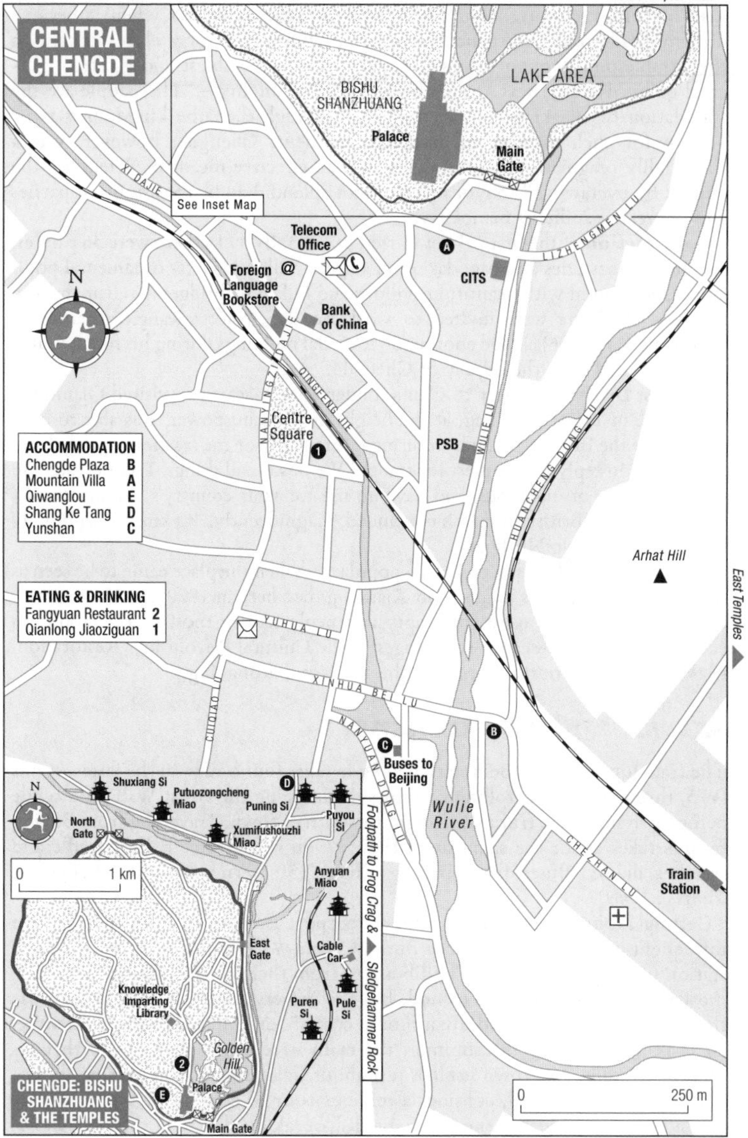

Some history

Originally called "Rehe", the town was discovered by the Qing-dynasty emperor **Kangxi** at the end of the seventeenth century, while marching his troops to the Mulan hunting range to the north. He was attracted to the cool summer climate and the rugged landscape, and built small lodges here from which he could indulge in a fantasy Manchu lifestyle, hunting and hiking like his northern ancestors. The building programme expanded when it became diplomatically useful to spend time north of Beijing, to forge closer links with the troublesome Mongol tribes. Kangxi, perhaps the ablest and most enlightened of his dynasty, was known more for his economy – "The people are the foundation of the kingdom; if they have enough then the kingdom is rich" – than for such displays of imperial grandeur. Chengde, however, was a thoroughly pragmatic creation, devised as an effective means of defending the empire by overawing Mongol princes with splendid audiences, hunting parties and impressive military manoeuvres.

Construction of the first palaces started in 1703. By 1711 there were 36 palaces, temples, monasteries and pagodas set in a great walled park, its ornamental pools and islands dotted with beautiful pavilions and linked by bridges. Craftsmen from all parts of China were invited to work on the project; Kangxi's grandson, **Qianlong** (1736–96), added another 36 imperial buildings during his reign, which was considered to be the heyday of Chengde.

The first **British Embassy** to China, under Lord Macartney, visited Qianlong's court here in 1793. Qianlong, at the height of Manchu power, was able to hold out against the British demands, refusing to grant any of the treaties requested and remarking, in reply to a request for trade: "We possess all things. I set no value on objects strange or ingenious, and have no use for your country's manufactures." His letter to the British monarch concluded, magnificently, "O king, Tremblingly Obey and Show No Negligence!"

Chengde gradually lost its imperial popularity when the place came to be seen as unlucky after emperors Jiaqing and Xianfeng died here in 1820 and 1860 respectively. The buildings were left empty and neglected for most of the twentieth century, but largely escaped the ravages of the Cultural Revolution. Restoration, in the interests of tourism, began in the 1980s and is ongoing.

Arrival and city transport

The train journey from Beijing to Chengde takes four hours on the fastest trains (¥75) through verdant, rolling countryside, hugging the Great Wall for a while before arriving at the **train station** in the south of town. Travelling from Beijing by **bus** takes about the same time, though you run greater risk of traffic and weather delays. Buses from Beijing Zhan (¥50) terminate just outside the *Yunshan Hotel*.

Getting around Chengde by public transport isn't easy, as **local buses** are infrequent and always crammed. Buses #5 and #11, which go from the train station to Bishu Shanzhuang, and bus #6, from there to the Puning Si, are the most useful. **Taxis** are easy to find, but the drivers are often unwilling to use their meters – a ride around town should cost ¥5, or ¥10 to an outlying temple. At peak hours during the summer, the main streets are so congested that it's quicker to walk. The town itself is just about small enough to cover on foot.

If your time is limited, consider a minibus **tour** to cram in all the sights. It's occasionally possible to arrange an English-speaking day-tour through CITS, though it's much easier to go through one of the larger hotels. Chinese tours, which leave sporadically from outside the train station, are slightly cheaper. A day-long organized tour is something of a trial of endurance, however, and the tours tend to overlook the less spectacular temples, which are also the most peaceful. Probably the best way to see everything in a short time is to take a minibus or a bike around the temples one day and explore the mountain resort the next. If you're travelling in a group you can charter a taxi or a minibus for around ¥200 a day.

Accommodation

There are plenty of hotels in **Chengde** town itself, plus a couple of expensive places inside **Bishu Shanzhuang**. Rates are highly negotiable; the price codes below apply to the peak summer season and weekends. At other times you can get discounts of up to two-thirds.

Chengde Plaza
承德大厦
chéngdé dàshà
Chezhan Lu ⓣ0314/2088808, ⓕ2024319. This fifteen-storey block is convenient for the train station, but in an uninteresting area of town. ¥688.

Mountain Villa
山庄宾馆
shānzhuāng bīnguǎn
127 Xiaonanmen (entrance on Lizhengmen Lu) ⓣ0314/2025588. This grand, well-located complex has huge rooms, high ceilings and a cavernous, gleaming lobby, and is extremely popular with tour groups. The large rooms in the main building are nicer but a little more expensive than those in the ugly building round the back, and there are some very cheap options in the basement. Buses #5 or #11 from the train station will get you here. ¥440.

Qiwanglou
倚望楼宾馆
yǐwànglóu bīnguǎn
Around the corner and uphill from the Bishu Shanzhuang main entrance ⓣ0314/2024385. A well-run hotel in a pleasing imitation Qing-style building. The grounds make for an interesting walk even if you're not staying here. ¥650.

Shang Ke Tang
上客堂宾馆
shàngkètáng bīnguǎn
Puning Si ⓣ0314/2058888. Staff at this interesting hotel wear period clothing and braided wigs – appropriate, given the adjoining Puning temple – and glide along the dim bowels of the complex to lead you to appealingly rustic rooms. ¥588.

Yunshan
云山饭店
yúnshān fàndiàn
2 Banbishan Lu ⓣ0314/2055588, ⓕ20558855. This modern block was the tour group favourite before being trumped by the *Mountain Villa*. The second-floor restaurant is good, the plushest in town, and not too expensive. A 10min walk from the train station and handy for the bus station. ¥900.

Bishu Shanzhuang

Surrounded by a 10km-long wall and larger than the Summer Palace in Beijing, **Bishu Shanzhuang** (避暑山庄, *bìshǔ shānzhuāng*; also referred to as the Mountain Resort) occupies the northern third of the town's area (daily 8am–5.30pm; April 16–Oct 15 combined ticket for the park and the palace ¥120; Oct 16–April 15 ¥90). This is where, in the summer, the Qing emperors lived, feasted, hunted, and occasionally dealt with affairs of state. The palace buildings just inside the main entrance are unusual for imperial China as they are low, wooden and unpainted – simple but elegant, in contrast to the opulence and grandeur of Beijing's palaces. It's said that Emperor Kangxi wanted the complex to mimic a Manchurian village, to show his disdain for fame and wealth, though with 120 rooms and several thousand servants he wasn't exactly roughing it. The same principle of idealized naturalness governed the design of the park. With its twisting paths and streams, rockeries and hills, it's a fantasy re-creation of the rough northern terrain and southern Chinese beauty spots that the emperors would have seen on their tours of inspection. The whole is an attempt to combine water, buildings and plants in graceful harmony. Lord Macartney noted its similarity to the "soft beauties" of an English manor park of the Romantic style.

The palace

The **main gate**, Lizhengmen, is in the south wall, off Lizhengmen Lu. The **palace quarter**, just inside the complex to the west of the main gate, is built on a slope, facing south, and consists of four groups of dark wooden buildings spread over an area of 100,000 square metres. The first, southernmost group, the Front Palace, where the emperors lived and worked, is the most interesting, as many of the rooms have been restored to their full Qing elegance, decked out with graceful furniture and ornaments. Even the everyday objects are impressive: brushes and ink stones on desks, ornate fly whisks on the arms of chairs, little jade trees on shelves. Other rooms house displays of ceramics, books and exotic martial-art weaponry. The Qing emperors were fine calligraphers, and examples of their work appear throughout the palace.

There are 26 buildings in this group, arranged south to north in nine successive compounds, which correspond to the nine levels of heaven. The main gate leads into the **Outer Wumen**, where high-ranking officials waited for a single peal of a large bell, indicating that the emperor was ready to receive them. Next is the **Inner Wumen**, where the emperor would watch his officers practise their archery. Directly behind, the **Hall of Frugality and Sincerity** is a dark, well-appointed room made of cedar wood, imported at great expense from south of the Yangzi River by Qianlong, who had none of his grandfather Kangxi's scruples about conspicuous consumption. Topped with a curved roof, the hall has nine bays, and patterns on the walls include symbols of longevity and good luck. The **Four Knowledge Study Room**, behind, was where the emperor did his ordinary work, changed his clothes and rested. A vertical scroll on the wall outlines the knowledge required of a gentleman, as written in the Chinese classics: he must be aware of what is small, obvious, soft and strong. It's more spartanly furnished, a little more intimate and less imposing than the other rooms.

The main building in the **Rear Palace** is the **Hall of Refreshing Mists and Waves**, the living quarters of the imperial family, and beautifully turned out in period style. It was in the west room here that Emperor Xianfeng signed the humiliating Beijing Treaty in the 1850s, giving away more of China's sovereignty and territory after their defeat in the Second Opium War. The **Western Apartments** are where the notorious Cixi (see p.100), lived when she was one of Xianfeng's concubines. A door connects the apartments to the hall, and it was through here that she eavesdropped on the dying emperor's last words of advice to his ministers, intelligence she used to force herself into power. The courtyard of the Rear Palace has a good **souvenir shop**, inside an old Buddhist tower reached by climbing a staircase by the rockery.

The other two complexes are much smaller. The **Pine and Crane Residence**, a group of buildings parallel to the front gate, is a more subdued version of the Front Palace, home to the emperor's mother and his concubines. In the **Myriad Valleys of Rustling Pine Trees**, to the north of here, Emperor Kangxi read books and granted audiences, and Qianlong studied as a child. The group of structures southwest of the main palace is the **Ahgesuo**, where male descendants of the royal family studied during the Manchurian rule; lessons began at 5am and finished at noon. A boy was expected to speak Manchu at 6, Chinese at 12, be competent with a bow by the age of 14, and marry at 16.

The grounds

The best way to get around the **lake area** of the park – a network of pavilions, bridges, lakes and waterways – is to rent a **rowing boat** (¥20/hour). Much of the architecture here is a direct copy of southern Chinese buildings. In the east, the

Golden Hill, a cluster of buildings grouped on a small island, is notable for a hall and tower modelled after the Golden Hill Monastery in Zhenjiang, Jiangsu Province. The **Island of Midnight and Murmuring Streams**, roughly in the centre of the lake, holds a three-courtyard compound which was used by Kangxi and Qianlong as a retreat, while the compound of halls, towers and pavilions on **Ruyi Island**, the largest, was where Kangxi dealt with affairs of state before the palace was completed.

Just beyond the lake area, on the western side of the park, is the grey-tiled **Wenjinge**, or Knowledge Imparting Library, surrounded by rockeries and pools for fire protection. From the outside, the structure appears to have two storeys. In fact there are three – a central section is windowless to protect the books from the sun. A fine collection is housed in the building, including *The Four Treasures*, a 36,304-volume Qing-dynasty encyclopedia, but sadly you can't go inside.

A vast expanse of **grassland** extends from the north of the lake area to the foothills of the mountains, comprising Wanshun Wan (Garden of Ten Thousand Trees) and Shima Da (Horse Testing Ground). Genuine Qing-dynasty **yurts** sit here, the largest an audience hall where Qianlong received visiting dignitaries from ethnic minorities.

The temples

The **temples** (daily 8am–5.30pm) in the foothills of the mountains around Chengde were built in the architectural styles of different ethnic nationalities, so that wandering among them is rather like being in a religious theme park. This isn't far from the original intention, as they were constructed by Kangxi and Qianlong less to express religious sentiment than as a way of showing off imperial magnificence, and also to make envoys from anywhere in the empire feel more at home. Though varying in design, all the temples share **Lamaist features** – Qianlong found it politically expedient to promote Tibetan and Mongolian Lamaism as a way of keeping these troublesome minorities in line.

The temples are now in varying states of repair, having been left untended for decades. Originally there were twelve, but two have been destroyed and another two are dilapidated. Present restoration work is being paid for by the high entrance fees charged in the large temples.

The best way to see the temples is to **rent a bicycle** (ask at your hotel; the *Qiwanglou* and *Mountain Villa* have bikes to rent): the roads outside the town are quiet, it's hard to get lost and you can dodge the tour groups.

The northern temples

Just beyond the northern border of Bishu Shanzhuang are five temples that were once part of a string of nine. Three of these deserve special attention, but the **Puning Temple** (普宁寺, *pǔníng sì*; April 1–Oct 31 ¥80; Nov 1–March 31 ¥60) is a must, if only for the awe-inspiring statue of Guanyin, the largest wooden statue in the world. This is the only working temple in Chengde, with shaven-headed Mongolian monks manning the altars and trinket stalls, though the atmosphere is not especially spiritual. There are rumours that the monks are really paid government employees working for the tourist industry, though the vehemence with which they defend their prayer mats and gongs from romping children suggests otherwise.

Puning Si was built in 1755 to commemorate the Qing victory over Mongolian rebels at Junggar in northwest China, and is based on the oldest Tibetan temple, the Samye. Like traditional Tibetan buildings, it lies on the slope of a mountain facing south, though the layout of the front is typically

Han, with a gate hall, stele pavilions, a bell and a drum tower, a Hall of Heavenly Kings, and the Mahavira Hall. In the **Hall of Heavenly Kings**, the statue of a fat, grinning monk holding a bag depicts Qi Ci, a tenth-century character with a jovial disposition, who is believed to be a reincarnation of the Buddha. Four gaudy *devarajas* (guardian demons) glare down at you with bulging eyeballs from niches in the walls. In the **West Hall** are statues of Buddha Manjusri, Avalokiteshvara and Samantabhadra. In the **East Hall**, the central statue, flanked by *arhats*, depicts Ji Gong, a Song-dynasty monk who was nicknamed Crazy Ji for eating meat and being almost always drunk, but who was much respected for his kindness to the poor.

The rear section of the temple, separated from the front by a wall, comprises 27 Tibetan-style rooms laid out symmetrically, with the **Mahayana Hall** in the centre. Some of the buildings are actually solid (the doors are false), suggesting that the original architects were more concerned with appearances than function. The hall itself is dominated by the 23m-high wooden **statue of Guanyin**, the Goddess of Mercy. She has 42 arms with an eye in the centre of each palm, and three eyes on her face, which symbolize her ability to see into the past, present and future. The hall has two raised entrances, and it's worth looking at the statue from these upper viewpoints as they reveal new details, such as the eye sunk in her belly button, and the little Buddha sitting on top of her head.

The **Xumifushouzhi Temple** (须弥福寿之庙, *xūmífúshòu zhīmiào*; April 1–Oct 31 ¥80; Nov 1–March 31 ¥60; joint ticket includes Putuozongcheng Miao), just southwest of Puning Si, was built in 1780 in Mongolian style for the sixth Panchen Lama when he came to Beijing to pay his respects to the emperor. Though he was lavishly looked after – contemporary accounts describe how Qianlong invited the Lama to sit with him on the Dragon Throne – he went home in a coffin, dead from either smallpox or poison.

The temple centrepiece is the **Hall of Loftiness and Solemnity**, its finest features the eight sinuous gold dragons sitting on the roof, each weighing over a thousand kilograms.

The Putuozongcheng Miao

Next door to the Xumifushouzhi Miao, the magnificent **Putuozongcheng Miao** (普陀宗乘之庙, *pǔtuó zōngchéng zhīmiào*) was built in 1771 and is based on the Potala Palace in Lhasa. Covering 220,000 square metres, it's the largest temple in Chengde, with sixty groups of halls, pagodas and terraces. The grand terrace forms a Tibetan-style facade screening a Chinese-style interior, although many of the windows on the terrace are fake, and some of the whitewashed buildings around the base are merely filled-in shapes. Inside, the West Hall is notable for holding a rather comical copper statue of the Propitious Heavenly Mother, a fearsome woman wearing a necklace of skulls and riding side-saddle on a mule. According to legend, she vowed to defeat the evil demon Raksaka, so she first lulled him into a false sense of security – by marrying him and bearing him two sons – then swallowed the moon and in the darkness crept up on him and turned him into a mule. The two dancing figures at her feet are her sons; their ugly features betray their paternity. The **Hall of All Laws Falling into One**, at the back, is worth a visit for the quality of the decorative religious furniture on display. Other halls hold displays of Chinese pottery and ceramics and Tibetan religious artefacts, an exhibition slanted to portray the gorier side of Tibetan religion and including a drum made from two children's skulls. The roof of the temple has a good view over the surrounding countryside.

The eastern temples

The three **eastern temples** (8.30am–4.30pm; ¥50 for a joint ticket to Pule and Anyuan) are easily accessible from a quiet road that passes through dusty, rambling settlements, some 3km or 4km from the town centre. From Lizhengmen Lu, cross over to the east bank of the river and head north. Note that the **Puren Temple** (溥仁寺, *pǔrén sì*), the first you'll reach and the oldest in the complex, is closed to tourists. It was built by Kangxi in 1713 as a sign of respect to the visiting Mongolian nobility who came to congratulate the emperor on the occasion of his sixtieth birthday.

The **Pule Temple** (普乐寺, *pǔlè sì*) farther north was built in 1766 by Qianlong as a place for Mongol envoys to worship, and its style is an odd mix of Han and Lamaist elements. The Lamaist back section, a triple-tiered terrace and hall, with a flamboyantly conical roof and lively, curved surfaces, steals the show from the more sober, squarer Han architecture at the front. The ceiling of the back hall is a wood and gold confection to rival the Temple of Heaven in Beijing. Glowing at its centre is a mandala of Samvara, a Tantric deity, in the form of a cross. The altar beneath holds a Buddha of Happiness, a life-size copper image of sexual congress; more cosmic sex is depicted in two beautiful mandalas hanging outside. In the courtyard, prayer flags flutter while prayer wheels sit empty and unturned. Outside the temple, the view from the car park is spectacular, and just north is the path that leads to **Sledgehammer Rock** and the cable car.

The less interesting **Anyuan Temple** (安远庙, *ānyuǎn miào*) is the most northerly of the group. It was built in 1764 for a troop of Mongolian soldiers who were moved to Chengde by Qianlong, and has a delightful setting on the tree-lined east bank of the Wulie river.

Eating and drinking

Chengde is located in Hebei's most fertile area, which mainly produces maize and sorghum but also yields excellent local chestnuts, mushrooms and apricots. This fresh produce, plus the culinary legacy of the imperial cooks, means you can eat very well here. The town is also noted for its **wild game**, particularly deer (*lurou*), hare (*yetou*) and pheasant (*shanji*), and its medicinal **juice drinks**: almond juice is said to be good for asthma; date and jujube juice for the stomach; and *jinlianhua* (golden lotus) juice for a sore throat. Date and almond are the sweetest and most palatable. Local **cakes**, such as the glutinous Feng family cakes, once an imperial delicacy but now a casual snack, can be found in the stalls on Yuhua Lu and Qingfeng Jie. Rose cakes – a sweet, crisp pastry cake and a particular favourite of Qianlong – are sold in Chengde's department stores.

There are plenty of **restaurants** catering to tourists on Lizhengmen Lu, around the main entrance to Bishu Shanzhuang. The small places west of the *Mountain Villa* hotel are fine, if a little pricey, and lively on summer evenings, when rickety tables are put on the pavement outside. A meal for two should cost about ¥60, and plenty of diners stay on drinking well into the evening. The best *jiaozi* in town are served at *Qianlong Jiaoziguan* (乾隆饺子馆, *qiánlóng jiǎoziguǎn*), just off Centre Square, a park at the heart of the shopping district. Nearby, **Qingfeng Jie** is an old, charmingly seedy street of restaurants and salons, and is a great place to have a satisfying *shaguo* – a veggie claypot costs ¥6, a meat-based one ¥10. Inside Bishu Shanzhuang itself, the *Fangyuan* (芳园居, *fāngyuán jū*) offers imperial cuisine, including such exotica as "Pingquan Frozen Rabbit", in an attractive environment.

Listings

Listings

8

Accommodation

Beijing hotels were once largely impersonal concerns, with standardized, rather nondescript, modern interiors. But newer accommodation options are placing more emphasis on design and character, the established places are sprucing themselves up, and now, whatever your budget, it's possible to stay somewhere that's not just functional but memorable. For information on finding **long-term accommodation** in the city, see p.39.

Central Beijing – anywhere within or just off the Second Ring Road – has plenty of luxury and a few mid-range hotels, while budget options have sprung up, including a number of good youth hostels. Beijing being the size it is, proximity to a subway stop is an enormous advantage, so accommodation on or near the Second Ring Road – and therefore the loop line – are often the most convenient. **Out of the centre**, the vast majority of hotels are on or near the Third Ring Road, a long way out in what is rather a dull area, though there are usually good transport connections to the centre. These hotels are mainly mid-range and comfortable, without many frills; all have a business centre.

The glitzy, expensive hotels are generally in or around the **Chaoyang** district, in the **east** of the city. Though anonymous architecturally, it's a cosmopolitan area with lively restaurants and nightlife: this is the place to stay if you are looking for international style and comfort.

The **north** of the city (south of the Second Ring Road) has some charmingly ramshackle (and newly fashionable) areas, particularly around Nanluogu Xiang and the Drum Tower. Head for this area if you want to stay in traditional Beijing; it's also good for the best budget and mid-range places.

The **west** and **south** of the city are, on the whole, less interesting – though there are plenty of accommodation options here, few are included below for this reason. A few **country retreats** are reviewed in the "Around Beijing" chapter.

Unless otherwise stated, the **prices** we quote in the reviews below represent the cost of the **cheapest double room** available to foreigners. Most places have a range of rooms, and staff will usually offer you the more expensive ones – it's always worth asking if they have anything cheaper. Almost all hotels, certainly all the more upmarket establishments, have high- and low-season rates; we have quoted rates at the higher end (April–Sept).

At all but the cheapest hotels, it's possible to **bargain** the price down, otherwise, you'll find discounted rates on the internet (see below). If you're on a tight budget, a little searching should turn up a bed in a clean dormitory for about ¥60 a night, or an en-suite double room for less than ¥250.

Reservations can be made by phone – generally someone on reception will speak English. You can reserve rooms from a counter at the airport (on the left as you exit customs), and they will usually offer a small discount – though you'll get a much better deal if you book the same room yourself. **Online** reservations are

Courtyard hotels

Beijing has many small **courtyard hotels** in all budgets. Reminiscent of B&Bs, these intimate back-alley guesthouses are atmospheric and distinctively Chinese, with the central courtyard becoming a venue for guests to mingle. They're often surprisingly well located too, usually just north of the centre. On the downside, the alleyways they are found on are generally inaccessible to taxis, and can be a bit earthy; rooms are a bit dark; and because of the age of the buildings, they're inevitably a little rough around the edges. They'll suffer from problems such as dodgy plumbing, and in winter you'll have to leave the heater on high.

Basically, go courtyard if you want atmosphere and local colour, but be aware that facilities and comfort may be slightly less than in a modern hotel at the same price. Some of the best are: *Qianmen Youth Hostel* (see opposite), *Leo Hostel* (see below), *Chinese Box Courtyard Hostel* (see opposite), *Fangzhuanchang Antique Courtyard* (see p.133), *Cote Cour* (see p.129), *Courtyard 7* (see p.131), *Double Happiness* (see p.131) and *Mao'er Hutong* (see p.133).

simple, and often give access to sizeable discounts: try Ⓦwww.hotelschina.net, www.elong.com or www.sinohotel.com; for cheaper options, check out Ⓦwww.hostelworld.com and www.hostelbookers.com, both of which require a small deposit.

Checking in involves filling in a form and paying a deposit. Remember to grab a few hotel business cards when you check in; these are vital for letting taxi drivers know where you're staying.

All hotels have **tour offices** offering trips to the obvious sights: the Great Wall, acrobatics and Beijing opera shows. These are usually good value, and the most convenient way to get to remote destinations such as Simatai Great Wall. Most hotels will also book train and plane tickets for you, for a small commission.

Youth hostels

Beijing's **hostels** are clean and professionally run. Unless otherwise mentioned in the reviews below, you can expect them to feature a lounge with a TV and a few DVDs, self-service laundry (¥15 or so) and bike rental (around ¥20 a day). They will also offer **tours** to sights outside the city such as the Great Wall, and will arrange train and plane tickets for a small commission (¥40 at most). They have to be given credit for offering **free wi-fi** and internet access, something the larger hotels charge for.

Don't be put off if you don't fit the backpacker demographic; they also have inexpensive double and some single rooms, (though sometimes with shared bathrooms). An added bonus of the places below is that they are actually rather better located than most of the larger mid-range hotels, in quiet neighbourhood *hutongs* not too far from the subway.

Note that any place billing itself a "youth hostel" will give you a ¥10 per night discount if you have a youth-hostel (ISIC) card, which they can sell you for ¥50.

South of the centre

The hostels reviewed below are marked on the "South of the centre" map on pp.62–63.

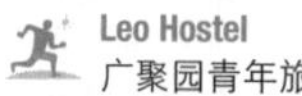

Leo Hostel
广聚园青年旅舍
guǎngjùyuán qīngnián lǚshè
52 Dazhalan Xi Jie ⓣ010/86608923, Ⓦwww.leohostel.com. With the dust finally settling

on the massive reconstruction of the Dazhalan area, this big, well-run hostel, ten minutes' walk from Tian'anmen Square, has come into its own. Extras such as a bar, pool table, DVD lounge and free maps play well with its youthful demographic, as does the wide range of day trips. Leafy and attractive communal spaces make up for rooms that are a bit tatty round the edges. It's easy to find, on the bustling, pedestrianized Dazhalan strip. Dorms ¥50–80; rooms ¥120.

Qianmen Youth Hostel
前门客栈
qiánmén kèzhàn
33 Meishi Jie ⓣ010/63132369. Though it's very well located, in a *hutong* just a couple of minutes walk from Tian'anmen Square and a minute from Qianmen subway stop, this little courtyard hostel doesn't impress on first sight, thanks to its poky, gloomy reception. Things improve greatly as you head inside – rooms are in a nineteenth-century building, overlooking a secluded courtyard, with attractive carved wooden balconies outside. Other original features include wood panelling and old tiled flooring – ask for one of the pricier heritage rooms, and insist on the second floor as ground-floor rooms are very dark. If you take a room without bath, be prepared for a long, chilly trip to the outside toilets and showers in winter. Some of the cheapest dorms in the city: ¥50 for a four- or six-bed option. Rooms start at ¥120.

North of the centre

The hostels reviewed below are marked on the "North of the centre" map on pp.84–85.

Chinese Box Courtyard Hostel
团圆四合院客栈
tuányuánsìhéyuàn kèzhàn
52 Xisi Bei Er Tiao ⓣ010/66186768, ⓦwww.chinesebox.hostel.com. A five-minute walk from Xisi subway stop, this charming little family-run courtyard hotel, hidden behind a sturdy red door in a *hutong*, is one of the best cheapies. Avoid it, though, if you're averse to cats – there are at least six slinking round, with guests invited to vote on which is their favourite. There are only a couple of rooms so you'll certainly need to book ahead. The dorms are on the pricey side but the two rather incongruously luxurious double rooms are excellent value, perhaps the best value in their price range. They feature huge beds with imperial touches in the wallpaper and cushions. They also offer free wi-fi, laundry for ¥15, and a room to watch DVDs in, along with a fairly minimal breakfast included in the rates. Dorms ¥80–100, rooms ¥340.

Lama Temple Youth Hostel
雍和宫青年旅舍
yōnghégōng qīngnián lǚshè
56 Beixinqiao Toutiao ⓣ010/64028663. Well-located courtyard hostel just south of Yonghe Gong. Rooms are spacious but dark, though at the price you can't really complain, and there's a large common room with a DVD collection. Staff are keen and friendly. Close to both Ghost Street and Nanluogu Xiang, it's handy for restaurants and nightlife. To get there, take the first *hutong* north of the Dongzhimennei and Yonghegong Dajie intersection, a few minutes south of Yonghe Gong subway stop; look for the yellow sign at the *hutong* entrance. Dorms ¥60, rooms ¥220.

Red Lantern House
红灯笼宾馆
hóngdēnglóng bīnguǎn
5 Zhengjue Hutong, Xinjiekou Nan Dajie ⓣ010/66115771, ⓦwww.redlanternhouse.com. The main feature here is an extraordinary courtyard overloaded with ornament, including two water features and a forest of red lanterns. Hidden amongst the jungle of kitsch are a cat, a dog and a receptionist. Rooms are good value and their plain white walls come as some relief. It's a fifteen-minute walk to Jishuitan subway stop. Six-bed dorms ¥60, rooms ¥200.

Sitting on the Walls Courtyard House
城墙客栈
chéngqiáng kèzhàn
57 Nianzi Hutong ⓣ010/64027805. Tucked away in a quiet *hutong*, this is another converted courtyard house that offers an intimate atmosphere, a bit of character, friendly staff, pets, and dodgy plumbing. It's very central, just behind the Forbidden City, though not near a subway stop. A good base for anyone who fancies cycling around (bike rental is ¥20 a day). It's a little tough to find first time, and taxi drivers don't know where it is; you'll have to wend your way through the alleyways, following the signs. Dorms ¥70, rooms ¥420.

Sleepy Town Inn
丽舍什刹海青年酒店
lìshě shíchàhǎi qīngnián jiǔdiàn
103 Deshengmennei Dajie ⓣ010/64069954, ⓦwww.sleepyinn.com.cn. This homely place has a great location, beside a canal just off Houhai Lake, but little in the way of facilities; there's no restaurant, for example. A good terrace and pleasant staff make up for slightly overpriced rooms; the dorms are good value, though. It's a 10min walk from Jishuitan subway station. Four- to eight-bed dorms ¥60; rooms ¥320.

Houhai Lake

The hostels reviewed below are marked on the "Houhai Lake & around" map on p.88.

Downtown Backpackers
东堂青年旅舍
dōngtáng qīngnián lǚshè
85 Nanluogu Xiang ⓣ010/84002429, ⓦwww.backpackingchina.com. One of the best backpacker places, with a location among the artsy boutiques of Nanluogu Xiang, Beijing's trendiest *hutong*; you won't be short of eating and nightlife options. Graffiti all over the walls extol the virtues of the staff, though perhaps they've let it go to their heads. There are a few single and double rooms – priced according to whether they have windows and bathrooms – which get rapidly booked up. A small breakfast is included. Light sleepers might find the gurgling plumbing in winter annoying. It's very popular, so you'll certainly have to book in advance. Six-bed dorms ¥70; rooms ¥150–225.

Drum Tower Youth Hostel
鼓楼青年旅舍
gǔlóu qīngnián lǚshè
51 Jiugulou Dajie ⓣ010/64037702. This three-storey hostel is in a good area, though right on a noisy main road. Rooms are spartan but clean, and the whole place looks a bit institutional. Still, staff are friendly and there's a mellow rooftop patio. There's a self-service kitchen and all the facilities you might expect but no free internet (¥8/hr). It's a 10min walk south from Gulou subway station. Dorms ¥50, rooms ¥140–220.

Hotels

The capital's **upmarket** hotels (from ¥900 per night for a double room in the high season) are legion, and more are appearing all the time. They offer amenities such as gyms, saunas, and business centres (though annoyingly, while cheap hotels have free internet, you have to pay for it at pricey ones). These establishments are comparable to their counterparts elsewhere in the world, though the finer nuances of service might well be lacking. If nothing else, they make useful landmarks, and some have pretty good restaurants that are, by Western standards at least, inexpensive. Some of them offer **off-season discounts** of up to seventy percent.

Mid-range hotels (¥350–900) are well equipped and comfortable, offering spacious double rooms, but are generally anonymous and unstylish – except for a few small hotels converted from old courtyard houses, which have an ambience that is recognizably Chinese, with quiet courtyards and period furniture (see p.126). Breakfast apart, it's recommended to eat out rather than in the hotel restaurant: hotel food is pretty mediocre at this level.

Budget hotels (up to ¥350) boast little in the way of facilities; you can expect your room to be clean, but it might be poky. There is, however, a lot of choice in this price range, thanks to Chinese chains such as *Home* and *Jinjiang Inn*. If you want a bit of atmosphere, however, go for a hostel instead.

Most hotels have a few single rooms, priced slightly cheaper than doubles. **Breakfast** is not usually included in the rate except in the classier places, where a choice of Western and Chinese food is available.

South of the centre

The following hotel is marked on the "South of the centre" map on pp.62–63.

Jianguo Qianmen
建国前门饭店
jiànguó qiánmén fàndiàn
175 Yong'an Lu ⓣ010/63016688, ⓦwww.qianmenhotel.com. The architecture is po-faced Soviet style, but this huge hotel, popular with tour groups, is given a glimmer of glamour by the on-site theatre, which has nightly performances of Beijing opera (see p.150). The huge lobby is quite stylish, but some of the rooms are in need of refurbishment and a bit of colour to leaven the incessant beige. It's quite far south, close to the Temple of Heaven but far from just about everything else. Bus #14 south from Hepingmen subway stop comes here – get off at the third stop. ¥700.

West of the centre

The following hotel is marked on the "West of the centre" map on pp.68–69.

Minzu
民族飯店
mínzú fàndiàn
51 Fuxingmen Dajie ⓣ010/66014466, ⓦwww.minzuhotel.com. Built in 1959, this Chinese-run behemoth is undeniably dated, but at least recent renovations mean they're still trying. There are more than 600 rooms, plus a gym, a billiards room and a good first-floor restaurant. The hotel is midway between Fuxingmen and Xidan subway stops, and not too far from some attractive parts of the city, though a little far from any of the tourist sites. ¥800.

East of the centre

The following hotel is marked on the "East of the centre" map on pp.74–75.

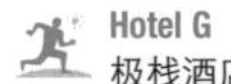
Hotel G
极栈酒店
jízhàn jiǔdiàn
A7 Workers' Stadium ⓣ010/65523600, ⓦwww.hotel-G.com. This slick, modern boutique hotel has a great gimmick – at night every window is lit up a different colour. If that seems a bit nightclubby, the impression is only reinforced by the sharp lines and subdued lighting in the lobby; rooms though, are cosy, with big, soft beds, and service standards are very high. Aimed at a hip young crowd who like to party in nearby Sanlitun. ¥1100.

Wangfujing

The following hotels are marked on the "Wangfujing" map on p.77.

Beijing
北京饭店
běijīng fàndiàn
33 Dongchang'an Jie ⓣ010/65137766, ⓦwww.chinabeijinghotel.com.cn. One of the most recognizable buildings in Beijing, this mansion just east of Tian'anmen Square – and very near the Wangfujing subway stop – was built in 1900. The view from the top floors of the west wing, over the Forbidden City, is superb. After the addition of a new wing in 1974, an office block had to be constructed nearby so that top-floor guests couldn't see into Zhongnanhai. Unfortunately, the hotel rested on its laurels for decades, and even though it's now trying to catch up with the competition, still has to be considered overpriced, more the home of cadres on junkets than businessmen. ¥880.

Cote Cour
北京演乐精品酒店
běijīng yǎnlè jīngpǐn jiǔdiàn
70 Yanyue Hutong, Dongcheng Qu ⓣ010/65128021, ⓦwww.hotelcotecourbj.com. This fourteen-room courtyard-style boutique hotel is bang in the middle of the city, near the Wangfujing subway station, but in a quiet *hutong*. Skilfully decorated in oriental chic (though oddly it doesn't have the Chinese name you'd expect), it's a place to consider if you would rather pay for style and character than lavish facilities. There's no restaurant, but a free breakfast is served in the lounge. If you are coming by taxi, note that some drivers won't go down the alley, so you'll have to walk for five minutes after being dropped off – best to call the hotel before you arrive and they'll arrange a taxi to pick you up. ¥1068–2688.

Crowne Plaza
国际艺苑皇冠饭店
guójìyìyuàn huángguān fàndiàn
48 Wangfujing Dajie ⓣ010/65133388, ⓦwww.crowneplaza.com. Well-established five-star chain hotel with arty pretensions (there's an on-site gallery), and a handy location for the shops and sights (it's near the Wangfujing

subway stop). The best of a number of pricey hotels in the area. ¥1240.

Grand Hotel Beijing
北京贵宾楼饭店
běijīng guìbīnlóu fàndiàn
35 Dongchang'an Jie ⓣ010/65130057, ⓦwww.grandhotelbeijing.com.cn. A central, if ageing, five-star palace near the Wangfujing subway stop and with splendid views over the Forbidden City. Rooms feature period rosewood furniture, and there's plenty of elegant calligraphy around. As well as a pool and gym and you can get a free *tai ji* lesson in the mornings. Service standards are high, making this a better bet than the *Beijing* next door. Doubles start at ¥950.

Haoyuan
好园宾馆
hǎoyuán bīnguǎn
53 Shijia Hutong ⓣ010/65125557. Near Beijing Zhan subway stop, and down a quiet alley off Dongsi Nan Dajie – look for the gates with two red lanterns hanging outside – this converted courtyard house features rooms kitted out with imitation Qing furniture, including four-poster beds. It's central and convenient, though the neighbourhood is rather anonymous. It's a small place, so book in advance. ¥850.

Hilton Wangfujing
王府井希尔顿酒店
wángfǔjǐng xī'ěrdùn jiǔdiàn
8 Wangfujing Dong Dajie ⓣ010/58128888. Newly refitted, luxurious and upscale, near the shopping district of Wangfujing, with an impressive gym and pool. You can see the Forbidden City from the upper floors and you're close to some decent restaurants. It's a safe international choice and there are some good discounts available. Good on detail – there's judicious use of incense, and rooms have iPod docks. Internet access is expensive at ¥3 a minute, however, which is a common gripe in this budget. ¥2200.

Kapok
木棉花酒店
mùmiánhuā jiǔdiàn
16 Donghuamen Dajie ⓣ010/65259988, ⓦwww.hotelkapok.com. A swish boutique hotel ten minutes' walk from the Forbidden City, with clean lines, glass walls and a bamboo theme giving it a distinctive, modish look. There aren't too many luxury extras, but overall it's clean, chic and not too pricey, which makes it very popular – you'll have to book. A fifteen-minute walk from Tian'anmen Dong subway station. Staff are friendly but don't always speak good English. ¥700.

Peninsula Palace
王府饭店
wángfǔ fàndiàn
Jingyu Hutong ⓣ010/65128899, ⓦwww.peninsula.com. A discreet, upmarket place with a very good reputation, though not quite up to the standard of its sister in Hong Kong. It's well located, within walking distance of the Forbidden City, and about fifteen minutes' walk from Wangfujing subway station, but if you need to get around quickly by taxi, be aware of the traffic snarls around here during rush hour. Nice touches include a non-smoking floor, and fresh fruit left in the room daily. Doubles start at ¥1800.

Jianguomen Dajie and around

The hotels reviewed below are marked on the "Jianguomen Dajie" map on p.79.

Jianguo
建国饭店
jiànguó fàndiàn
5 Jianguomenwai Dajie ⓣ010/65002233, ⓦwww.hoteljianguo.com. Popular, thanks to its convenient (if hardly atmospheric) location just down the road from the Silk Market, this old stalwart has rooms of varying quality – ask to stay on the newly renovated executive floor or on a lower floor with a view of the garden. The restaurant, *Justine's*, has pretty good French food, and there are plenty of drinking and dining options outside. It's near the Yong'an Li subway stop. ¥1100.

New Otani
长富宫饭店
chángfùgōng fàndiàn
26 Jianguomenwai Dajie ⓣ010/65125555. Get seriously pampered in this five-star, Japanese-managed modern mansion – and pay heftily for the privilege. There's a decent-sized swimming pool, saunas and a squash court. It's near the Jianguomen subway stop. ¥1200.

Ritz Carlton
北京丽思卡尔顿酒店
běijīng lìsīkǎěrdùn jiǔdiàn
83A Jianguomen Dajie ⓣ010/59088131. Compact five-star hotel in the slick but rather anonymous, high-end Guomao – it's

handy for the subway (Guomao stop) and expensive shops. Rooms are spacious and decorated, in opposition to the usual "modern luxe" you get in this district, in a chintzy, English manor house style. There are all the facilities you might expect, and the pampering is very professional. ¥2400.

St Regis
国际俱乐部饭店
guójìjùlèbù fàndiàn
21 Jianguomenwai Dajie ⓣ010/64606668, ⓦwww.starwoodhotels.com. This, the plushest hotel in the city, is the first choice of visiting dignitaries, having housed both George Bush and Quentin Tarantino. It features real palm trees in the lobby, and there's a personal butler for guests. ¥2500.

Sanlitun and the northeast

The hotels reviewed below are marked on the "Sanlitun & the northeast" map on p.81.

Great Wall Sheraton
长城饭店
chángchéng fàndiàn
6 Dongsanhuan Bei Lu ⓣ010/65005566, ⓦwww.sheraton.com. An ageing compound out on the Third Ring Road towards the airport. Built around a seven-storey atrium, it's not only architecturally impressive but also very comfortable, with a good ground-floor teahouse that hosts jazz performances. There are plenty of excellent restaurants and some lively bars nearby. ¥1300.

Kempinski
凯宾斯基饭店
kǎibīnsījī fàndiàn
Lufthansa Centre, 50 Liangmaqiao Lu ⓣ010/64653388, ⓦwww.kempinski.com/Beijing. On the Third Ring Road, this luxurious business hotel is a little out of the way, though the huge attached shopping complex means there's no shortage of diversions on site. The deli (see p.136) is great for a quick breakfast. ¥1600.

Opposite House
瑜舍
yúshè
Building 1, 11 Sanlitun Lu ⓣ010/64176688, ⓦwww.theoppositehouse.com. This trendy modern hotel is bright, white and decorated with modern Chinese art; you could have walked into a gallery. Rooms offer minimalist chic with no stinting on comfort; bathrooms have oakwood tubs and waterfall showers. It's just around the corner from Sanlitun, so there's no shortage of restaurants and nightlife in the area – what it doesn't have, however, is a subway stop anywhere nearby. There's no sign on the outside – look for the green building next to the 3.3 mall. ¥2560.

North of the centre

The hotels reviewed below are marked on the "North of the centre" map on pp.84–85.

Beijing Templeside Deluxe Hutong House
广济.邻青年旅舍
guǎngjì.lín qīngnián lǚshè
2 Baita Xiang, inside Anping, Zhaodengyu Jie ⓣ010/ 66172571, ⓦwww.templeside.com. This renovated courtyard house has really gone for a Chinese feel; everything, from the designs on the carpets to the latticework windows, is red, tassled, or plastered with characters. Even the cisterns are decorated with Chinese motifs. But if you don't mind a bit of chintz, this is a pretty successful marriage of *hutong* house and comfy pad. The central courtyard has been turned into a sociable lounge by the addition of a glass roof, and it's cute and quiet with friendly staff. A fifteen-minute walk from Fuchengmen subway stop, it's just a little out of the way. Rooms ¥650–880; a bed in the five-bed basement dorm costs ¥100.

Courtyard 7
秦唐府客栈七号院
qíntángfǔ kèzhàn qīhàoyuàn
7 Qian Gulou Yuan Hutong ⓣ010/64060777, ⓦwww.courtyard7.com. Rooms in this courtyard hotel off Nanluogu Xiang might be on the small side, and the restaurant isn't up to much, but it more than makes up for it with a peaceful ambience and good location. It's single storey so all the rooms face the courtyard, and elegantly furnished throughout, with four-poster beds and colourful tiled bathrooms. The *hutong* is pleasant and clean but you won't get a cab to go down there. ¥550–1100.

Double Happiness Courtyard Hotel
阅微庄四合院宾馆
yuèwēizhuāng sìhéyuàn bīnguǎn
37 Dongsi Sitiao ⓣ010/64007762, ⓦwww.doublehappinesshotel.com. A courtyard hotel boasting larger rooms than most, with wooden floors and the usual traditional Chinese carved and

lacquered decor. The courtyards are attractive, with red lanterns and plenty of foliage. It's central, but a couple of hundred metres down a narrow alley that taxis won't drive down – still, Dongsi Shitiao subway station is only a couple of minutes' walk away. It can get a bit chilly in winter. ¥550.

Green Tea
格林豪泰酒店
gélín háotài jiǔdiàn
46 Fangjia Hutong ⓣ010/64032288. A typical example of one of the new business hotel chains – efficient, clean, cheap and characterless. But this branch scores for its location at the back of the Yongjia Hutong complex of trendy arts venues, restaurants and bars. It's a fifteen-minute walk from Yonghe Gong subway stop. ¥180.

Lüsongyuan
侣松园宾馆
lǚsōngyuán bīnguǎn
22 Banchang Hutong, off Jiaodaokou Nan Dajie ⓣ010/64040436. Converted from a Qing dynasty mansion, this hotel, though it's aimed at tour groups, has a little more charisma than most such places. Rooms vary, so try to check a few. They might all be rather old-fashioned but they are arranged around quiet courtyards which feature red lanterns, caged birds and even statues of famous Chinese figures. The area is good, a quiet alley just around the corner from fashionable Nanluogu Xiang, so there are plenty of places to eat nearby. Avoid the expensive breakfast. To get there from Beijing Zhan, take bus #104 and get off at the Beibingmasi stop. Walk 50m south and you'll find a sign pointing you down an alley to the hotel. A few dorm beds in the basement for ¥60–100; rooms start at ¥550.

Michael's House
迈克之家旅馆
màikèzhījiā lǚguǎn
1 Nanyuan, Zhiqiang Beiyuan, Haidian ⓣ010/62225620, ⓦwww.michaels-houses.com. This inexpensive but stylish boutique courtyard hotel is far up in the northwest, in studenty Haidian, ten minutes' walk from Jishuitan subway stop. Bric-a-brac and pot plants make the courtyards feel cosy and each room is distinctively, if rather quirkily, furnished with chinoiserie – and with its friendly staff it feels more like a B&B. Breakfast isn't much good, but overall this has to be considered one of the best deals in its price range. ¥320–650.

Red Capital Residence
新红资客栈
xīnhóngzī kèzhàn
9 Dongsi Liu Tiao ⓣ010/84035308, ⓦwww.redcapitalclub.com. Formerly a state guesthouse, this discreet *hutong* hotel now has five rooms tricked out with Cultural Revolution artefacts. The courtyard rock formation hides the entrance to a bomb shelter-turned-bar and Madame Mao's old Red Flag limousine is available for tours. It's frankly more a novelty than a luxury experience, rather like staying in an eccentric museum, and pricey for what you get. Still, you'll need to book in advance as it remains popular. It's neatly hidden away: look for the red doors and the little "9". ¥1650.

Zhong Tang Hotel
中堂客栈
zhōngtáng kèzhàn
12 Xi Si Bei Er Tiao Hutong, off Deshengmennei Dajie ⓣ010/66171369. Another courtyard hotel with period furniture – lots of dark wood and lacquer, and plenty of quirky detail. But rooms are a little poky, plumbing unreliable and breakfast isn't very good. Still, it's in a quiet lane a couple of minutes walk from Xisi subway stop. The better rooms have four-poster beds and wooden bath tubs. ¥360–880.

Houai Lake

The hotels reviewed below are marked on the "Houhai Lake & around" map on p.88.

Bamboo Garden
竹园宾馆
zhúyuán bīnguǎn
24 Xiaoshiqiao Hutong, Jiugulou Dajie ⓣ010/64032299, ⓦwww.bbgh.com.cn. This hotel was converted from the residence of a Qing official and today the courtyards and bamboo-filled gardens are by far its best features. It's an old hotel, not musty thanks to recent refurbishment, but perhaps service standards are a little behind the times. The more expensive suites boast period furniture, but the standard rooms are fine and pretty good value, with garden views. It's tucked into an alley in an agreeable part of the city, near Houhai but still quiet. Head south from Gulou subway for about 250m down Jiugulou Dajie and take the fourth alley to the right; continue along for 100m, turn left and you're there. Rooms start at ¥680.

Fangzhuanchang Antique Courtyard
方砖厂6号院私人会馆
fāngzhuānchǎng liùhàoyuàn sīrénhuìguǎn
6 Fangzhuanchang, Di'Anmenwai Dajie ⓣ010/64035469. A refined little *hutong* hotel given character by all the old wooden furniture, fittings and slightly spooky "tree root" sculptures – there's something of a teahouse feel to the place. There are only five rooms, all arranged around a leafy courtyard, and all packed with period furniture, including big four poster beds. Rooms ¥780.

Guxiang 20
古巷20号商务会
gǔxiàng èrshí hào shāngwùhuì
20 Nanluogu Xiang ⓣ010/64005566. Slick hotel well located right in the nightlife area of Nanluogu Xiang – though note that it's on a pedestrianized street far from a subway, so you'll need to do some walking. It's done out in that discreet, orientalist style perennially popular in restaurants – dark, red and minimal. The best doubles have four-poster beds and there's a tennis court on the roof too. It seems aimed at young locals, and not much English is spoken. It doesn't maintain much presence on the street and looks rather like a club; hence, presumably, the English sign outside announcing that there's no entrance fee. Rooms start at ¥640.

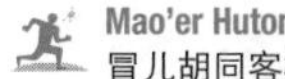

Mao'er Hutong
冒儿胡同客栈
mào'er hútóng kèzhàn
28 Mao'er Hutong, off Nanluogu Xiang ⓣ13661219901 (mobile), ⓦwww.bb-china.com. There are just four rooms in this intimate courtyard hotel, stuffed with chinoiserie – one of them is a single and another is deluxe. It's more of a B&B; service is highly personal and Angela the owner is eager to please, offering an excellent breakfast that changes daily. There's no restaurant, but as you're round the corner from nightlife district Nanluogu Xiang, you don't need one. Note that the alley is too narrow for taxis, so expect to walk for five minutes or so after the taxi drops you off. Uniquely for Beijing, the whole place is non-smoking. You'll certainly need to book in advance. ¥350–900.

Qing Zhu Yuan
青竹园
qīngzhú yuán
113 Nanluogu Xiang ⓣ010/64013961. The no-frills, cheap rooms and gloomy lobby are all forgiven as it's on party central Nanluogu Xiang – you won't want to stay in much. A good option for when the *Downtown Backpackers* (see p.128) is booked up, or if you find the hostel's demographic tiresome. Doubles without bathroom ¥140, with bathroom ¥220.

Eating

The Chinese are a nation of foodies: even pleasantries revolve around the subject. One way of asking "how are you?" – *nǐ chīfàn le ma?* – translates literally as "have you eaten rice yet?", and they talk food like the British talk about the weather, as a social icebreaker. It follows then, that China boasts one of the world's most complex **cuisines**, from market-stall buns and soup through to intricate varieties of regional cooking.

The culinary wealth of Beijing is unique; it encompasses every style of Chinese food available, along with just about any Asian fare and most world cuisines. It's no surprise that, for some visitors, eating becomes the highlight of their trip. Prices are low in comparison with the West, and it's possible to eat well for less than ¥50 a head, although you can spend a lot more if you dine lavishly in palatial surroundings. Meals are considered social events, and the Chinese like their restaurants to be *renao* – hot and noisy.

As for **opening hours**, note that the Chinese tend to eat early, sitting down to lunch at noon and dinner at six. By 2pm most restaurants are empty and the staff impatient to begin their afternoon break, and as a general rule, if you want to eat very late in the evening head to a place that sees a lot of foreign custom; their kitchen may well have longer hours.

Tipping isn't expected; if there is a service charge, it will be on the bill. **Chopsticks** aren't obligatory: all restaurants have knives (*da-ozi*) and forks (*cha-zi*). Tofu dishes should be eaten with a spoon.

Among China's varied cuisines, **Sichuan cooking** and **hotpot meals** are perhaps the most popular in Beijing. Among faddish foodies, Yunnan cuisine from China's far south has recently become popular, as has malatang from Sichuan – a kind of dry hotpot. As for cuisines from elsewhere in Asia, Japanese, Thai and Korean food are widely available and well worth trying. You'll also find Indian, Russian and Middle Eastern cooking, generally in upmarket areas.

There's also ample opportunity to eat **Western food** in the city, though this generally costs a little more than a Chinese meal in a comparable restaurant. If you really want the home comforts, try international fast-food chains, many of which are well established here.

Many visitors find the Chinese **breakfast** of dumplings and glutinous rice bland and unappealing, but the classic Beijing breakfast snack *jianbing guozi* (seasonal vegetables wrapped in an omelette wrapped in a pancake), deftly made in thirty seconds by street vendors, is definitely worth trying (¥3). Most large hotels offer some form of Western breakfast; alternatively, head to a branch of *Delifrance* for cheap croissants, or to one of the many international coffee shops that offer coffee, croissants and muffins. Coffee is generally a drink of the cosmopolitan elites, so coffee shops tend to cluster in expensive areas.

Beijing is well stocked with **supermarkets**, especially useful if you want to get a picnic, or have self-catering facilities. Finally, you could even forego the whole tedious business of leaving your room by contacting Beijing Goodies (Ⓣ010/64167676, Ⓦwww.beijinggoodies.com) who, for a small service charge, deliver from many of the city's popular restaurants.

Fast food and street food

The Chinese version of **fast food** (found in department stores or at street stalls), is usually a serving of noodles or dumplings, or rice with meat, in a polystyrene carton. The best Asian fast food chains are *Yoshinoya* (noodles), *Ajisen* (Japanese noodles), *Dayang Dumplings, Kungfu Catering* (simple dishes with chicken soup), *Yongfu King* (noodles and fried bread sticks), and *Chamate* (Cantonese style).

Street food, sold by stalls parked by the roadside, is widely available, though not in the city centre, where vendors are shooed away by the police. The best place to try street fare is at one of the designated **night markets** (see below), which begin operating around 5pm and start to shut down around 10pm; they're at their busiest and best in the summer. Generally, what's on offer is hygienic – you can feel confident of food cooked in front of you. Most popular are the skewers of heavily spiced, barbecued meat, often served up by Uigurs from Xinjiang, China's far west. For cheap and filling suppers, try *huntun* (wonton) soup; *xianer bing* (savoury stuffed pancake); or the plentiful varieties of noodles. However, you should avoid anything that's eaten cold, such as home-made ice cream, which is often of a dubious standard.

It's also worth knowing that every shopping centre, mall and plaza also holds a **food court** –generally in the basement, but sometimes on the top floor – which offers inexpensive meals from a cluster of outlets. Food courts are good places to start sampling simple Chinese food – the environment may not be very atmospheric but it's clean, and prices are fixed. Paying can be a little confusing at first; you have to buy a plastic card at a central booth (¥20 is usually the lowest denomination), which is debited at the food counters when you order – you can claim back the remainder at the end. There's always a good range of dishes, and as the food is displayed on the counter it's easy to choose. Good, substantial food courts can be found at the Parkson Building on Fuxingmennei Dajie (see p.69); in the Xidan stores (see p.68); and, on Wangfujing, on the fifth floor of the Sun Dong'an Plaza or the basement of the *Oriental Plaza* (see p.76). The best food court in town, however – for choice and comfort – has to be the new one in the basement of Shin Kong Place (see p.159).

Ajisen
味千拉面
wèiqiān lāmiàn
Shop 0102, SOHO A, 39 Dongsanhuan Zhonglu, Guomao Ⓦwww.ajisen.com. Superior fast food from this Japanese chain offering ramen, noodles, miso soup and basic curries. Daily 10.30am–10pm.

Chamate
一茶一坐
yīcháyīzuò
B1, Oriental Plaza, Chang'an Dong Dajie; Third Floor, Shin Kong Place, 87 Jianguomennei Dajie; Ⓦwww.chamate.cn. Cheap Cantonese dishes such as barbecued ribs and fried rice. Daily 10am–10pm.

Dong'anmen night market
东华门夜市
dōnghuámén yèshì
Dong'anmen Dajie, off Wangfujing Dajie; see "Wangfujing" map on p.77. Set up along the street, the red-canopied stalls here offer *xiǎo chī* – literally, "little eats" – from all over China. Nothing costs more than a few yuan, except the odd delicacy, such as chicken hearts. Daily 5.30–10.30pm.

Goubuli
狗不理
gǒubùlǐ
29 Dazhalan Dajie; 88 Dongdan Bei Dajie. The original fast food: delicious steamed buns with various fillings for a few yuan. You can

eat them here – the downstairs canteen is cheaper than upstairs – or take away, as most customers do. Daily 10am–10pm.

Kempi Deli

First Floor, *Kempinski Hotel* (see p.131); Lufthansa Centre, 50 Liangmaqiao Lu. Produces the city's best bread and pastries. It's not cheap (a croissant is ¥12) but prices halve after 8pm. Daily 7am–11pm.

Kungfu Catering

真功夫

zhēn gōngfū

FF10, Basement, Oriental Plaza, 1 Cang'an Dong Dajie; 105, Building A, Jianwai Soho, Sanhuan Dong Lu; Basement, Xidan Shopping Mall, 120 Xidan Bei Dajie. Simple, cheap steamed Chinese food from an aggressively expanding chain; they'll surely get into trouble eventually for their Bruce Lee rip-off logo. Try the fragrant sauce ribs (¥20). Daily 9am–10pm.

Xian Lao Man

馅老满

xiànlǎomǎn

5 Anhu Beili Yayuan, Gulou. An earthy little dumpling restaurant that's always busy and does a lot of takeaway business. Good for a quick, tasty lunch. Daily 9am–9.30pm

Xiaochi Jie

小吃街

xiǎochī jiē

Xiagongfu Jie, running west off the southern end of Wangfujing; see "Wangfujing" map on p.77. This alley is lined with stalls where pushy vendors sell exotic food – skewers of fried scorpions, silkworm pupae, crickets and sparrows – none of it tastes of much, to be honest, and the only reason to try it is for the bragging rights. Daily 9am–11pm.

Yonghe King

永和大王

yǒnghé dàwáng

22 Jianguomenwai Dajie; 8 Meishuguan Dong Jie; Third Floor, Shin Kong Place, 87 Jianguomennei Dajie. Fast food chain known for its *youtiao* (fried dough sticks). Daily 9am–10pm.

Yoshinoya

吉野家

jíyějiā

Fourth Floor, Sun Dong'an Plaza, Wangfujing; outside the main gate of the Yiheyuan (Summer Palace); and in the New World Plaza, Jianguomennei Dajie; Ⓦ www.yohsinoya.com. A Japanese chain offering bowls of rice topped with slices of meat or fish and vegetables – healthy fast food that's cheap, hygienic and tasty. Daily 10am–10pm.

Cafés

As well as those places listed below, note that some bars are also great spots to linger over a cappuccino, notably *Pass By Bar* (see p.147), *No Name* (see p.147) and *Drum and Gong* (see p.147). The places below, almost all of which are in the north of the city, all have **free wi-fi**.

Bookworm

书虫

shū chóng

Sanlitun Nan Jie, back of building 4 Ⓦ www.chinabookworm.com. See "Sanlitun & the northeast" map on p.81. This classy bistro-cum-café-cum-library is full of hipster types musing. There are regular literary events and lectures, and a literary festival every March; check the website. Daily 9am–2am.

Cafe Zarah

飒哈

sàhā

42 Gulou Dongdajie, near Jiaodaokou Ⓦ www.cafezarah.com. See "North of the centre" map on pp.84–85. This bright, cosy art café, attractively converted from a courtyard house, hosts regular exhibitions. There's a good Western breakfast and plenty of snacks, including tasty home-made ice cream. Daily except Tues 10am–midnight.

Sculpting In Time

雕刻时光

diāokè shíguāng

7 Weigongcun Lu, outside the southern gate of the Beijing Insititute of Technology Ⓦ www.sitcoffee.com. See "North of the centre" map on pp.84–85. A relaxed, attractive café with a largely student clientele. Follow by example and sip on lattes, browsing the book collection and gazing thoughtfully out of the window. They serve good muffins and pasta dishes, too. Daily 9am–12.30am.

Starbucks
星巴克
xīngbākè
First Floor, China World Trade Centre, Jianguomenwai Dajie; COFCO plaza, 8 Jianguomennei Dajie; Chaoyangmenwai Dajie, opposite the Dongyue Temple; Sun Dong'an Plaza (basement) and Oriental Plaza (First Floor, A307) on Wangfujing Dajie; north side of Xidan Plaza, Xidan. The coffee colonizers have overtaken *McDonald's* as the most potent symbol of Westernization in town. A medium-sized cup of their caffeinated mud is ¥15. The branch at the north end of Qianmen is interesting – the three-storey building has been comprehensively Sinified, and even the baristas are in traditional Chinese clothes. This is the brand's attempt to prove its sensitivities after having been perceived as insulting Chinese culture by opening a branch inside the Forbidden City (which has since closed).

Timezone 8
东八时区艺术书屋
dōngbāshíqū yìshū shūwū
4 Jiuxianqiao Lu, 798 Arts District ⓦwww.timezone8.com. This fashionable bookshop-cum-café/restaurant is the best pit-stop for anyone schlepping round the galleries of 798. Daily 8.30am–9pm.

Vineyard Café
葡萄院儿
Pútáoyuàn'er
31 Wudaoying Hutong, south of Yonghe Gong Bridge ⓦwww.vineyardcafe.cn. **See "North of the centre" map on pp.84–85.** Good Western wine and food, including pizza, makes this popular with the local expats. Cross the Second Ring Road onto Yonghe Gong Dajie and take the first *hutong* on the right. Serves good brunches, a perfect combination with a trip to the Yonghe Gong. Daily 11.30am–midnight.

Xiaoxin's
小新的店
xiǎoxīn de diàn
103 Nanluogu Xiang. **See "Houhai Lake & around" map on p.88.** This cosy hideaway is one of the better Nanluogu Xiang cafés, though the staff could be a little more alert. Limited menu; try their smoothies and cheesecakes. Daily 9am–2am.

Restaurants

All of Beijing's expensive **hotels** have several well-appointed restaurants, where the atmosphere is sedate and prices are sometimes not as high as you might expect. Look out for their **special offers** – set lunches and buffets, usually – advertised in the city's listings magazines. Note, too that some of the best restaurants are in shopping malls, and that they often have several branches.

South of the centre

The restaurant reviewed below is marked on the "South of the centre" map on pp.62–63.

Lichun
利群烤鸭店
lìqún kǎoyādiàn
11 Bei Xiang Hutong ⓣ010/67025681. Deep in a *hutong*, this place is tough to find but offers decent duck at half the price of the chains (¥80). From Qianmen subway stop walk east along Qianmen Dong Dajie, take the first right into Zhengyi Lu, and turn right at the end. Then follow the English sign to the "Lichun Roast Duck Restaurant" and it's on the left. If in doubt, ask a passer-by – they're well used to pointing the place out to foreigners. The restaurant is in an old courtyard house, and it's small, so you'd be wise to reserve. Daily 10am–10pm.

East of the centre

The restaurants reviewed below are marked on the "East of the centre" map on pp.74–75.

The estimated **prices** of meals in our restaurant reviews are calculated on the basis of each person ordering a couple of dishes plus rice, or a main course and dessert. We've included phone numbers where it's wise to book a table.

Bellagio

鹿港小镇

lùgǎng xiǎozhèn

Raffles City Shopping Mall, 1 Dongzhimen Nei; Shin Kong Place, 87 Jianguo Lu; ⓣ010/84098075. This bright and cheery Taiwanese chain is popular with the hipster crowd, though they can be outcooled by the staff, who all, somewhat cultishly, sport the same haircut. There's a good range of Sichuan dishes and Taiwanese specialities such as *migao*, steamed glutinous rice flavoured with shrimp and mushroom, and *caipu dan* – a turnip omelette. It's open till the early hours, so good for late night, post-club snacks. Daily 11am–4am.

Dadong

大董烤鸭店

dàdǒng kǎoyādiàn

1–2/F Nanxincang International Building, Á2, Dongsi Shi Tiao, southwest of Dongsi Shitiao Bridge ⓣ010/51690328. A bright, modish place that's garnered a good reputation for its crispy-skinned, succulent Beijing duck. Don't restrict yourself to these signature dishes though; the rest of the Chinese food is fine too. Daily 11am–10pm.

Dongbei Ren

东北人

dōngběirén

A1 Xinzhong Jie, Dongzhimenwai Dajie ⓣ010/64152855. Colourful and boisterous, this popular place brings to the capital the hale and hearty dining style of northeastern China; honest, rustic grub and chirpy waitstaff. Stick to staples such as stew, dumplings, sweet-and-sour crispy pork and home-made tofu in a basket – or be adventurous and try the grilled donkey. Be warned that if you order the fish the staff break into song. Daily 10am–10pm.

Golden Thaitanium

泰合金

tàihéjīn

Dongsanhuan Bei Lu, next to the Chaoyang Theatre. Spicy and inexpensive Thai food in a relaxed setting and with a picture menu to order from. It's a handy option if you're headed to the acrobatics show at the theatre next door (see p.152), as the restaurant stays open after the performance. Daily 10am–10pm.

Jiajingdu Peking Duck

嘉靖都烤鸭店

jiājìngdū kǎoyādiàn

8 Hot Spring Chamber, Chaoyang Park West Gate, east of Zhanghong Qiao, near Jingchao Building ⓣ010/65918008, ⓦwww.afunti.com.cn. Go south, past *Suzie Wong's* bar, turn right after 50m and you'll see a building standing alone; the restaurant is on its north side. This place is pure food theatre; your chair is a throne, located in what looks like an imperial hall, and the waitstaff are dressed as palace servants. During your meal, emperors and concubines from various dynasties come out to greet you. It's impressively lavish and the banquets are pretty good – the duck is the last of many courses, so arrive hungry. Set meals only, starting at ¥299. Daily 11am–10.30pm.

Wangfujing and around

The restaurants reviewed below are marked on the "Wangfujing" map on p.77.

The Courtyard

四合院

sìhé yuàn

95 Donghuamen Dajie, outside the east gate of the Forbidden City ⓣ010/65268883, ⓦwww.courtyardbeijing.com. An elegant, modish place within spitting distance of the Forbidden City's moat. The fusion cuisine – continental French food with a Chinese twist – will set you back at least ¥250. There's a contemporary art gallery downstairs (see p.158) and a cigar lounge upstairs. Daily 6pm–1am.

Crystal Jade

翡翠酒家

fěicuì jiǔjiā

BB78–BB82, Oriental Plaza basement, 1 Dongchang'an Jie ⓣ001/85150238, ⓦwww.crystaljade.com. This classy Singapore chain has grown very popular thanks to a winning formula: delicious Cantonese food served up in a dark, palatial interior. It's tasty but not cheap; expect to pay around ¥300 a head. Great for lunchtime *dim sum*, and their barbecued meats are sumptuous. Daily 11am–10pm.

Hong Kong Food City

香港美食城

xiānggǎng měishíchéng

18 Dong'anmen Dajie ⓣ010/65136668. A big, bright Cantonese restaurant good for seafood and *dim sum*. It's popular with Chinese tourists, so it gets noisy. Reasonably priced at around ¥80 per person – if you avoid the shark's fin, abalone and the like. Daily 11am–2.30pm & 5pm–midnight.

Lei Garden
利苑酒家
lìyuàn jiǔjiā
Third Floor, Jinbao Tower, 89 Jinbao Jie, behind the *Regent Hotel* ⓣ010/85221212, ⓦwww.leigarden.hk. This upmarket and well-established Cantonese restaurant really comes into its own at lunchtime, thanks to its big selection of reasonably priced *dim sum*. Speciality dishes include crab with egg yolk. Daily 11am–2.30pm & 5–10.30pm.

Made in China
***Grand Hyatt*, 1 Dong Chang'an Jie ⓣ010/65109608.** An element of drama is added to this crisp, modish restaurant by the spectacle of chefs toiling over the giant woks and ovens in the open kitchen. Situated in the gleaming *Grand Hyatt* hotel, it's one of the swankiest places in town, and the food is reliably excellent. A great place to try Beijing duck with a date. Daily 7–10am, 11.30am–2.30pm & 5–10pm.

Jianguomen Dajie and around

The restaurants reviewed below are marked on the "Jianguomen Dajie" map on p.79.

Bellagio
See p.138 for a review of this small chain.

Ding Ding Xiang
鼎鼎香
dǐngdǐngxiāng
Sixth Floor, Shinkong Place, 87 Jianguo Lu ⓣ010/65305997; 1/F, 14 Dongzhong Jie, Dongzhimenwai ⓣ010/64172546 (for this branch see "East of the centre" map on pp.74–75). The gig at these upmarket hotpot restaurants is that everyone gets their own pot, which is handy if one of your party can't take spice or meat. Choose from a wide variety of broths – chicken is recommended – then pick the raw ingredients to cook up. For a hotpot place, the ambience here is a little rarefied – the white tablecloths are a surprise, considering how messy a hotpot dinner always gets – but it shouldn't set you back more than ¥250 per head. Daily 11am–12midnight.

Din Tai Fung
鼎泰丰
dǐngtàifēng
Sixth Floor, Shin Kong Place, 87 Jianguo Lu ⓣ010/65331536, ⓦwww.dintaifung.com. Slick, upscale Taiwanese restaurant where the speciality is *xiaolong bao* – juicy buns with a filling of crab, pork or seafood. Make sure to leave space for the delectable red bean paste buns for dessert. Daily 11.30am–10pm.

Dong Lai Shun Fan Zhuang
东来顺饭庄
dōngláishùn fànzhuāng
Xiaoyangmao Jie, just off Jianguomennei Dajie. This venerable old Bejing brand is a great, inexpensive place to sample hotpot, with a very good reputation among locals and an English menu. Stick to the staples – glass noodles, vegetables, tofu and piles of thinly sliced lamb and beef – for a plentiful feed. It's just around the corner from the ancient observatory. Around ¥50 per person. Daily 10.30am–2.30pm & 5–10pm.

The Elephant
大笨象
dàbènxiàng
Courtyard 39, Shenlu Jie Ritan Shang Jie, near Ritan Bei Lu. A popular, reasonably priced restaurant that keeps the city's sizeable Russian population happy; decor and service are ordinary but there's nothing wrong with staples such as borscht, caviar and chicken Kiev. The signature "Elephant fish" and Ukrainian stew come recommended. Daily noon–2am.

Justine's
***Jianguo hotel*, 5 Jianguomenwai Dajie ⓣ010/65002233 ext 8039.** Beijing's oldest French restaurant still has the best wine list in the capital. Try the lobster soup or grilled lamb. Service is attentive. Around ¥250 per person. Daily 6.30am–10.30am, noon–2pm & 6–10.30pm.

Makye Ame
玛吉阿米
mǎjí āmǐ
Second Floor, A11 Xiushui Nan Jie ⓣ010/65069616. Hearty Tibetan food in a cosy atmosphere, rather more upscale than anywhere in Tibet. Try the *tashi delek* (a yak meat lasagne) and wash it down with butter tea. Tibetan singing and dancing on Wed & Fri nights. It's behind the Friendship Store. Daily 10am–2am.

Nadaman
滩万
tānwàn
Third Floor, *China World Hotel*, China World Trade Centre ⓣ010/65052266. Discreet, minimalist and seriously expensive Japanese restaurant with a set meal of lots of small dishes

priced at ¥260–450 per person. Most of the ingredients are flown in from Japan. Take someone you want to impress. Daily 11.30am–2pm & 5.30–9.30pm.

Sichuan Government
川京办餐厅
chuānjīngbàn cāntīng
5 Gongyun Tou Tiao, off Jianguomennei Dajie ☎010/65122277. Authentic Sichuan restaurant designed to serve homesick bureaucrats. Head north up the alley that passes the east side of the Chang'an Theatre, and after 200m there's an alley to the right with a public toilet opposite. Around 50m down the alley a set of green-and-gold gates on the left mark the entrance to the Sichuan government building. Pass through these into the compound and you'll see the restaurant on the left. No English menu, no concessions to wimpy palettes, no fancy decor – just great, inexpensive food. Note that it's state-owned, so service isn't great, and they stop serving lunch at 2pm. Daily 10.30am–2pm & 4.30–10pm.

Steak and Eggs
喜来中
xǐláizhōng
Xiushui Nan Jie, behind the Friendship Store. Good-value American-diner food has made this an expat favourite, especially for Sunday brunch. Daily 7am–midnight.

Sanlitun and the northeast

The restaurants reviewed below are marked on the "Sanlitun & the northeast" map on p.81.

Alameda
茵茵西餐厅
yīnyīn xīcāntīng
Sanlitun Bei Jie, inside Nali Studios ☎010/64178084. This bright and cheery Brazilian restaurant is a firm expat favourite, so be sure to reserve. Set lunches (¥60) are good value, but watch out for that little dish of olives – they aren't complimentary. It's in an alley 100m south of the 3.3 Mall. Mon–Sat 11.30am–3pm & 6pm–12midnight; Sun 11.30am–10pm.

Bei
北
běi
***Opposite House* 11 Sanlitun Lu ☎010/64105230, Ⓦwww.beirestaurant.com.** Sleek, modernist destination restaurant *du jour*, housed in the basement of the trendy *Opposite House* hotel (see p.131). Stick with one of the three tasting menus (which, bizarrely, are named after David Bowie songs; ¥300/¥400/¥500), for a range of stylish, tasty north Asian food with a twist. Good choices include bacon and miso soup and salmon cooked in green tea. Daily 5.30–10.30pm.

Berena's Bistro
柏瑞娜中国菜
bóruìnà zhōngguócài
35 Lucky Street Mall, Zaoying Lu, Sanyuanqiao, opposite 21st Century Center ☎010/58670266. Foreigner-friendly but a little pricier than elsewhere, serving Sichuan food (not too spicy, unless you insist). Try their *gongbao jiding* or the sweet-and-sour pork. Reckon on ¥70 per head. Daily 11am–11pm.

Element Fresh
新元素餐厅
xīnyuánsù cāntīng
S8–31 Sanlitun Village Complex, 19 Nan Sanlitun Ⓦwww.elementfresh.com. All right, it's not very Chinese – the decor is straight out of the IKEA school – but if you're craving a salad and a smoothie, head for this trendy health food chain from Shanghai and expect to pay about the same as you would at home; the Asian sets such as pepper chicken salad are the best value for money. It's also the place to come if you need a hearty Western breakfast. Mon–Fri 10am–10pm, Sat & Sun 8am–10pm.

Hai Di Lao
海底捞
hǎidǐlāo
Á Baijiazhuang Lu ☎010/65950079. This reasonably priced chain is a great place for spicy Sichuan hotpot, with a good choice of broths and a make-your-own-dipping-sauce counter. You can order half portions, so you don't have to get a big group together. If you order the *la mian* noodles the waiter will pull them while dancing in front of you; and you get a free manicure while you're waiting for a table. Daily 10am–3am.

Hatsune
隐泉日本料理
yǐnquán rìběnliàolǐ
S8–30, Third Floor, Sanlitun Village Complex, 11 Bei Sanlitun Lu ☎010/64153939. Hip, young, American-styled Japanese restaurant with a reputation for good sashimi, which will cost you around ¥200 per head. Daily 11.30am–2pm & 5.30–10pm.

Karaiya Spice House
辣屋
làwū
Third Floor, Building 8, Sanlitun Village Complex, 19 Sanlitun Lu ⓣ010/64153535. Spicy Hunanese fine dining from the owner of *Hatsune* (see opposite). Specialities at this expat favourite are the hot and sour pork ribs and steamed Mandarin fish – a meal will set you back about ¥150 per person. Watch out for the trick front door. Daily 10.30am–2pm & 5.30–10pm.

Middle 8th
中8楼
zhōngbālóu
Building 8, Sanlitun Dong Lu, the alley running east from 3.3 Mall ⓣ010/64130629. This classy Yunnan restaurant is not as pricey as its frosty modernist decor might have you believe; you can fill up for less than ¥150. Specialities are the mushroom dishes, but the goats' cheese and wild herb salad are also very good. Wash it down with rice wine. There is even a selection of fried insects for the adventurous. Daily 11am–11pm.

One Thousand and One Nights
一千零一夜
yīqiān língyīyè
21 Gongrentiyuchang Bei Lu ⓣ010/65324050. Bus #118 comes here from Dongsi Shitiao subway stop. Beijing's oldest Middle Eastern restaurant is still popular both with Western bigwigs who come here to fill up on kebabs before or after hitting the bars, and with homesick diplomats who puff on hookahs on the pavement outside. There's nightly music and belly dancing. It's open till late (2am) but some dishes sell out early: try the hummus as a starter and the baked chicken for a main course, and leave enough room for some baklava. About ¥100 per head. Daily 11am–11pm.

Serve the People
为人民服务
wèi rénmín fúwù
1 Sanlitun Xiwujie ⓣ010/64153242. Trendy Thai restaurant, going for a postmodern Soviet look, presumably ironically. Thai staples such as green curry, pork satay with peanut sauce and *tom yum* seafood soup are all worth trying, and you can ask them to tone down the spices. The stylish T-shirts worn by the staff are available to buy. About ¥80 per person. Daily 10.30am–10.30pm.

Sureno
瑜舍地中海餐厅
yúshè dìzhōnghǎi cāntīng
Sanlitun Village Complex, 11 Sanlitun Bei Lu ⓣ010/64105240, ⓦwww.surenorestaurant.com. This expat favourite, featuring an open kitchen and a wood-fired oven, is the city's best venue for Mediterranean-style fine dining. A meal will set you back about ¥400 per person. Mon–Fri noon–10.30pm, Sat 6–10.30pm, Sun noon–10.30pm.

Three Guizhou Men
三个贵州人
sāngè guìzhōurén
8 Gongti Xilu (behind Bellagio) ⓣ010/65518517 or 9. This artsy joint has carved itself a niche by offering hearty Guizhou cusine in a stylish environment. Try house specialities such as rice tofu and vermicelli with pork, and leave some room for the steamed ribs too. It's open around the clock, and makes a good place to sate post-drink peckishness. A meal should come to around ¥150 a head. Daily 24hr.

Xinjiang Red Rose
新疆红玫瑰餐厅
xīnjiāng hóngméiguì cāntīng
7 Xiang Xingfu Yicun, Gongti, opposite the north gate of the Workers' Stadium ⓣ010/64155741. This is not a place for a quiet meal; not only is there a boisterous floorshow, with bellydancers and a live band, but diners are encouraged to get involved. Still, the hearty Xinjiang food is pretty decent, with good roast goat and lamb kebabs, and you can finish with a hookah pipe. Daily 11am–11pm.

North of the centre

The restaurants reviewed below are marked on the "North of the centre" map on pp.84–85.

Aimo Town
埃蒙小镇
aìméng xiǎozhèn
46 Fangjia Hutong, off Andingmennei Dajie ⓣ010/64001725. Yunnan food is all the rage right now, and this quiet spot serves it up well. The grilled fish and the mint with beef are recommended. The walls are covered with batik prints and photos from the province, and the waitstaff are in minority dress. Daily 11am–11pm.

Ghost Street (簋街 *guǐ jiē*)

Nicknamed "Ghost Street", a 1km-long stretch of **Dongzhimennei Dajie**, from Dongzhimen Bridge to Jiaodaokou Dongdajie, is lined with hundreds of restaurants – one after the other, and all festooned with red lanterns and neon – creating a colourful and boisterous scene, particularly on weekends. Take the subway to Yonghegong and walk south for ten minutes. Note that staff in these restaurants will probably speak little or no English; few places will have an English menu, but plenty have a picture menu. Many venues specialize in hotpot and *shuishuyu* (spicy Sichuan-style fish served in oil on a heated metal tray). You can't go too far wrong just picking somewhere busy, but recommended is famous hotpot brand **Xiao Fei Yang** (小肥羊, *xiǎo féiyáng*; 209 Dongzhimen Neidajie, north side) and duck restaurant **Huajia Yiyuan** (花家怡园, *huājiā yíyuán*; 235 Dongzhimennei Dajie, north side; ⓣ010/51283316). For spicy fish, try **Dumencchong** (独门冲, *dúmén chòng*; 208 Dongzhimen Neidajie, south side). For *malatang*, a dry, spicy hotpot, try **Xiao Dong Tian** (小洞天, *xiǎo dòngtiān*; 269 Dongzhimen Neidajie, north side). **Ming Hui Fu** (明辉府, *mínghūi fǔ*; 199–201 Dongzhimen Neidajie, north side) serves most staples and is open 24 hours.

Crescent Moon
弯弯月亮
wānwānyuèliàng
16 Dongsi Liu Tiao (just off Dongzhimen Nan Xiao Jie), Dongcheng district ⓣ010/64005281. You can't really go wrong at a decent Xinjiang restaurant as long as you eat meat. Stick with classics such as roast leg of mutton, hand-pulled noodles and kebabs and you won't be disappointed. There's no floorshow; service can be moody. Daily 10am–11.30pm.

Dali Courtyard
大理院子
dàlǐ yuànzi
67 Xiaojingchang Hutong, Gulou Dong Dajie ⓣ010/84041430, ⓦwww.dalicourtyard.com. A charming courtyard restaurant tucked down a *hutong*. It has no menu – you simply turn up, pay the fixed price (¥100/¥200/¥300) then the chef gives you whatever Yunnanese food he feels like cooking. Call to reserve, and ask for a table outside (at least in summer). Daily 11am–2pm & 6–11pm.

Huajia Yiyuan
花家怡园
huājiā yíyuán
Beixinqiao Toutaio, first *hutong* north of the Dongzhimennei and Yonghegong Dajie intersection ⓣ010/64058440. This secluded courtyard restaurant, with songbirds and pleasant outdoor seating, is an excellent place to sample Beijing duck, a bargain at ¥88. It's a few doors east of the *Lama Temple Youth Hostel*. Note that there's a second branch on Ghost Street (see above). Daily 10.30am–4am.

Li Family Restaurant
历家菜
lìjiā cài
11 Yangfang Hutong ⓣ010/66180107. Tucked away in a *hutong*, this little courtyard restaurant has a big rep for imperial-style dining, and it's popular with foreigners. They have set menus only, which start at ¥200 per person – it's best to stay at the cheaper end, as paying more simply gets you dodgy delicacies such as shark's fin. Each menu is made up of a vast number of small-portioned courses. Highlights include sweet-and-sour fish, fried scallops and lotus roots cake. Don't expect a cabbie to be able to find the place; ask to be dropped at Deshengmennei Dajie. Daily 6am–10.30pm.

Private Kitchen 44
细管胡同44号
xìguǎnhútóng sìshísìhào
44 Xiguan Hutong ⓣ010/64001280. Head north from Zhangzizhong subway stop, turn left into Sishisitiao *hutong* and you'll come across this cosy courtyard restaurant serving home-style Guilin food, which is strong on pickles and tart flavours. Stick to the set meal (¥68) or splash out on sour fish, which you'll have to ring and order in advance as it takes some preparation, and wash it down with rice wine with osmanthus. Relaxed, tasty, and a good find. Daily 11am–2pm & 4.30–10pm.

Red Capital Club
新红资俱乐部
xīnhóngzī jùlèbù
66 Dongsijiu Tiao ⓣ010/84018886, ⓦwww.redcapitalclub.com.cn. Imperial cuisine in an environment of pure communist kitsch – an old state guesthouse decorated with Mao memorabilia; there's even a red-flag limo parked out front. The dishes are all the favourites of Chinese modern and historical leaders; don't miss the roast beef favoured by Genghis Khan. All this irony and decadence will set you back about ¥350 a head. Daily 6–11pm.

The Source
都江源
dūjiāng yuán
14 Banchang Hutong ⓣ010/64003736. Foreigner-friendly Sichuan set-meals, starting at ¥120 per person, in a courtyard restaurant next to the *Lüsongyuan* hotel. They'll go easy on the spices if you ask. Daily 11am–2pm & 5–10pm.

Houhai Lake and around

The restaurants reviewed below are marked on the "Houhai Lake & around" map on p.88.

Drum and Gong
锣鼓洞天
luógǔ dòngtiān
104 Nanluogu Xiang. Foreigner-friendly, cheap Sichuan and home-style food, with big portions. Always busy and a little cramped. Daily 10am-midnight.

Fish Nation
鱼邦
yú bāng
31 Jiaodaokou, Nanluogu Xiang ⓦwww.fishnation.cn. You wouldn't guess from the decor, but this is an English restaurant, with a surprisingly authentic fish 'n' chips for ¥40. Shame about the lacklustre service, but there's a good rooftop balcony. Daily 10am–2pm.

Gong Wang Fu Restaurant
恭王府四川饭店
gōngwángfǔ sìchuān fàndiàn
14 Liuyin Jie, just north of Prince Gong's Palace ⓣ010/66156924. Fiery Sichuan food in a lavishly re-created traditional setting with bamboo chairs and a lot of rosewood – but with pop art on the walls. It sees plenty of tourist traffic, so there's an English menu and they'll tone down the spices if asked. Around ¥60 per head. Daily 11am–2pm & 5–9pm.

Hutong Pizza
胡同批萨
hútóng pīsà
9 Yindingqiao ⓣ010/66175916. A charming little courtyard restaurant serving up delicious, square pizzas. It's hidden away in an alley; go to the *hutong* directly opposite *Kaorouji* (see below) and follow the signs. Daily 11am–11pm.

Kaorouji
烤肉季
kǎoròujì
14 Qianhai Dong Yuan ⓣ010/64045921. From the Drum Tower, continue south down Di'anmenwai Dajie, then take the first *hutong* on the right; the restaurant is a short walk down here, just before the lake bridge. In the *hutongs* close to the Drum Tower, this Muslim place, run by the same family for 150 years, takes advantage of its great lakeside location with big windows and, in summer, balcony tables. The beef and barbecued lamb dishes are recommended. You'll spend around ¥50 a head. Daily 11am–2pm & 5–11pm.

No Name Restaurant
无名云南餐吧
wúmíng yúnnán cānbā
1 Dajinsi Hutong ⓣ010/8328360. A new venture from the owner of the *No Name* bar (see p.147), this classy courtyard restaurant is well hidden down an alley by Yinding bridge. Follow the signs or phone ahead and they'll pick you up. The stone-flagged, covered courtyard is filled with low-lit sofas, chests and picnic tables, with a fountain centrepiece; it feels like a cantina. The food, from Yunnan in the far south, is excellent, with the speciality roast duck (¥108) being rather lighter than its Beijing equivalent, and lots of ingedients you won't see elsewhere in Chinese cooking, such as mint and goats' cheese. "Over the bridge" noodles (¥88) are fun – the bowl arrives with a host of ingredients for you to throw in the stock. Daily 11am–midnight.

Nuage
庆云楼
qìngyún lóu
Just east of Kaorouji, at 22 Qianhai Dong Zhao ⓣ010/64019581. Decent Vietnamese food served in a smart but cosy upstairs bar-restaurant. Try the steamed garlic prawns and battered squid, and finish with super-strong Vietnamese coffee if you don't intend to sleep in the near future. You'll

Koreatown

Beijing's large population of Korean expats is amply catered for in the strip of restaurants, shops and bars at "**Koreatown**", in Wudaokou, Haidian district, outside the Beijing Language and Culture Insititute. Prices for meals are pretty inexpensive, around ¥30 per head. The other Koreatown, opposite the *Kempinski Hotel* (see p.131), is more upmarket. At either, pick any restaurant that looks busy and order *nayng myon*, cold noodles; *bibimbap*, a clay pot of rice, vegetables, egg and beef; or *pulgoki* barbecued beef, which you cook yourself on the table grill.

spend around ¥100 per head. Don't miss the extraordinary tropical fantasy toilets. Daily 11am–2pm & 5.30–10.30pm.

Old Character Hakka Restaurant
老汉子客家菜馆
lǎohànzi kèjiā càiguǎn
12 Qianhai Nanyan ⓣ010/64042259.
Harassed, shouty staff reveal how popular this place is, and deservedly so – it's cramped but atmospheric, and the food, Hakka dishes from the south, is delicious and not expensive. Try the "three cup duck". Daily 11am–3.30pm & 5–10.30pm.

Sauveurs de Coree
韩香馆
hánxiāng guǎn
29 Nanluogu Xiang ⓣ010/64016083, ⓦwww.sauveursdecoree.com.cn. A comfortable Korean bistro, with keen-to-please staff. If you're new to spicy Korean cuisine, go for one of the set meals, which start at ¥59 for *bibimbap* (rice, vegetables, egg and beef) accompanied by fiery ginseng-flavoured *baekseju* and finishing with iced cinnamon tea. Daily 11am–11pm.

Supermarkets

All **supermarkets** sell plenty of Western food alongside all the Chinese, though few have a decent range of dairy products. The **CRC Supermarket** in the basement of the China World Trade Centre is impressive, though Western goods cost a little more here than they would at home. **Park'n'Shop**, in the basement of the COFCO Plaza on Jianguomen Dajie, is a little cheaper. The supermarket on the first floor of the **Friendship Store**, Jianguomenwai Dajie, is very pricey but a good place to find imported cheese and canned goods. Meanwhile, the Parkson Store, Lufthansa Centre and CVIC Plaza also have large basement supermarkets, and Carrefour has stores at 6 Dongsanhuan Bei Lu, just west of the zoo, and on Xizhimenwai Dajie.

But for the best range of Western produce, including hard-to-find items such as oregano and hummus, head for **Jenny Lou's** outside the west gate of Chaoyang Park in the east of the city, where prices are half those of the Friendship Store.

Capital cuisine

Forget spice, oil and rice; Beijing food is heavy and hearty, with steamed buns and noodles as staples. It's delicious and nourishing, and perfect for the harsh climate. You'll find plenty of places to sample it, along with every other Chinese cuisine. The following section lays out a taster of the capital's unmissable culinary delights, recommending the best places to sample them.

Beijing duck ▲

Stuffed prawns ▼

Beijing duck

Succulent **roast duck** is Beijing's big hitter, and deservedly so. Locals love to debate the merits of convection roasters over peach-wood ovens and the like, and every venerable restaurant has a different preparation technique.

Once the duck has been brought to your table and carved, however, the routine is always the same; slather dark, tangy bean sauce onto pancakes, pop in a few scallions, add shreds of duck with your chopsticks, roll it up and prepare for the local taste sensation. Nothing is wasted; you finish off your meal with rich, filling and delicious **duck soup**.

Imperial cuisine

Pity the poor emperor. At mealtimes he wasn't allowed to take more than one mouthful of any one dish, for fear that if he showed a preference a poisoner might take advantage. As a lowly citizen however, you are under no such compunction, and the city has some great places where you can indulge in the **imperial cuisine** that originated in the Qing dynasty kitchens.

As well as meticulously prepared dishes created with extravagant ingredients such as **birds' nests** and **sharks' fins**, imperial cuisine is noted for fish that's so fresh it's still flapping (it's all about keeping the nerves intact) and **fine pastries** such as pea-flour cakes and kidney bean-flour rolls.

Although you'll find dishes made with exotic meats such as **calf** and **camel**, these days you won't come across bear or wolf on the menu. Thankfully, one other ingredient is also no longer included: traditionally, imperial food always came with a strip of silver inside, as it was thought to turn black in the presence of poison.

Mongolian hotpot

Mongolian hotpot is Beijing's classic winter warmer, but makes for a fantastic communal meal at any time of year. The brass pot in the centre of the table has an outer rim around a chimney with a charcoal-burner underneath. Stock is boiled in the rim, and diners dip in slices of raw meat, vegetables, bean noodles, mushrooms and bean curd. **Lamb** is the traditional highlight, and it's sliced so finely that it takes only a few seconds to cook between your chopsticks. Shake to get rid of excess water, then dunk into the sesame-based dipping sauce, and it's ready to eat. There are hotpot restaurants all over town; just look for the steamed-up windows.

▲ Mongolian hotpot

Other Chinese cuisines

Of course, Beijing being the capital, you can try every kind of Chinese cuisine here. Boisterous **Sichuan food**, with its extravagant use of fiery chillies and pungent flavours, is a particular favourite. Try **mapo dofu** (beancurd with pork), **gongbao jiding** (chicken and peanuts), and **suan cai yu** (fish with pickles) for a classic spicy meal.

The joke that the Chinese will eat anything with four legs that isn't a table refers to **Cantonese** cuisine. Snake, dog and guinea pig are among the more unusual dishes, but more conventionally, there's also plenty of lightly seasoned, fresh vegetables. **Dim sum** (*dianxin* in Mandarin), a meal of tiny buns, dumplings, and pancakes is a favourite for a long leisurely lunch.

Food from the **Turkic** peoples of Xinjiang, in the far northwest, is perennially popular; it has a Central Asian flavour, with lamb kebabs, handmade noodles and some great mutton dishes on the menu.

▼ *Mapo dofu*

Market food ▲

Eating noodles at a street stall ▼

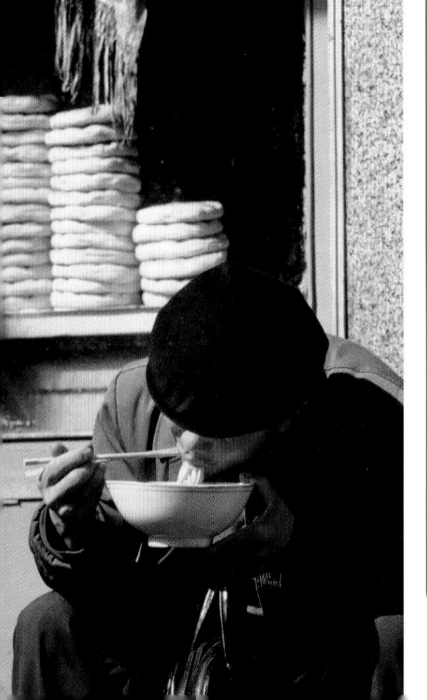

Beijing street snacks

Street snacks are the ultimate convenience food – cheap, tasty, available at all hours, and cooked in front of you in a few seconds. **Jiaozi** are little dumplings of meat paste or vegetables, packaged in a thin skin of dough, and steamed or fried. Savoury crêpes – **jianbing** – are the best breakfasts in the capital – and at around ¥3, they're the cheapest, too. Vendors put the whole thing together in seconds – cooking up a pancake on a hotplate, cracking an egg onto it, sprinkling cilantro and onion, adding a wedge of fried dough and bean paste, and finally folding the thing up. Street food vendors are common in the backstreets but rare in the centre.

Don't-miss dining

For the most satisfying and authentic dining experiences, make sure to try the following dishes at the following places. For more on where to eat the best in Chinese cuisine, see pp.134–144.

▶▶ **Beijing duck** *Dadong* (see p.138), *Lichun* (see p.137), *Made in China* (see p.139).

▶▶ **Imperial cuisine** *Red Capital Club* (see p.143).

▶▶ **Mongolian hot pot** *Ding Ding Xiang* (see p.139), *Dong Lai Shun Fan Zhuang* (see p.139).

▶▶ **Sichuan food** *Sichuan Government Restaurant* (see p.140), *The Source* (see p.143).

▶▶ **Cantonese food** *Lei Garden* (see p.139).

▶▶ **Turkic food** *Crescent Moon* (see p.142), *Xinjiang Red Rose* (see p.141).

▶▶ **Street food** *Dong'anmen night market* (see p.135).

Drinking and nightlife

In 1995, **Sanlitun Lu** in the east of the city had just one bar, and it was losing money. A new manager bought it, believing the place had potential but that the *feng shui* was wrong – the toilet was opposite the door and all the wealth was going down it. He changed the name, moved the loo, and – so the story goes – the city's bar scene took off from there. Now the area is choked with drinking holes, and new bars open all the time. Many mimic their popular neighbours; if one does well, a couple more will open around it, and before you know it, the original will have closed down.

Most **clubs** these days have embraced a slickly international style, and import their DJs from abroad. The city's **indie music** scene is cool, fun, and thriving – for more, see p.153.

Bars

Beijing bars pop up fast, multiply, then die as suddenly as they appeared. For the most up-to-date information on all the comings and goings, check the listings in one of the expat magazines (see p.29).

Despite recent demolitions, **Sanlitun Lu** remains as popular as ever. Head up the main strip (avoiding the touts, beggars, neon and sleaze); just off it lie a fascinating array of diverse venues, from cheap and cheerful pick-up joints to exclusive jazz bars.

A mellower scene exists around attractive **Houhai**, where venues have ambient music and no dancefloors, though the place is getting crowded. For an even more relaxed drink head off here into the *hutongs* around the Drum and Bell towers. The heritage district **Nanluogu Xiang** attracts an artsier crowd, and a group of expat-oriented bars around the west gate of **Chaoyang Park** in the far east of the city is increasingly popular. For something a bit edgier – and the heart of the rock scene – head to **Wudaokou**; the student clientele means that bars here tend to be cheaper and grungier.

Hours are flexible – a bar tends to close only when its last barfly has lurched off – though everywhere will be open until at least midnight (and well into the early hours at weekends). We've listed the **phone numbers** of bars that can be tough to find (just get your cabbie to ring them) or have regular gigs; usually there's a cover charge to get in (around ¥30) when a band is playing.

Though Chinese **beer** can be cheaper than bottled water if bought in a shop, a 350ml bottle of Tsingtao or the local Yanjing at a bar will usually cost ¥20–40. Many bars also sell Western draught beers such as Guinness and Boddingtons, which cost at least ¥40. The *Tree* (see below) has an impressive collection of Belgian brews.

East of the centre

Just inside the northeast section of the Third Ring Road, this busy area can be reached by taking the subway to Dongsi Shitiao, then bus #113 east; get off at the third stop. The main strip – **Sanlitun Lu** – is sometimes called **Jiuba Jie**, literally "bar street".

Q Bar
Q吧
Qbā
Sixth Floor, *Eastern Hotel*, corner of Sanlitun Nan Lu and Gongti Nan Lu; see "East of the centre" map on pp.74–75. Sleek and well-run lounge bar with good cocktails; it is at its best in summer when drinkers spill out onto the terrace.

Jianguomen Dajie and around

The places reviewed below are marked on the "Jianguomen Dajie" map on p.79.

Centro
炫酷酒廊
xuànkù jiǔláng
First Floor, *Kerry Centre Hotel*, 1 Guanghua Lu. Slinky lounge bar whose lavish cocktails will cost the best part of a red bill. Dress up.

Ichikura
一藏酒吧
yīcáng jiǔbā
36 Dong San Huan Bei Lu, on the right side of the Chaoyang Theatre building. This two-storey Japanese whisky bar is as tasteful and understated as the acrobatic shows next door are glitzy and vulgar. A great range of single malts – including superb Japanese varieties – and great attention to detail (check out the round ice cubes) make this dark, cosy venue a hidden gem.

Sanlitun and the northeast

We've listed the best bars below, but there are plenty more in this area from which to choose. In addition to drinks, a few offer Western food, and there are plenty of decent places to eat hereabouts too (see p.140). Venues with a cover charge are listed under "Nightclubs" opposite.

The places reviewed below are marked on the "Sanlitun & the northeast" map on p.81.

Jazz Ya
爵士屋
juéshì wū
18 Sanlitun Bei Lu ⓣ010/64151227. This mellow Japanese place, with its rough-hewn wooden tables and moody music, has a better drinks menu than most of its neighbours. It's set back from the road; look for the yellow sign down an alley next to *Bella Coffee*. Occasional live jazz.

Kai
开吧
kāi bā
Sanlitun Bei Jie, behind 3.3 Mall. An unpretentious little bar, popular with young foreigners for its ¥10 beers.

Punk
***Opposite House*, 11 Sanlitun Lu.** Cosy, classy cocktail bar in the basement of a chic hotel (see p.131) that attracts a trendy international crowd. Dress up, order a jasmine iced tea (¥70), and try and look sophisticated. Closed Sundays and Mondays.

Tree
树酒吧
shù jiǔbā
43 Sanlitun Nan Lu, behind 3.3 Mall ⓣ010/64151954. Relaxed and unassuming little bar, with a selection of Belgian white beers and decent pizza.

Around Chaoyang Park

Bus #113 comes to this district from Dongsi Shitiao subway – get off at the fourth stop.

Juicy Spot
Chaoyang Park west gate. See "East of the centre" map on pp.74–75. The bar may be in a converted boat, but the decor is otherwise rather restrained. Reasonably priced drinks and loud tunes draw a studenty crowd; it's best in summer when the rooftop terrace provides respite from the sweaty dancefloor.

North of the centre

As well as the obvious strip that runs alongside **Houhai**, there are plenty of chilled-out venues sunk in the *hutongs* all around. To reach the area, take bus #107 from Dongzhimen subway stop, get off at the north entrance to Beihai Park and walk north around the lake. In addition to the places reviewed below, you will also find a number of relaxed venues around the Drum and Bell towers, and off Nanluogu Xiang.

Houhai Lake and around

The places reviewed below are marked on the "Houhai Lake & around" map on p.88.

Bed Bar
床
chuáng
17 Zhangwang Hutong ⓣ010/84001554. A simple courtyard nightspot, rather hidden away from the action and all the better for it. Lined with rugs and traditional beds, it is aimed at the horizontally inclined, so perhaps better for a second date than a first. They also serve good tapas.

Drum and Bell
鼓钟咖啡馆
gǔzhōng kāfēiguǎn
41 Zhonglouwan Hutong ⓣ010/84033600. With welcoming staff and a great location between the Drum and Bell towers, this little place is always crowded. The rooftop patio is an added bonus in summer, and they serve decent thin-crust pizza. It's very popular on a Sunday afternoon, when there's an all-you-can-drink for ¥50 deal.

East Shore Live Jazz Café
东岸咖啡
dōng'àn kāfēi
Second Floor, 2 Qianhai Nanyan Lu ⓣ010/84032131. Dark, mellow jazz bar, with a view of the lake and live shows from Thursday to Sunday.

Huxleys
德比酒吧
débǐ jiǔbā
16 Yandai Xiejie. Cheap booze, no attitude and approachable staff make this drinking hole a winner with young expats.

No Name Bar
3 Qianhai Dongyuan, just east of the *Kaorouji* restaurant. A hippy-ish café bar that thinks it's special because it doesn't have a sign. Look for the red walls and the out-of-control foliage. This was the first lakeside bar, and its trendy anonymity and bric-a-brac-style interior design has informed every other establishment in the area. They also serve Yunnan cuisine.

Pass By Bar
过客酒吧
guòkè jiǔbā
108 Nan Luo Guo Xiang, off Di'anmen Dong Dajie ⓣ010/84038004. A renovated courtyard house turned comfortable bar/restaurant, popular with backpackers and students. There are lots of books and pictures of China's far-flung places to peruse, and well-travelled staff to chat to – if you can get their attention. Free wi-fi.

Sex and da City
欲望都市
yùwàng dūshì
Lotus Lane. A pick-up joint with bar-top dancing; Carrie might not approve but Samantha probably would.

Nightclubs

Gone are the days when everything stopped at 10pm for a raffle; Chinese **clubs** are pretty slick these days, with hip-hop and house music proving enduringly popular. There's a dense concentration of clubs around the west side of the Workers' Stadium, and on Saturday night the car park here is full of white Mercedes dropping off the *dakuans* (big moneys) and their *xiaomis* (little honeys). African guys work the crowds, selling the shaky head drug (ecstasy). Welcome to the new China.

All places listed here have a **cover charge**, quoted in our reviews, which generally increases at weekends. If you just want to dance, and aren't too prissy about the latest music, check the bar reviews above for venues with their own dancefloor.

East of the centre

Most of the classier clubbing venues are northeast of the centre, in two clusters – around distant **Chaoyang Park** and **Sanlitun**.

Around Chaoyang Park

Bus #113 comes here from Dongsi Shitiao subway – get off at the fourth stop. The places reviewed overleaf are arrowed off the "East of the centre" map on pp.74–75.

Bling

Solana 5–1, 6 Chaoyang Park Lu ⓣ010/59056999, ⓦwww.all-starclub.com. Aimed, as the name might suggest, at those captivated by shiny things, heavy bass and exposed flesh. Beijing's newest hip-hop venue wows its beautiful, vapid clientele with features such as a DJ booth made out of a Rolls-Royce. Closed Mon & Tues; ¥50 cover charge.

World of Suzie Wong

苏西黄酒吧

sūxīhuáng jiǔbā

Outside the west gate of Chaoyang Park, above the *Mirch Masala* restaurant – look for the discreet yellow neon sign outside; ⓦwww.suziewong.com.cn. Not as fashionable as it was, but still a stalwart with its striking neo-Oriental decor – think lacquer and rose petals. Dancing downstairs and a cocktail bar above. ¥50 cover charge.

Jianguomen Dajie

The following club is marked on the "Jianguomen Dajie" map on p.79.

GT Banana

赛特饭店

sàitè fàndiàn

***Scitech Hotel*, 22 Jianguomenwai Dajie ⓣ010/65283636.** Huge, gaudy and in-your-face, this megaclub has three sections – techno, funk and chill-out – and features go-go girls, karaoke rooms and an enthusiastic, young crowd. Mon–Fri 8.30pm–4am, Sat & Sun until 5am. Cover charge ¥30, or more when a big-name DJ is playing.

Sanlitun and the northeast

The places reviewed below are marked on the "Sanlitun & the northeast" map on p.81.

The Boat

船吧

chuánbā

Opposite 8 Liangmahe Nan Lu ⓣ010/64605512, ⓦtheboatbeijing.ning.com. This smart and trendy venue is, literally, a boat, sitting in a canal on the Liangma river, accessible via a gangplank. The upper deck is a bar, the lower deck a dance floor, and all the waitstaff are dressed in sailor suits. Thursday is gay night, so feel free to make your own "cruising" jokes. Drinks start at a reasonable ¥30. No cover.

Vics

威克斯

wēikèsī

Inside the Workers' Stadium's north gate ⓣ010/52930333, ⓦwww.vics.com.cn. Long-running hip-hop club, with a sweaty dancefloor filled with enthusiastic booty grinders. The low cover charge and cheapish drinks (bottled beer is ¥15) make it popular with students and embassy brats. On Wednesdays women get in free and receive free drinks until midnight. Thursday is ragga/reggae night, with hip-hop, R&B and techno all weekend. ¥30 except Thurs, when it's free.

White Rabbit

大白兔

dàbáitù

Tongli Studio, Sanlitun Jie ⓦwhiterabbitclub.blogspot.com. Underground dive bar run by DJs, with a good sound system that blasts out techno most nights. It's a cut above other clubs, at least musically, and it attracts a crowd more interested in dancing than posing. Open Wed–Sun. ¥60 cover charge includes one drink.

Gay Beijing

Official attitudes towards **homosexuality** have softened in China – it's been removed from the official list of psychiatric disorders and is no longer a national crime, though gay men have occasionally been arrested under public disturbance statutes. That's unlikely to happen in cosmopolitan Beijing however, where pink power is a big influence on fashion and the media.

Beijing's **gay scene** is vibrant but discreet, with bars for the *tongzhi* (literally, comrades) no longer required to hand out pamphlets urging clients to go home to their wives. *Destination* (see "East of the Centre" map on pp.74–75) at 7 Gongti Xi Lu, opposite the Workers' Stadium West Gate, is the liveliest venue, with a busy dance floor (目的地, *mùdìdì*; ⓦwww.bjdestination.com). Clubs *GT Banana* and *The Boat* (see above) are also popular with the young gay crowd.

Entertainment and art

Most visitors to Beijing make a trip to see **Beijing opera** and the superb Chinese **acrobatics displays** – both of which remain timeless arts. Fewer investigate the equally worthwhile contemporary side of the city's entertainment scene – the **indie music**, theatre and **art** events. There are also a number of **cinemas** where you can check out the provocative movies emerging from new, underground filmmakers.

For mainstream cultural events – visiting ballet troupes, large-scale concerts and so forth – check the **listings** in the *China Daily*, available at most hotels; but for a more in-depth view and comprehensive listings, including gigs and art happenings and the like, check the expat magazines (see p.29).

Tickets for all big shows are available at the venue's box office or from China Ticket Online (Ⓣ010/64177845, Ⓦwww.piao.com.cn).

Traditional opera

Beijing opera (*jingxi*) is the most celebrated of China's 350 or so regional operatic styles – a unique combination of song, dance, acrobatics and mime. Highly stylized, to the outsider the performances can often seem obscure and wearying, as they are punctuated by a succession of crashing gongs and piercing, discordant songs. But it's worth seeing once, especially if you can acquaint yourself with the story beforehand. Most of the plots are based on historical or mythological themes – two of the most famous sagas, which any Chinese will explain to you, are

Shows at teahouses

Beijing has a small number of **teahouse theatres** where you can sit and snack while watching performances of Beijing opera, sedate zither music and martial arts. All are aimed at tourists rather than locals.

You can watch a ninety-minute variety show – comprising all three genres – at the **Lao She Teahouse**, 3rd floor, Dawancha Building, 3 Qianmen Xi Dajie (daily 7.40pm; ¥60–380; Ⓣ010/63036830). Popular with tour groups, the show gives a gaudy taste of traditional Chinese culture.

The **Tianqiaole Teahouse Theatre**, set in a mock-traditional building at 113 Tianqiao Nan Dajie (Ⓣ010/63040617), aims to create an authentic atmosphere, right down to the Qing costumes worn by the staff. Performances begin at 7pm and last two hours, and mostly comprise segments of traditional opera with a little acrobatics in between. The ticket price of ¥180 includes tea and snacks; for ¥330, you get a duck dinner, too. Buying tickets a day in advance is advised as the place is sometimes booked out with tour groups.

The White Snake and *The Water Margin* – and full of moral lessons. Offering an interesting, if controversial, variation on the traditions are those operas that deal with contemporary themes – such as the struggle of women to marry as they choose. Apart from checking out the venues below, you could also visit a **teahouse** for your opera fix (see p.149). Teahouse performances are short and aimed at foreigners; you can also slurp tea or munch on snacks – often Beijing duck as well – while being entertained.

The **colours** used on stage, from the costumes to the make up on the players' faces, are highly symbolic: red signifies loyalty; yellow, fierceness; blue, cruelty; and white, evil.

Chang'an Grand Theatre
长安大戏院
cháng' ān dàxìyuàn
7 Jianguomennei Dajie ⓣ010/65101309. A modern, central theatre putting on nightly performances at 7.15pm. ¥40–150.

Huguang Guild Hall
湖广会馆
húguǎng huìguǎn
3 Hufang Lu, a 20min walk south from Hepingmen subway stop ⓣ010/63518284, ⓦwww.huguanghuiguan.com. This reconstructed theatre with a fine performance hall also has a small opera museum on site, with costumes and pictures of famous performers, though no English captions. Nightly performances at 7.15pm. ¥180–380.

Liyuan Theatre
梨园剧场
líyuán jùchǎng
First Floor, *Jianguo Qianmen hotel* (see p.129), 175 Yong'an Lu ⓣ010/63016688 ext 8860, ⓦwww.qianmenhotel.com/en/liyuan.html. Pricey, but perhaps the best place to see opera, with an emphasis on accessibility; as you go in you pass the actors putting on their make-up – a great photo op. The opera itself is a visitor-friendly bastardization, lasting an hour and jazzed up with some martial arts and slapstick. A display board at the side of the stage gives an English translation of the few lines of dialogue. Nightly performances at 7.30pm; tickets can be bought from the office in the front courtyard of the hotel (daily 9–11am, noon–4.45pm & 5.30–8pm; ¥70–180). The more expensive seats are at tables at the front, where you can sip tea and nibble pastries during the performance. Take bus #66 from Hepingmen subway stop.

National Centre for the Performing Arts
国家大剧院
guójiā dàjùyuàn
2 Xichang'an Jie ⓣ010/66550000, ⓦwww.chncpa.org. This is one venue you can't miss; it's that giant egg west of Tian'anmen Square. Designed by French architect Paul Andreu and opened in 2007, this huge dome at the centre of a lake is meant to showcase the best of Chinese performance art for the delectation of its political elites. The opera hall seats over 2000, with fantastic acoustics and lighting to capture every nuance of the performance. There's an English subtitle screen too. You'll probably be in elevated company; Wen Jiabao is a big fan. There is a performance every night at 7.30pm. The box office is open daily from 9.30am or you can ring to reserve. Ticket prices vary, but cost at least ¥150.

Prince Gong's Mansion
恭王府
gōngwáng fǔ
Liuyun Jie ⓣ010/66186628. Opera is put on every night for tour groups in the grand hall at the Prince Gong mansion. Call to book a seat. Performances start at 7.30pm and cost ¥80–120.

Zhengyici Theatre
正义祠剧场
zhèngyìcí jùchǎng
220 Qianmen Xiheyan Jie ⓣ010/63189454. The genuine article, performed in the only surviving wooden Beijing opera theatre and worth a visit just to check out the architecture. Duck dinners cost an additional ¥110. Performances nightly at 7.30pm (2hr; ¥150).

Drama and dance

Spoken **drama** was only introduced into Chinese theatres in the twentieth century. The People's Art Theatre in Beijing became the best-known company and, prior to the Cultural Revolution, staged Chinese-language translations of European plays – Ibsen and Chekhov were among the favourite playwrights. But in 1968, Jiang Qing, Mao's third wife, declared that "drama is dead". The company, along with most of China's cinemas and theatres, was almost completely out of action for nearly a decade afterwards, with a corpus of just eight plays (deemed socially improving) continuing to be performed. Many of the principal actors, directors and writers were banished, generally to rural hard labour. In 1979 the People's Art Theatre reformed and quickly re-established its reputation.

Most evenings you can catch Chinese **song and dance** simply by turning on the TV, though there's plenty of opportunity to see it live. One revue not to miss is the regularly staged Red Detachment of Women, a classic piece of retro communist pomp that celebrates a revolutionary women's fighting outfit – the dancers wear guerilla uniform and carry hand grenades and rifles. Some venues, such as the Beijing Exhibition Theatre, occasionally stage performances, in the original language, of imported musicals like *The Sound of Music*, which, with tickets at ¥50–100, are a lot cheaper to watch here than at home.

Dance is popular in Beijing, generally more so at the traditional end of the spectrum, though you can see more contemporary forms at a few small venues. In addition to the venues listed below, check the Poly Theatre (see p.153) for its programme of theatre and dance.

Beijing Exhibition Theatre
北京展览馆剧场
běijīng zhǎnlǎnguǎn jùchǎng
135 Xizhimenwai Dajie ⓣ010/68354455, ⓦwww.bjexpo.com. This giant hall with nearly 3000 seats stages classical ballet, folk dance and large-scale song-and-dance revues.

Beijing Modern Dance Company Theatre
北京现代舞团实验剧场
běijīng xiàndàiwǔtuán shíyàn jùchǎng
8 Majiabao Dongli, in the south of the city beyond the Third Ring Road ⓣ010/67573879. A small but dedicated dance troupe performing modern pieces. Tickets are cheap, at around ¥40.

Capital Theatre
首都剧场
shǒudū jùchǎng
22 Wangfujing Dajie ⓣ010/65121598, ⓦwww.bjry.com. Look out for the People's Art Theatre company here – their photo archive, documenting their history, is displayed in the lobby. Tickets generally start at ¥40 and can cost as much as ¥300. Most performances are in Chinese.

Penghao Theatre
蓬蒿剧场
pénghāo jùchǎng
35 Dongmianhua Hutong, off Nanluogu Xiang ⓣ010/64006452, ⓦwww.penghaoren.com/cn/index.asp. In a *hutong* just behind the Central Academy of Drama, this intimate, privately run theatre set in a beautifully converted courtyard house also has a rather nice rooftop bar.

Puppet Theatre
中央木偶剧院
zhōngyāng mùǒu jùyuàn
A1, Section 1, Anhua Xi Li, Bei Sanhuan Lu (Third Ring Road), opposite the Sogo Department Store ⓣ010/64254798, ⓦwww.puppetchina.com. Once as important for commoners as opera was for the elite, Chinese puppetry usually involves hand puppets and marionettes. Occasionally, shadow puppets made of thin translucent leather and supported by rods are used. Beijing opera, short stories and Western fairy tales, aimed at kids. Shows daily at 6.30pm; ¥40.

Acrobatics and martial arts

Certainly the most accessible and exciting of the traditional Chinese entertainments, **acrobatics** covers anything from gymnastics through to magic tricks and juggling. The tradition of professional acrobatics has existed in China for two thousand years and continues today at the country's main training school, Wu Qiao in Hebei province, where students begin training at the age of 5. The style may be vaudeville, but performances are spectacular, with truly awe-inspiring feats of dexterity – sixteen people stacked atop a bicycle and the like. Just as impressive are martial arts displays, which usually involve a few mock fights and feats of strength, such as breaking concrete slabs with one blow.

Chaoyang Theatre
朝阳剧场
cháoyáng jùchǎng
36 Dongsanhuan Bei Lu ⓣ010/65072421, ⓦwww.chaoyangtheatre.com. If you want to see acrobatics, come to one of the shows here. At the end, the Chinese tourists rush off as if it's a fire drill, leaving the foreign tour groups to do the applauding. There are plenty of souvenir stalls in the lobby – make your purchases after the show rather than during the interval, as prices reduce at the end. Shows nightly (1hr 15min); tickets cost ¥180, though they can work out cheaper if you arrange them through your hotel.

Red Theatre
红剧场
hóng jùchǎng
44 Xingfu Dajie, east of the Temple of Heaven ⓣ010/67142473, ⓦwww.redtheatre.cn. A lively kung fu routine, taking place daily at 7.30pm. Tickets ¥180–680.

Tianqiao Theatre
天桥杂技剧场
tiānqiáo zájì jùchǎng
95 Tianqiao Lu, Xuanwu, east end of Beiwei Lu ⓣ010/63037449, ⓦwww.tianqiaoacrobatictheater.com. One of the old staples for acrobatics, in an old-fashioned but newly renovated theatre. Nightly performances begin at 7.15pm. Tickets ¥180.

Live music venues

Traditional Han Chinese music is usually played on the *erhu* (a kind of fiddle) and *qin* (a seven-stringed zither). Contemporary compositions tend to be in a pseudo-romantic, Western-influenced style; easy on the ear, they can be heard live in upmarket hotels and restaurants. To hear traditional pieces, visit the concert halls. Western classical music is popular – the best place to catch it is the Beijing Concert Hall – as is jazz, which you can hear at a few venues, notably *Jazz Ya* (see p.146).

Mainstream **Chinese pop** – mostly slushy ballads sung by Hong Kong or Taiwanese heartthrobs – is hard to avoid; it pumps out of shops on every street and can be heard live at the Workers' Stadium (see p.153). For details of Beijing's thriving underground scene and **edgy rock** see opposite.

Beijing Concert Hall
北京音乐厅
běijīng yīnyuètīng
1 Beixinhua Jie, just off Xichang'an Jie ⓣ010/66057006. South of Zhongnanhai, this hall seats 1000 people and hosts regular concerts of Western classical and Chinese traditional music by Beijing's resident orchestra and visiting orchestras from the rest of China and overseas.

Tickets, usually priced in the ¥30–150 range, can be bought here, at the CVIK Plaza (see map on p.79), and at the Parkson Department Store (see p.69).

Century Theatre
世纪剧院
shìjì jùyuàn
Sino-Japanese Youth Centre, 40 Liangmaqiao Lu, 2km east of the *Kempinski hotel* ⓣ010/64663311. An intimate venue for

soloists and small ensembles. Mostly Chinese modern and traditional classical compositions. Evening performances. ¥120–150.

Forbidden City Concert Hall
北京中山公园音乐堂
běijīng zhōngshāngōngyuán yīnyuètáng
Zhongshan Park, Xi Chang'an Jie ⓣ010/65598285, ⓦwww.fcchbj.com. A stylish hall, with regular performances of Western and Chinese classical music. Tickets from ¥40.

National Centre for the Performing Arts
国家大剧院
guójiā dàjùyuàn
2 Xichang'an Jie ⓣ010/66550000, ⓦwww.chncpa.org. The giant egg-shaped structure just west of Tian'anmen Square hosts the best international performances in its huge concert hall. Note that you can't bring a camera. For more on the centre, see p.67.

Poly Theatre
保利大厦国际剧场
bǎolìdàshà guójì jùchǎng
Poly Plaza, 14 Dongzhimen Nan Dajie, near Dongsi Shitiao subway stop ⓣ010/65001188, ⓦwww.polytheatre.com. A gleaming hall that presents diverse performances of jazz, ballet, classical music, opera and modern dance for the edification of Beijing's cultural elite. Tickets start at around ¥100 and performances begin 7.30pm.

Workers' Stadium
工人体育场
gōngrén tǐyùchǎng
In the northeast of the city, off Gongren Tiyuchang Bei Lu ⓣ010/65016655. This is where giant gigs are staged, mostly featuring Chinese pop stars, though the likes of Björk have also played here (though, given her views on Tibet, that'll never happen again).

Indie music

Controversial local legend **Cui Jian**, a sort of Chinese Bob Dylan, was China's first real rock star, giving up a job as a trumpeter in a Beijing orchestra to perform gravel-voiced guitar rock with lyrics as risky as he could get away with – look out for his albums *Power to The Powerless* and *Egg Under the Red Flag*.

Cui Jian is now seen as the granddaddy of Beijing's thriving **indie music** scene. Nobody makes any money, as venues and bands struggle to survive against all-pervasive pop pap, and when an act does take off, piracy eats up any profits the recordings might have made – but fierce dedication keeps the scene alive. Most **bands** of note are on the Scream, Badhead or Modern Sky labels and the best new electronic music is on Shanshui Records.

Many **bands** perform in English, or have a mixed set. Bands to look out for include Rolling Stones-wannnabes Joyside, indie noise merchants Carsick Cars, Mongolian rockers Voodoo Kungfu, indie pros Lonely China Day, and electro popsters Pet Conspiracy. Veteran punks Brain Failure are still going strong, though the mantle of nuttiest punks has passed to younger bands like Demerit. For electronica, look out for iLoop and Sulumi. Not so well represented is **hip-hop** (odd, as it has made plenty of inroads in fashion) though old favourites CMCB carry it off pretty well.

The **Midi Rock Music** festival is held at the beginning of May in Haidian Park, just west of Beijing University campus (ⓦwww.midifestival.com); it has always been controversial, banned in 2008 and with foreign acts refused permission to play in 2009, a stricture which looks likely to continue. Still, plenty of local talent is on display, and the audience is enthusiastic. You can even camp, for the full-on "Chinese Glastonbury" experience. Tickets are ¥100 for the four-day event, ¥50 for one day.

Overleaf we have reviewed the best live music venues; there will generally be a cover of around ¥30–80.

2 Kolegas
两个好朋友
liǎnggè hǎopéngyǒu
21 Liangmaqiao, inside the drive-in movie cinema park ⓣ010/81964820, ⓦwww.2kolegas.com. See "Sanlitun & the northeast" map on p.81. This dive bar in the far northeast of the city is great for checking out the indie rockers and their fans, though it's a fair way out. In summer the crowd spill out onto the lawn.

D22
242 Chengfu Lu; come out of Wudaokou subway and walk towards the Beijing University East Gate ⓣ010/62653177, ⓦwww.d22beijing.com.cn. See "Haidian & the Summer Palaces" map on p.98. In-your-face bar in Wudaokou that attracts an energetic student crowd. Try and catch hugely popular Carsick Cars and Hedgehog. Rival rock venue, *Club 13* (ⓣ010/82619267, ⓦwww.myspace.com/13clubinchina), is two doors down.

Mao Livehouse
Mao现场
mào xiànchǎng
111 Gulou Dong Dajie, at the north end of Nanluogu Xiang ⓣ010/64025080, ⓦwww.maolive.com. See "Houhai Lake & around" map on p.88. Managed by Japanese music label Bad News, who know their stuff, this great, decent-sized venue hosts all the best local rock and punk bands. There may be no frills – not even a cloakroom – but it has the best sound system around, and drinks are refreshingly cheap (¥10).

What Bar
什么酒吧
shénme jiǔbā
72 Beichang Jie, north of the Forbidden City west gate ⓣ13341122757 (mobile). See "Tian'anmen Square & the Forbidden City" map on p.48. Oddly, this rock and punk gig venue is within spitting distance of the Forbidden City. It's so small you'll probably get spattered with the guitarist's sweat. A good introduction to the local rock scene.

Yugong Yishan
愚公移山
yúgōngyíshān
3–2 Zhangzigong Lu (on Ping'an Dajie 100m west of Zhangzizhong Lu subway stop) ⓣ010/64042711, ⓦwww.yugongyishan.com. See "North of the centre" map on pp.84–85. With a big dance floor, an up-for-it crowd and an eclectic mix of live acts, this has to be the best all-round venue in town.

Cinemas

There are plenty of **cinemas** showing Chinese and dubbed Western films, usually action movies. Just twenty Western films are picked by the government for release every year, and when they're too popular, they get pulled: *Avatar* disappeared from Chinese screens to give homegrown borefest *Confucius* a chance, for example. Despite such restrictions, these days most Beijingers have an impressive knowledge of world cinema, thanks to the prevalence of cheap, pirated DVDs.

Some of the **largest screens** in Beijing, showing mainstream Chinese and foreign films, are the old *Dahua Cinema* at 82 Dongdan Bei Dajie (ⓣ010/65274420, ⓦwww.dhfilm.cn), *Star City* in the Oriental Plaza Mall (BB65, 1 Dongchang'an jie; ⓣ010/85186778, ⓦwww.xfilmcity.com); the *Xin Dong'an Cinema* on the fifth floor of the Sun Dong'an Plaza, at 138 Wangfujing (ⓣ010/65281838, ⓦwww.b-cinema.cn); the *UME Huaxing Cinema* at 44 Kexueyuan Nan Lu, Haidian, next to the Shuang Yu Shopping Centre, just off the Third Ring Road (ⓣ010/62555566, ⓦwww.bjume.com) and the slick new *Megabox* in Sanlitun Village (ⓣ010/64176118, ⓦwww.imegabox.com). **Tickets** cost ¥50 or more. There are usually two showings of foreign movies; one dubbed into Chinese, the other subtitled. Ring to check.

Space for Imagination at 5 Xi Wang Zhuang Xiao Qu, Haidian, opposite Qinghua University's east gate (ⓣ010/62791280) is a charming cineastes' bar that shows **avant-garde films** every Saturday at 7pm. The best **arthouse** venture, though, is *Cherry Lane Movies*, which organizes showings at *Yugong Yishan* (see above; ⓣ010/64042711, ⓦwww.cherrylanemovies.com.cn). Their screenings, which include obscure and controversial underground Chinese films, usually with

Beijing on film

Foreigners are likely to be familiar with acclaimed "fifth generation" films, made in the 1980s, such as **Chen Kaige**'s *Farewell My Concubine*, the epic tragedy of a gay Beijing opera singer, and **Zhang Yimou**'s hauntingly beautiful *Raise the Red Lantern*. However, these films were criticized at home as being overly glamorous and made only for foreigners. In the 1990s, the new "sixth generation" of directors subsequently set out to make edgier work. Their films, usually low-budget affairs, shot in black-and-white – and difficult to catch in China – depict what their makers consider to be the true story of modern urban life: cold apartments, ugly streets, impoverished people. The best-known of these films is *Beijing Bastards*, the story of apathetic, fast-living youths, which included a role for rebel rocker Cui Jian (see p.153). The satirical *In The Heat of The Sun* was scripted by **Wang Shuo**, the bad boy of Chinese contemporary literature (see p.181), and perfectly captures the post-revolutionary ennui of 1970s Beijing in its tale of a street gang looking for kicks.

Commercial films have been influenced by this social-realist aesthetic; look out for *Beijing Bicycle* (2001), the story of a lad trying to get his stolen bike back, and **Liu Fendou**'s *Spring Subway* (2002) which employs the capital's gleaming subway stations as a backdrop to the main character's soul-searching.

The biggest box office director is **Feng Xiaogang**. Sadly, he's started making overwrought historical confections like *The Banquet* (2006) but his early works, made in the 90s – *Be There or Be Square*, *Sorry Baby*, *A World Without Thieves* and *Big Shot's Funeral* – are his best: light, clever comedies set in Beijing.

Finally, China has a promising new **documentary movement**; look out for Li Hong's *Out of Phoenix Bridge* (2007), which follows the lives of four young women who move from the coutryside to Beijing in search of a new life, and Jian Yi's *New Socialist Climax* (2009), which explores the way in which revolutionary sites have been turned into tourist attractions.

English subtitles, take place every Sunday at 8pm (¥50), followed by a discussion, sometimes featuring the director or cast members.

Art galleries

Chinese **painting** has an ancient history. The earliest brush found in China, made out of animal hairs glued to a hollow bamboo tube, dates from about 400 BC. The Chinese used silk for painting on as early as the third century BC, with paper being used as early as 106 AD. **Traditional** Chinese paintings are light and airy, with empty spaces playing an important element in the design, and rich in symbolism; they're decorated with a few lines of poetry and several names in the form of seals – the marks of past owners.

The best places to see fine **classical** Chinese paintings are the galleries in the Forbidden City (see p.52); examples from the Sui, Song and Tang dynasties are the highlights. Respectable examples of Chinese painting are for sale at the Traditional Painting Store, at 289 Wangfujing Dajie. However, be wary in general of private art galleries selling classical-looking paintings. They're aimed at tourists, and almost all the images are worthless prints or produced en masse in art sweatshops.

Due to the recession in the West, the **contemporary art** scene has been through a rocky few years, but that has also served to winnow out some of the less talented artists. Contemporary art is still flourishing in Beijing, and worth checking out. Chinese art schools emphasize traditional crafts, but many students have been

Contemporary Chinese art

The **contemporary art scene** in China began in earnest in the 1990s, with a group who, with little chance of selling their work or even exhibiting, banded together to form an arts village in the suburbs of Beijing, near the old summer palace. These artists developed a school of painting that expressed their individualism and their sceptical, often ironic and jaundiced view of contemporary China; this was, of course, the generation that had seen its dreams of change shot down at Tian'anmen Square. Nurtured by curator **Li Xianting**, known as "the Godfather of Chinese art", as well as sympathetic foreign collectors, they built the foundations of the art scene as it is today.

The most famous of these so-called **cynical realists** is **Fang Lijun**, whose images of disembodied heads against desolate landscapes are some of the most characteristic images of modern Chinese art. Other art stars who began their career here include **Yue Minjun**, who paints sinister laughing figures, and the satirists **Wang Jinsong** and **Song Yonghong**.

Artists such as Wang Guangyi developed a second, distinctly Chinese school of art called **political pop**, where the powerful iconography of the Cultural Revolution was co-opted to celebrate consumerism – workers wave iPods instead of little red books. This kind of thing, perennially popular with foreign visitors, is regarded these days as pretty hackneyed in China. Rather more interesting was the deliberately brash "**gaudy art**" movement of the 1990s, whose aesthetic celebrated the tacky and vulgar; look out for **Xu Yihui**'s ceramic confections and the **Luo Brothers**' kitsch extravaganzas.

It's much harder to pick out trends in today's ferment of activity, but many artists are unsurprisingly preoccupied with documenting the destruction of the Chinese urban landscape and the gutwrenching changes that have accompanied **modernization**. As spaces for viewing art have increased, artists have diversified into new media such as **performance** and **video**; two to look out for are **Cao Fei**, who films and photographs fantasy tableaux, and **Yang Fudong**, who makes wistful images of modern life. With all the noise, you need to shout to make yourself heard – and the loudest modern artists are the impresario **Zhang Huang**, who produces witty sculptures on an enormous scale, and art celebrity **Ai Weiwei**, who helped design the concept behind the Bird's Nest Olympic stadium (see p.92).

quick to plug themselves into international trends. At its best, this leads to art that is technically proficient and conceptually strong. Artists and photographers have fewer problems with censorship and counterfeiting than writers or musicians and the scene has been nurtured by considerable foreign interest – the best galleries are owned by expats, and Chinese art is seen as an attractive investment by foreign buyers. The scene is particularly lively during the **Beijing biennale** (Ⓦwww.bjbiennale.com.cn), which will be held in late September 2012 and 2014.

798 District

The classic arty stomping ground is **798**, an old electronics factory in the northeast of the city that's been redeveloped as a sprawl of studios and more than a hundred galleries (see p.82). Addresses aren't much help, but do indicate which of the two main east–west roads to head for: "2 Liuxianqiao Lu" means the northernmost, "4 Liuxianqiao Lu" the southernmost. To find your way around, study the **maps** dotted around the complex, or head to the *Timezone Bookstore Café* (see p.162) and pick up the handy little **RedBox art guide** (¥10), whose maps show all the best galleries. Note that just about everywhere is **closed** on a Monday.

The area is particularly lively during the **798 Art Festival** – though the size of the festival, its dates, and, indeed, whether it happens at all, are dependent on the precarious political climate. It should be scheduled for the autumn.

Beijing Commune
北京公社
běijīng gōngshè
4 Jiuxianqiao Lu ⓣ010/86549428, ⓦwww.beijingcommune.com. Known for having the most imaginatively curated shows. Tues–Sun 10am–6pm.

Beijing Tokyo Art Projects
北京东京艺术工程
běijīngdōngjīng yìshùgōngchéng
4 Jiuxianqiao Lu ⓣ010/84573245, ⓦwww.tokyo-gallery.com. The first gallery to set up shop here, and still one of the best, with a large elegant space for challenging shows. Tues–Fri 11am–7pm, Sat 11am–5pm.

Galeria Continua
常青画廊
chángqīng huàláng
2 Jiuxianqiao Lu ⓣ010/64361005, ⓦwww.galeriacontinua.com. Shows international and homegrown art stars. Tues–Sun 11am–6pm.

Long March Space
长征空间
chángzhēng kōngjiān
4 Jiuxianqiao Lu ⓣ010/64387107, ⓦwww.longmarchspace.com. This space is popular for its attempts to reach out to the masses with education programmes (as its name hints). Tues–Sun 11am–7pm.

Ullens Centre for Contemporary Art (UCCA)
尤伦斯当代艺术中心
yóulúnsī dāngdài yìshùzhōngxīn
4 Jiuxianqiao Lu ⓣ010/64386675, ⓦwww.ucca.org.cn. This huge nonprofit space is more of a museum than a gallery; nothing is for sale and it is the only space that charges an entrance fee (¥15). There are three exhibition halls and a programme of regular events (all detailed on the website). Tues–Sun 10am–6pm.

White Space
空白空间
kòngbái kōngjiān
2 Jiuxianqiao Lu ⓣ010/84562054, ⓦwww.alexanderochs-galleries.de. This well-run space, owned by a German curator, has a reputation for putting on challenging shows by up-and-coming artists. Tues–Sat 10am–6pm.

Caochangdi Art District

Even further out along the airport expressway than 798, by the Fifth Ring Road, a new and even hipper art zone has recently emerged. **Caochangdi Art District** was set up by Ai Weiwei and friends when they felt that 798 was getting too commercial.

It's another tough place to get to – far better to take a cab from Dongzhimen subway station (¥30) than even attempt the buses (though if you do, it's #402 or #973 from Dashanzi Lukou Nan on Jiuxianqiao Lu to the Caochangdi stop on Nangao Lu).

There are a couple of dozen galleries here, with new ones opening all the time, but unlike 798, they are not quite densely packed enough to make walking around worthwhile. Addresses are basically useless and the streets are a maze, so the best way to get around is to hire a taxi for the afternoon (¥300 or so, from anywhere in town), and get the cabbie to call the galleries for instructions on getting there. If you do want to try to navigate yourself, you'll need the map from the **RedBox art guide** (see p.156). As in 798, everything is shut on a Monday.

The four **can't-miss** spaces here are the cutting-edge **Platform** (319-1, Caochangdi A; ⓣ010/64320169, ⓦwww.platfromchina.org; Tues–Sun 10am–6pm); the huge **Boers-Li Gallery** (8A Caochangdi; ⓣ010/64322620, ⓦwww.boersligallery.com; Tues–Sun 10am–6pm) which also has a coffee-shop; the **Three Shadows Photography Art Centre** (155 Caochangdi; ⓣ010/64322663, ⓦwww.threeshadows.cn; Tues–Sun 10am–6pm), and Ai Weiwei's own **China Art and Archives Warehouse** (100 Tiedaoqiao ⓣ010/84565152, ⓦwww.archivesandwarehouse.com; Tues–Sun 2–6pm).

City centre galleries

Galleries in the **city centre** are rather more commercial than those in the suburban artsy areas; they tend to focus on selling paintings rather than making a splash with a themed show. Still, there are some that display interesting and challenging work.

Courtyard Gallery

四合苑画廊

sìhéyuàn huàláng

95 Donghuamen Dajie ⓣ010/65268882, ⓦwww.courtyard-gallery.com. In an old courtyard house by the east gate of the Forbidden City, this little basement gallery has frequent shows; it's something of a meeting point for the cultural elite. There's also a cigar lounge and restaurant (see p.138). Mon–Sat 11am–7pm, Sun noon–7pm.

National Art Museum of China

中国美术馆

zhōngguó měishùguǎn

1 Wusi Dajie ⓣ010/84033500, ⓦwww.namoc.org. Bus #2 from Qianmen or trolleybus #104 from Beijing Zhan. At the northern end of Wangfujing Dajie, this grand building usually holds a couple of shows at once. There's no permanent display; past exhibitions have included specialist women's and minority people's exhibitions, and even a show of Socialist-Realist propaganda – put up not to inspire renewed zeal but as a way to reconsider past follies. Once regarded as a stuffy academy, it now embraces modern trends such as installation and video art. In July, the art colleges hold their degree shows here. Daily 9am–5pm, last entry at 4pm; entrance ¥20 (though this can vary depending on what's on).

Red Gate Gallery

红门画廊

hóngmén huàláng

Dongbianmen watchtower, Chongwenmen Dong Dajie ⓣ010/65251005, ⓦwww.redgategallery.com. Commercial gallery, run by a Western curator, inside one of the last remnants of the old city wall. A little more adventurous than other Beijing galleries, it has a good reputation among overseas curators. Daily 10am–5pm.

Today Art Museum

今日美术馆

jīnrì měishùguǎn

Building 4, Pingod Community, 32 Baiziwan Lu ⓣ010/58621100, ⓦwww.todayartmuseum.com. This promising new gallery is one of China's first privately owned museums, with a focus on promoting contemporary Chinese art. Daily 10am–5pm.

Shopping

Appropriately for the capital of a major commercial power, Beijing has some great shopping. Much of it concentrated in four main shopping districts: **Wangfujing** has mostly mid-range shops and malls, and famous Chinese brands; **Xidan** hosts giant department stores; **Dongdan** sells mainly brand-name clothes; and **Qianmen** has been reinvented as an open-air mall. **Liulichang** (see p.61), a street of imitation Qing buildings aimed especially at visitors, is a good spot to furnish yourself with souvenirs, while **Jianguomenwai Dajie** is the place to head for clothes, and **Guomao** is where you'll find the really high-end stuff. Shopping is more exciting, and cheaper, in the city's many **markets**, even though they offer no guarantee of quality; you can – and should – **bargain** (aim to knock at least two thirds off the starting price).

China has a massive industry in **fakes** – nothing escapes the counterfeiters. You'll no doubt hear assurances to the contrary, but you can assume that all antiques and

Department stores and malls

For general goods, check out the city's **department stores**, which sell a little of everything, and give a general idea of current Chinese taste. A prime example is the Beijing Department Store at 255 Wangfujing Dajie. The newer Landao Store on Chaoyangmenwai Dajie is more impressive, as is the Chung Yo Department Store at 176 Xidan Bei Dajie and the nearby Xidan Department Store. All are aimed at the Chinese middle-class; you'll find more international and aspirational brands at the Parkson Building on Fuxingmenwai Dajie, the Lufthansa Centre on Liangmaqiao Lu in the northeast of the city, or the Japanese SOGO Store at 8 Xuanwumenwai Dajie. The **Friendship Store** on Jianguomenwai Dajie, built in the late 1970s, was the first modern department store in China; it was the only place in the city selling imported goods, and Chinese shoppers, barred from entering, would bribe foreigners to buy things for them. The store has since failed to reinvent itself, and is known for high prices and insouciant staff.

But the newest shopping trend is for **malls** – maybe it's the air of exclusivity and sophistication, or just a reaction to Beijing's bad weather, but the appetite for vast and sterile shopping warrens seems insatiable. The new giant malls sell goods (clothes mostly) that cost as much as they do in the West, and also have supermarkets, coffee shops, restaurants, chemists and food courts, and sometimes cinemas and bowling alleys. The most convenient to visit are **Sun Dong'an and Oriental plazas** on Wangfujing Dajie, the **China World Plaza** in the World Trade Centre on Jianguomenwai Dajie, and the new **Raffles City** at Dongzhimen. The shiniest, newest and highest-end malls are the **Shin Kong Place** at 87 Jianguomen Dajie, the **Solana Lifestyle Shopping Park** at Chaoyang Park, and **Season's Place** at 2 Jinchengfang Jie, opposite the *Westin Hotel*; but probably the most successful, with its winning mix of elegant dining and high-end consumerism, is the showcase **Sanlitun Village**, off Sanlitun Lu.

collectable stamps, coins and posters are replicas, the paintings are prints, and that Rolex watches will stop working as soon as you turn the corner. If you don't mind robbing artists of their livelihood, pirated CDs and DVDs are very cheap. Even more of a bargain are the widely available fake designer-label clothes and accessories.

Shops generally stay **open** from Monday to Saturday from 9am to 6pm or 7pm, closing earlier on Sunday; the large shopping centres are open every day until around 9pm. When they differ markedly, specific opening hours are given in the reviews below. Outdoor **markets** don't have official opening times, but tend to trade from about 7am to 6pm. **Phone numbers** are given for shops that are particularly out of the way – head there in a taxi and ask the driver to call them for directions.

Antiques, curios and souvenirs

There's no shortage of **antique stores** and **markets** in the capital, offering opium pipes, jade statues, porcelain Mao figurines, mahjong sets, Red Guard alarm clocks, Fu Manchu glasses, and all manner of bric-a-brac – pretty much all of it fake. The jade is actually soapstone, inset jewels are glass, and that venerable painting is a print stained with tea. There are very few real antiques for sale in Beijing, and no bargains.

Liulichang, south of Hepingmen subway stop, has the densest concentration of curio stores in town, with a huge selection of wares, particularly of art materials, porcelain and snuff boxes, though prices are steep. Chairman Mao's Little Red Book is ubiquitous (and only costs about ¥10), and the most popular memento is a soapstone **seal** for imprinting names in either Chinese characters or Roman letters (starting at around ¥40); to see ancient traditions meeting modern technology, go round the back and watch them laser-cut it. For contemporary curios, try **Yandai Xiejie**, a *hutong* full of little stores selling souvenir notebooks, matchboxes and the like, at the north end of Houhai Lake.

Good, widely available, inexpensive **souvenirs** include seals, kites, art materials, papercuts (images cut into thin card), tea sets, jade bracelets, mahjong sets and ornamental chopsticks (try any department store). For something a little unusual, you could get some Cultural Revolution kitsch (antique stores); a specialist tea blend (stores on Dazhalan); a drily witty T-shirt (try Plastered, p.164); a riot cop keyring (from the Police Museum, p.76); a model ear marked with acupuncture points, or a perhaps goat-penis aphrodisiac (Tongrentang pharmacy, p.61).

Beijing Curio City
北京古玩城
běijīng gǔwánchéng
21 Dongsanhuan Nan Lu, west of Huawei Bridge in the southeast of the city. Bus #300 from Guomao subway stop. A giant arcade of more than 400 stalls, best visited on a Sunday, when other antique traders come and set up in the surrounding streets. Daily 9.30am–6.30pm.

Gongyi Meishu Fuwubu
工艺美术服务部
gōngyì měishù fúwùbù
200 Wangfujing Dajie. Bus #111 from Wangfujing subway stop. A huge and well-reputed store selling art supplies. Soft Chinese brushes (some with tips up to 15cm long) and decorated blocks of solid ink are good value. Daily 9am–10pm.

Hongqiao Department Store
红桥百货中心
hóngqiáo bǎihuò zhōngxīn
Northeast corner of Tiantan Park. Bus #41 from Qianmen. The top floor of this giant mall is packed with stalls selling antiques and curios. One shop is given over solely to Cultural Revolution kitsch, such as alarm clocks with images of Red Guards on the face, porcelain Red Guards and Mao badges. The Socialist Realist posters are great (replicas, of course) though it's tough getting a sensible price for anything. The stalls are set up alongside a pearl and jewellery market. Clothes and fake bags are

sold on the second floor; the first floor is the place to go for small electronic items, including such novelties as watches that speak the time in Russian when you whistle at them. Daily 9am–8pm.

Huaxia Arts and Crafts Store
华夏工艺品店
huáxià gōngyìpǐndiàn
293 Wangfujing Dajie. Stocks a decent selection of expensive objets d'art. The selection upstairs is better, with clocks, rugs and woodcarvings. Mon–Sat 8.30am–8pm.

Liangma Antique Market
亮马收藏品市场
liàngmǎ shōuchángpǐn shìchǎng
27 Liangmaqiao Lu; take subway line 10 to Liangmaqiao. This market is small but also less picked over than others, with good carpet and furniture sections. One for the serious collector, with time to root around; you might even find the odd real antique.

Panjiayuan Market
潘家园市场
pānjiāyuán shìchǎng
Panjiayuan Lu, one of the roads connecting the southeastern sections of the Second and Third ring roads, east of Longtan Park. Bus #300 from Guomao subway stop or take a taxi. Also called the "Dirt Market", this is Beijing's biggest antique market, with a huge range of souvenirs and secondhand goods on sale (sometimes in advanced states of decay) including plenty of traders from Tibet. It's at its biggest and best at weekends between 6am and 3pm, when the surrounding streets are packed with stalls – worth a visit even if you're not buying. The initial asking prices for souvenirs are more reasonable than anywhere else. Mon–Fri 8am–6.30pm, with earlier opening at weekends.

You An Kite
右安风筝坊
yòu'ān fēngzhēngfǎng
63 You'anmenwai Dajie, just off the Second Ring Road. A specialist kite shop; all the wares have bamboo frames and colourful designs.

Yunhong chopsticks
韵泓筷子店
yùnhóng kuàizidiàn
277 Wangfujing Dajie. This little shop sells decorative and gift-set chopsticks.

Carpets and furniture

Created mainly in Xinjiang, Tibet and Tianjin, the beautiful handmade **carpets** on sale in Beijing aren't cheap, but are nevertheless pretty good value. Tibetan carpets are yellow and orange and usually have figurative mythological or religious motifs; rugs from Xinjiang in the northwest are red and pink with abstract patterns, while weaves from Tianjin are multicoloured. Check the colour for consistency at both ends – sometimes, large carpets are hung up near a hot lamp, which causes fading.

As well as the places reviewed below, you can get carpets at the Friendship Store (see p.159; bargain hard here), Yuanlong Silk Corporation (see p.165), and on Liulichang.

Khawachen Tibetan Rugs
喀瓦坚西藏手工地毯
kèwǎnjiān xīzàng shǒugōng dìtǎn
3–2FA, Solana Shopping Park, Chaoyang Park ⓣ010/59056311. Handmade Tibetan rugs from about ¥2000, plus custom designs produced to order. Daily 10am–10pm.

Qianmen Carpet Company
前门地毯厂
qiánmén dìtǎnchǎng
59 Xingfu Jie, just north of the *Tiantan hotel* ⓣ010/67151687. Bus #8 from Dongdan subway stop. A converted air-raid shelter selling carpets mostly from Xinjiang and Tibet; the silk carpets from Henan in central China are very popular. A typical 2m by 3m carpet can cost around ¥50,000, though the cheapest rugs start at around ¥2000. Mon–Fri 8.30am–5pm.

Zhaojia Chaowai Market
兆佳朝外市场
zhàojiā cháowài shìchǎng
43 Huawei Bei Lu, off Dongsanhuan Lu, 100m north of Panjiayuan Junction. Some carpets and enormous quantities of reproduction traditional Chinese furniture in all sizes and styles, for those whose lives lack lacquer. Daily 10am–5.30pm.

Books

Plenty of English-language **books** on Chinese culture – many hard to find in the West – are on sale in Beijing, ranging from giant coffee-table tomes celebrating new freeways in China to comic-book versions of Chinese classics. Even if you're not buying, Beijing's **bookshops** are pleasant environments in which to browse – Chinese customers spend hours reading the stock, sometimes bringing along their own stool and cushions to make themselves comfortable. Some bookshops have cafés and art galleries attached.

In addition to the outlets reviewed below, there's a bookshop within the Friendship Store (see p.144), selling foreign newspapers (¥50) – a few days out of date – as well as a wide variety of books on all aspects of Chinese culture, though rather overpriced. The *Bookworm* (see p.136) also functions as a library and bookshop.

Charterhouse

B107, The Place, 9 Guanghua Lu Ⓦwww.charterhouse.com.cn. A good selection of imported books and magazines. Daily 10am–10pm.

Foreign Language Bookstore

外交书店

wàiwén shūdiàn

218 Wangfujing Dajie Ⓦwww.bpiec.com.cn. The main store has the biggest selection of foreign-language books in mainland China. An information desk on the right as you go in sells listings magazines; opposite is a counter selling maps, including an enormous wall map of the city (¥80). The English books on offer downstairs include fiction, textbooks on Chinese medicine, and translations of Chinese classics. The upper floors, too, have more fiction in English, magazines, wall hangings, and Japanese *manga*. Sometimes, the same book is cheaper upstairs than downstairs. Daily 8am–5pm.

Garden Books

韬奋西文书局

tāofènxīwén shūjú

44 Guanghua Lu, opposite the Brazilian Embassy Ⓦwww.gardenbooks.cn. Charming bookstore and expat favourite, with an eclectic selection of imported novels, children's books and cookbooks. Daily 8am–9pm.

Timezone8 Bookstore Café

东八时区艺术书屋

dōngbāshíqū yìshū shūwū

4 Jiuxianqiao, 798 Art District Ⓦwww.timezone8.com. This chic art bookstore with attached café is the most civilized venue in the bobo (bohemian-bourgeois) playground that is the 798 Art District. Tote a laptop to truly fit in; they have free wi-fi. Daily 8.30am–9pm.

Tushu Daxia

图书大厦

túshū dàshà

Xichang'an Jie. Bus #22 from Qianmen. Beijing's biggest bookshop, with the commercial feel of a department store. English fiction is on the third floor. Mon–Sat 9am–7pm.

Clothes and fabrics

Clothes are a bargain in Beijing, but be sure to check the quality carefully. Head for **Jianguomen Dajie**, where the silk and cotton markets, the Friendship Store and the plazas offer something for every budget. If you're particularly tall or have especially large feet, you'll generally have difficulty finding clothes and shoes to fit you, though there's a reasonable chance of finding clothes in your size at the Silk Market. One big Asian trend that seems unlikely to catch on in the West is the phenomenon of matching T-shirts for couples – if you want to check out the "his and hers" T-shirts that are all the rage among the kids, take a look in the clothes shops near the universities.

Tailors

At **Yaxiu Market**, a suit should cost around ¥800 and tailored shirts around ¥150; they will take about a week to make, three days at the shortest. Shop assistants will speak basic English. Aim to barter about a third off the asking price, and if you want to be certain of getting exactly what you want, be prepared to be assertive about asking for issues to be sorted out when you pick up your clothes. Turn up with any design, or even just a picture from a fashion magazine, and they'll gamely give it a go. Try Alice My Tailor at no. 3186, or Tailor Ma on the third floor (mobile ⓣ13910095718).

Another good bet for bargain tailoring is **Lisa Tailor** (Shop 3066, Third Floor, 3.3 Mall, 33 Sanlitun Bei Lu; mobile ⓣ13910578826), where a suit starts at around ¥1000. Similar services are available at the **Silk Market**, and in some of the shops reviewed below.

For more reliably good men's tailoring, head to **Senli and Frye** at 46 Liangmaqiao Lu, inside the Yaxing Dasha (mobile ⓣ13910092410); suits here start at about ¥3000 and take ten days to make. For real quality men's tailoring, Chinese-style, try **Hongdu Tailor**, at 28 Dongjiao Minxiang, just west of the *Capital Hotel*, which once tailored Chairman Mao himself (not that he was any kind of fashion icon). A suit at this famous Chinese brand will set you back about ¥10,000, and take a month to make.

A You
阿尤
āyóu
Xinjiekou Bei Dajie. Trendy, ethnic-style designer clothes from an established local design brand. Prices start at around ¥180 for striking summer dresses.

Aliens Street Market
老番街
lǎofān jiē
Yabao Lu, south of the Fullink Plaza. This bustling warren of stalls is where the Russian expats come en masse. There's a vast range of (cheap) goods, but it's particularly worth picking over for clothes and accessories.

Beijing Silk Store
北京谦祥益丝绸商店
běijīng qiānxiángyì sīchóu shāngdiàn
50 Dazhalan Jie ⓣ010/63016658. This is an excellent place to buy quality silk clothes in Chinese styles, with a wider selection and keener prices than any of the tourist stores. The ground floor sells silk fabrics, while clothes can be bought upstairs.

Dong Liang Studio
栋梁
dòngliáng
26 Wudaoying Hutong ⓣ010/84047648. Chic, elegant and affordable clothes by local designers; look out for beautiful dresses by JJ, Ye Qian and Shen Ye.

Dong Xi Hui
东西会
dōngxīhuì
3.3 building, Sanlitun Bei Jie. This shop sells secondhand clothes once worn by movie stars – the *qipao* that Zhang Ziyi wore in the film *Banquet* was on sale here – though you pay a price for the garments' history.

Dongwuyuan Wholesale Market
动物园服装批发市场
dòngwùyuán fúzhuāng pīfā shìchǎng
Xizhimenwai Daijie, south of the zoo, above the bus depot. This giant, hectic indoor market is full of stalls selling very cheap non-branded clothes, shoes and accessories to locals in the know. Almost everything has a price tag so you won't have to bargain. Note that there won't be anything in large sizes.

The First Outdoor
第一户外
dìyī hùwài
6 Zhushikou Dong Dajie ⓣ010/67071365. Decent-quality outdoors and trekking gear. It's pricey, but at least it's all genuine, and the shop has a camping club. Small discounts are available if you ask.

Five Colours Earth
五色土
wǔsètǔ
1505, Building 5, Jianwai SOHO, 39 Dongsanhuan Zhong Lu ⓣ010/58692923, ⓦwww.fivecolours earth.com. Interesting and unusual collections, often incorporating fragments of old

embroidery, by a talented local designer. Not too expensive either; you can pick up a coat for ¥500.

Lan

21 Yandai Xie Jie. Imaginatively designed, vaguely ethnic women's clothes, all handmade, between ¥200 and ¥500.

Mingxing Clothing Store

明星中式服装店

míngxīng zhōngshì fúzhuāngdiàn

133 Wangfujing Dajie ⓣ010/65257945. Well-made Chinese-style garments, such as *cheongsams* and *qipaos*, with an on-site tailor.

Neiliansheng Shoes

内联升布鞋

nèiliánshēng bùxié

34 Dazhalan, Qianmen ⓣ010/63013041, ⓦwww.nls1853.com. Look out for the giant shoe in the window. All manner of handmade flat, slip-on shoes and slippers in traditional designs, starting from ¥100 or so – they make great gifts.

NLGX Design

NLGX设计

NLGXshèjì

33 Nanluogu Xiang ⓣ010/64048088, ⓦwww.nlgx.com. Hipster streetwear from local designers, with much made from recycled materials. Their airport code series of T-shirts is perennially popular. There's a small coffee shop upstairs with free wi-fi. Daily 10am–11pm.

Plastered T-Shirts

创可贴T恤

chuàngkětiē tīxù

61 Nanluogu Xiang ⓦwww.plasteredtshirts.com. Hipster T-shirts and sweatshirts whose witty designs reference everyday Beijing life – subway tickets, thermoses and so on.

Ruifuxiang Store

瑞蚨祥丝绸店

ruìfúxiáng sīchóudiàn

5 Dazhalan, off Qianmen Dajie ⓣ010/63035313, ⓦwww.ruifuxiang.cn; also at 190 Wangfujing Dajie. Silk and cotton fabrics and a good selection of shirts and dresses, with a tailor specializing in made-to-measure *qipaos*. You should aim to barter a little off the quoted price. Daily 9am–9pm.

Shanghai Tang

上海滩

shànghǎi tān

B1, *Grand Hyatt Hotel*, 1 Dong Chang'an Jie ⓦwww.shanghaitang.com. This Chinese designer label offers brightly coloured luxury chinoiserie. Nice bags and cufflinks, especially, though it's all a bit pricey.

Sheng Xifu Hat Store

盛锡福帽店

shèngxīfú màodiàn

196 Wangfujing. China's most famous hat brand, with a display in the store of hats worn by luminaries; a cap of cotton is ¥128, rabbit fur ¥680.

Silk Market

秀水市场

xìushuǐ shìchǎng

Xiushui Jie, off Jianguomenwai Dajie, very near Yong'anli subway stop ⓦwww.xiushui.com.cn. This huge six-storey mall for tourists has electronics, jewellery and souvenirs, but its main purpose is to profit through flouting international copyright laws, with hundreds of stalls selling fake designer labels. You'll need to haggle hard; you shouldn't pay more than ¥80 for a pair of jeans, ¥70 for trainers, ¥25 for T-shirts, ¥20 for ties, ¥150 for jackets and ¥80 for shirts. There are also a few tailors – pick out your material, then bargain, and you can get a suit made in 24hr for ¥800 or so. It's incredibly busy, attracting over 50,000 visitors a day on weekends, and vendors are tiresomely pushy. There is a huge toy market on the third floor, a branch of the Tongrentang Pharmacy on the fourth floor, and a Quanjude roast duck restaurant on the sixth. Daily 9am–9pm.

Ullens Centre for Contemporary Art (UCCA)

尤伦斯当代艺术中心

yóulúnsī dāngdài yìshùzhōngxīn

4 Jiuxianqiao Lu, 798 Art District ⓦwww.ucca.org.cn. This artsy gallery (see p.157) sells limited-edition fashions by local designers for around ¥1000 and handwoven bags for ¥300. Tues–Sun 10am–6pm.

Yansha Outlets Mall

燕莎奥特莱斯购物中心

yànshā àotèláisī gòuwù zhōngxīin

9 Dongsihuannan Jie, at the southern end of the eastern section of the Fourth Ring Road ⓣ010/67395678, ⓦwww.yansha.com.cn. A huge outlet for genuine designer clothes and bags, all old lines, at discounts of between thirty and fifty percent. Very popular with expats. Daily 10am–10pm.

Yaxiu Clothing Market (also called Yashow)

雅秀服装市场

yǎxiù fúzhuāng shìchǎng

58 Gongrentiyuchang Bei Lu. A four-storey mall of stalls selling designer fakes, very like the

Silk Market but a little less busy. The third floor is filled with tailors, and the fourth is for souvenirs. Daily 9.30am–8pm.

Yuanlong Silk Corporation
元隆顾绣绸缎商场
yuánlóng gùxiù chóuduàn shāngháng
55 Tiantan Lu ⓣ010/67052451. A good selection of silk clothes, blankets and bedding from this century-old shop. Mon–Sat 9am–6.30pm.

Yuexiu Clothing Market
越秀市场
yuèxiù shìchǎng
99 Chaoyangmennei Dajie. A market with a little bit of everything and a great deal of fake clothes. It's much less well known than the Silk Market, so the shopping experience is somewhat more pleasant. Daily 9.30am–8pm.

CDs and DVDs

Pirated CDs and DVDs are sold by chancers who approach foreigners around the Silk Market, on Dazhalan and in bars in Houhai and Sanlitun. The discs generally work, though sometimes the last few minutes are garbled. You can get DVDs for as little as ¥8, CDs for ¥5, though the asking price starts out at ¥15. Note that with DVDs of newly released films, you're likely to get a version shot illicitly in a cinema, with heads bobbing around at the bottom of the screen.

Otherwise, music shops selling **legitimate CDs** can be found throughout the city; FAB, in the basement of the Orient Plaza Mall, close to the west entrance, is a good, central store, but there's a particularly dense cluster around Xinjiekou Dajie in the northwest. A couple of the best are reviewed below.

Fusheng
福声唱片店
fúshēng chàngpiàndiàn
Xinjiekou Dajie, 50m east of the Ping'anli intersection. Local rock and a few imports.

Hongyun
宏运音象中心
hóngyùn yīnxiàng zhōngxīn
62 Xinjiekou Bei Dajie. A huge collection of legitimate CDs; Western imports, Mando-pop and local rock.

Computer equipment

You can pick up memory sticks, an MP3 player, a webcam or a medium-spec laptop for less than at home, if you go for unglamorous Korean or Chinese brands such as Acer and Lenovo, but be aware that there is little after-sales support. **Pirated software**, though a steal in more ways than one, should be given a wide berth. The main area for electronic goodies is **Zhongguancun** in northwest Beijing, nicknamed "Silicon Alley" for its plethora of computer shops and hi-tech businesses.

Hailong Electronics Market
海龙大厦
hǎilóng dàshà
1 Zhongguancun Dajie, Haidian. A veritable bazaar, piled high with all manner of gadgetry. One of a few in the area, and the biggest, with six storeys. There is a little leeway for bargaining. Mon–Sat 9am–6pm.

Hi-Tech Mall
百脑汇
bǎinǎohuì
10 Chaoyangmenwai Dajie, opposite the Dongyue Temple. Convenient and orderly four-storey mall of stores, some of which will build you a PC for around ¥5000. You can barter, but this isn't the Silk Market; you might get at most a quarter off. Daily 9am–8pm.

Tea

There are **tea shops** all over the city, including chains such as Zhang Yiyuan (22 Dazhalan ⓣ010/63034001) and Wu Yutai (44 Dongsi Bei Dajie ⓣ010/64041928), but for all your tea needs, check out **Maliandao Lu** (马连道茶叶街, *mǎliándào cháyèjiē*), behind the train station, which hosts hundreds of tea shops along a 1.5km-long stretch. They all offer free **tastings**, but remember that you're expected to bargain for the actual product. You're spoilt for choice, of course, but check out four-storey Tea City, about halfway down. There's plenty of tea paraphernalia around, too, much of which makes good gifts – look for porous Yixing ware **teapots**.

Jewellery and accessories

Jewellery is a good buy in Beijing, and often much cheaper than at home. Handmade pieces by minorities such as the Miao and Tibetans are perennially popular with foreigners, and are currently trendy with the Chinese.

Dragon House
East side of Yaxiu Market ⓣ010/64132929. Lovely silver and gold jewellery in Chinese and Western styles.

D-SATA
Unit A116, Nali Patio, 81 Sanlitun Bei Lu ⓦwww.d-sata.com. Stylish, quirky fashion bags and jewellery, made from recycled materials (such as snakeskin that's been discarded from restaurants). Daily 1–9pm.

Jia Na Ma Ni
嘉纳玛尼藏饰中心
jiānàmǎní zàngshìzhōngxīn
6 Fangyuan Si Lu. Tibetan curiosities, including carpets.

Miao Wang Zhai
21 Yandai Xiejie. Intricate Miao jewellery and hand-dyed fabrics.

Yu Hai Cui Yuan
玉海翠圆
yùhǎicuìyuán
Fatou Xi Lu, close to the Temple of Heaven East Gate. Everything to do with jade, with a few stunning showcase pieces on display.

13

Sports and fitness

During the **2008 Olympics**, a passion for athletic activity became a patriotic duty. Now the dust has settled, the legacy of the games includes a range of good sports facilities across the capital, from the outdoor workout machines placed in every neighbourhood to the showpiece stadiums.

But the most visible kinds of exercise need no fancy equipment; head to any park in the morning and you'll see citizens going through all sorts of **martial arts** routines, as well as performing popular exercises deemed good for the *qi* (life force), such as walking backwards, chest slapping, and tree hugging. Plenty of people play **table tennis** (often with a line of bricks as a net) and **street badminton** (no net at all), while in the evening many public spaces (such as the square at the south end of Houhai Lake) become the venue for mass **ballroom dancing**.

Spectator sports

The Chinese excel at "small ball" games such as **squash**, **badminton** and particularly **table tennis**, at which they are world champions (you can see kids being coached at the outdoor tables in Ritan Park), but admit room for improvement in the "big ball" games, such as **soccer**.

Nevertheless, European football leagues have a surprisingly strong following, and English, Spanish and German games are shown on CCTV5 and BTV. The domestic football league is improving, and decent wages have attracted a fair few foreign players and coaches, though it continues to be rocked by match fixing scandals. In season (mid-March to mid-Oct), **Guo'an**, Beijing's team and current league title holders, play at the Workers' Stadium on Sunday afternoons. The squad includes a Brazilian, a couple of Africans and even a Scot, Maurice Ross. **Tickets** cost ¥30–100 and can be bought up to three days in advance from the office at the stadium's west gate, from the ticket line ⓣ4008101887, online at ⓦwww.228.com.cn, or on the day from a tout. Games with local rivals Tianjin Teda and title challengers Shanghai Shenhua are the liveliest, but even at these, the atmosphere is relaxed, and there's no trouble; no one sees the need to segregate fans, for example. Glamorous foreign teams often include Beijing on their pre season warm up tours; they usually play at the National (Bird's Nest) Stadium.

American basketball is as popular as soccer, and getting more so, thanks to shrewd marketing by the NBA. It helps that Shanghai-born **Yao Ming**, who plays for the Houston Rockets, is one of the league's biggest stars. At 2.29m tall (7' 6") he's the tallest player in the league and also China's wealthiest celebrity; you'll see his face on billboards everywhere. Chinese league teams, including Beijing's **Shougang**, play at the Workers' Stadium from October to March; tickets cost

¥30. Exhibition matches are played at the superb Wukesong Arena, built for the Olympics (Ⓦwww.wukesongarena.com; Wukesong subway stop).

Gyms

Gyms are becoming as popular as they are in the West. Most large hotels have **gyms**; the *International Hotel* (see p.78) at 1 Jianguomen Dajie has a good one (Ⓣ010/65126688), as does the *China World Hotel* in the China World Trade Centre on Jianguomenwai Dajie (Ⓣ010/65052266), though it's pricey. The best **private gym** is the Evolution Fitness Centre (Ⓦwww.evolution-fitness.com); there's a branch at Dabeiyao Centre, Sanhuan Dong Lu, behind the Motorola building (Ⓣ010/65670266; ¥100 for one visit, ¥2000 for three months membership). There's another at the Blue Castle Centre, 3 Xidawang Lu, 300m north of Soho New Town (Ⓣ010/85997650).

Hiking and biking

Beijing Hikers (Ⓣ010/64322786, Ⓦwww.beijinghikers.com) is an expat-run group organizing frequent, imaginative **hikes** in the city's environs, to dilapidated sections of the Great Wall, caves and the like. Adults pay ¥250 and reservations are required. Meet every Saturday at the *Starbucks* in the *Lido Holiday Inn*.

Mountain bikers **MOB** meet most Sundays for rides in and around the city (mobile Ⓣ13401145438, Ⓦhttp://groups.google.cm/group/beijingmob).

Ice skating

In winter, try Qianhai (see p.87), the Summer Palace (see p.99) or the Shicha Lakes for **ice skating**. Otherwise, there's Le Cool in Basement 2 of the China World Trade Centre (Mon, Wed, Fri & Sat 10am–7pm, Tues & Thurs 10am–5.50pm, Sun 10am–8pm; ¥30 for 90 minutes). You wouldn't want to visit any of these places as a novice, as Chinese skaters are very good and expect a certain degree of confidence.

Martial arts

Beijing has some good places to study Chinese martial arts such as *tai ji*, Shaolin kung fu and *bagua*. At the Beijing Language and Culture Institute (15 Xueyuan Lu, Haidian; Ⓣ010/66629493), classes begin at 5pm and cost ¥50. Two schools with good reputations are the Beijing Milun School of Kung Fu (33 Xitangzi Hutong, off Wangfujing; mobile Ⓣ13811706568, Ⓦwww.kungfuinchina.com), and the Wuzhizhun Martial Arts Centre (Yangming Square, 10 Xiaoying Lu, Chaoyang; mobile Ⓣ15010242278, Ⓦwww.dadahe.com; daily 9am–9pm). Both schools have teachers who speak English, take their classes in Ritan Park, and charge ¥100 a session.

For **kick boxing** and other non-Chinese martial arts, try the Evolution Fitness Centre (see "Gyms" above).

Skiing

Beijing has a number of decent **ski resorts**; best is **Nanshan** (Ⓣ010/89091909, Ⓦwww.nanshanski.com), northeast of the city, with thirteen 1500m-long runs. For snowboarders there are two kickers, a mini pipe, and more than a dozen boxes and rails, and there's also sledging and cable gliding. Entrance is ¥20, and skiing costs ¥100 for two hours on weekdays, ¥150 on weekends; gear rental is ¥20. To get there, take a bus from Dongzhimen bus station to Miyun Xidaqiao (¥10), then a taxi the rest of the way (¥10).

The city's best **indoor snowboard slope** is the Buront Qiaobo Mellow Park, at 6 Shun'an Lu, in Sunyi (Ⓣ010/84972568, Ⓦwww.mellowparks.cn). A two-hour session costs ¥180 from Monday to Friday, ¥230 at weekends, and a little less at night; equipment rental is ¥30 for the set.

Snooker and pool

Pool and **snooker** are very popular; you can take on the local sharks at the Chengfeng Pool Hall, Olympic Stadium East Gate, 1 Anding Lu (Ⓣ010/64929199; snooker ¥36/hr, pool ¥20/hr), or at the Xuanlong Pool Hall, 179 Hepingli Xi Jie (Ⓣ010/84255566; snooker ¥25/hr, pool ¥16/hr).

Swimming

Avoid **swimming pools** at the weekends, when they're full of teenagers doing just about everything but swimming. If you just want a cheap swim, try the Ditan Swimming Pool at 8 Hepingli Zhong Jie (Ⓣ010/64264483; ¥30); but serious swimmers should check out the Olympic-size pool in the Sino Japanese Centre, 40 Lianmaqiao Lu, by the Century Theatre (Ⓣ010/64683311; ¥88). For family pool fun, visit the Splash recreation Club at the *Sino Swiss Hotel* (9 Xiao Tianzhi Nan Lu; Ⓣ010/64565588, Ⓦwww.sinoswisshotel.com; ¥130/day), which has hot springs and the capital's only indoor-outdoor pool. Some hotels open their lavish pools and gym facilities to non-guests; most impressive are the pools at the *Westin Chaoyang* (1 Xinyuan Nan Lu; Ⓣ010/59228888; ¥250 for a weekend pass), the *Ritz-Carlton* (1 Jinchengfang Dong Jie; Ⓣ010/66016666; ¥220) and the *Doubletree by Hilton* (168 Guang'anmen Wai Dajie; Ⓣ010/63381888; ¥150).

Since the games, the famous **Olympic Water Cube** has re-opened as a water theme park, featuring spas, slides and a wave pool (daily 10am–9.30pm; ¥200).

Contexts

Contexts

History

A centre of power for nearly a thousand years, Beijing is the creation of China's turbulent political history. Its pre-eminence dates back to the mid-thirteenth century, and the formation of **Mongol China** under **Genghis Khan**, and subsequently **Kublai Khan**. It was Kublai who took control of the city in 1264, and who properly established it as the capital, replacing the earlier power centres of Luoyang and Xi'an. **Marco Polo** visited him here and was impressed with the city's sophistication: "So great a number of houses and of people, no man could tell the number…", he wrote. "I believe there is no place in the world to which so many merchants come, and dearer things, and of greater value and more strange, come into this town from all sides than to any city in the world…"

The wealth he depicted stemmed from Beijing's position at the start of the **Silk Road**, the trading route that stretched all the way to Central Asia: Marco Polo described "over a thousand carts loaded with silk" arriving in the city "almost each day". It allowed the Khans, who later proclaimed themselves emperors, to aspire to new heights of grandeur, with Kublai building himself a palace of astonishing proportions, walled on all sides and approached by great marble stairways; sadly, nothing remains of it now.

With the accession of the **Ming dynasty**, who defeated the Mongols in 1368, the capital shifted temporarily to **Nanjing**. However, the second Ming emperor, Yongle, returned to Beijing, building around him prototypes of the city's two great monuments, the Forbidden City and the Temple of Heaven. It was during Yongle's reign, too, that the city's basic layout took shape, rigidly symmetrical, extending in squares and rectangles from the palace and inner-city grid to the suburbs, much as it is today. An inward-looking dynasty, the Ming also began constructing the **Great Wall** in earnest, in a grandiose but ultimately futile attempt to stem the incursions of northern Manchu tribes into China.

The Qing dynasty

The city's subsequent history is dominated by the rise and eventual collapse of the **Manchus** who, as the **Qing dynasty**, ruled China from Beijing from 1644 to the beginning of the twentieth century. Three outstanding Qing emperors brought an infusion of new blood and vigour to government early on. **Kangxi**, who began his 61-year reign in 1654 at the age of 6, was a great patron of the arts – as is borne out by the numerous scrolls and paintings blotted with his seals, indicating that he had viewed them – you'll see plenty in the Forbidden City. His fourth son, the Emperor **Yongzheng** (1678–1735), ruled over what is considered one of the most efficient and least corrupt administrations ever enjoyed by China. This was inherited by **Qianlong** (1711–99), whose reign saw China's frontiers greatly extended and the economy stimulated by peace and prosperity. In 1750, the capital was perhaps at its zenith, the centre of one of the strongest, wealthiest and most powerful countries in the world. It was at this time that the extraordinary **Summer Palace** was constructed. With two hundred pavilions, temples and palaces, and immense artificial lakes and hills, it was the world's most remarkable royal garden, and, along with the Forbidden City, a magnificent symbol of Chinese wealth and power.

China confronts European expansionism

In the late eighteenth century expansionist European nations were sniffing around Asia, looking for financial opportunities. China's rulers, immensely rich and powerful and convinced of their own superiority, had no wish for direct dealings with foreigners. When a British envoy, **Lord Macartney**, arrived in Chengde in 1793 to propose a political and commercial alliance between King George III and the emperor, his mission was unsuccessful. This was partly because he refused to kowtow to the emperor, but also because the emperor totally rejected any idea of allying with one whom he felt was a subordinate. Macartney was impressed by the vast wealth and power of the Chinese court, but later wrote perceptively that the empire was "like an old crazy first-rate man-of-war which its officers have contrived to keep afloat to terrify by its appearance and bulk".

Foiled in their attempts at official negotiations with the Qing court, the British decided to take matters into their own hands and create a clandestine market in China for Western goods. Instead of silver, they began to pay for tea and silk with **opium**, cheaply imported from India. As the number of addicts escalated during the early nineteenth century, China's trade surplus became a deficit, as silver drained out of the country to pay for the drug. The emperor suspended the traffic in 1840 by ordering the destruction of more than twenty thousand chests of opium, an act that led to the outbreak of the first **Opium War**. This brought

Historical chronology

21C–16C BC	Xia dynasty
16C–11C BC	Shang dynasty
11C–771 BC	Zhou dynasty
770 BC–476 BC	Spring and Autumn Period – China fragments into city states and small kingdoms
457 BC–221 BC	Warring States – China's fragmentation continues
221 BC–207 BC	Qin dynasty
206 BC–220 AD	Han dynasty

The Three Kingdoms: China is divided into three competing territories

220–265	Wei kingdom
221–263	Shu Han kingdom
222–280	Wu kingdom
265–420	Jin dynasty
420–581	Southern dynasties and Northern dynasties – rapid succession of short-lived dynasties
581–618	Sui dynasty – China united for the first time since Han dynasty
618–907	Tang dynasty
907–960	Five dynasties – a period of discord and instability
960–1271	Song dynasty
1271–1368	Yuan dynasty
1368–1644	Ming dynasty
1644–1911	Qing dynasty
1911–45	Short-lived republic founded, its fall followed by civil war between Nationalists and Communists, and Japanese occupation
1945–49	Further period of civil conflict between Guomindang and the Communist People's Liberation Army
1949	Communists take power over all China; establishment of People's Republic

British and French troops to the walls of the capital, and the Summer Palace was first looted, then burned, more or less to the ground, by the British.

The fall of the Qing dynasty

While the imperial court lived apart, within the gilded cage of the **Forbidden City**, conditions for the civilian population, in the capital's suburbs, were starkly different. Kang Youwei, a Cantonese visiting in 1895, described this dual world: "No matter where you look, the place is covered with beggars. The homeless and the old, the crippled and the sick, with no one to care for them, fall dead on the roads. This happens every day. And the coaches of the great officials rumble past them continuously."

The indifference spread from the top down. China was now run by the autocratic, out-of-touch **Cixi** (see p.100), who could hardly have been less concerned with the fate of her people. She squandered money meant for the modernization of the navy on building a new Summer Palace of her own. Her project was really the last grand gesture of imperial architecture and patronage – and, like its predecessor, was badly burned by foreign troops, in another outbreak of the Opium War. By this time, in the face of successive waves of occupation by foreign troops, the empire and the city were near collapse. The **Manchus abdicated** in 1911, leaving the northern capital to be ruled by warlords.

A short-lived republic, under the idealistic **Sun Yatsen**, failed to unify the country, and the post-imperial period was initially characterized by chaos and factionalism. In 1928, Beijing came under the military dictatorship of **Chiang Kaishek**'s nationalist **Guomindang** party, who held the city until the Japanese seized it in 1939. At the end of World War II, Beijing was controlled by an alliance of Guomindang troops and American marines.

The Communist era

It wasn't until 1949, when **Mao Zedong**'s Communist People's Liberation Army defeated the Guomingdang, that the country was again united, and Beijing returned to its position at the centre of Chinese power. The city that Mao inherited for the Chinese people was in most ways primitive. Imperial laws had banned the construction of houses higher than the official buildings and palaces, so virtually nothing was more than one storey high. The roads, although straight and uniform, were narrow and congested, and there was scarcely any industry.

The rebuilding of the capital, and the erasing of symbols of the previous regimes, was an early priority for the Communists. The Communists wanted to retain the city's sense of ordered planning, with **Tian'anmen Square**, laid out in the 1950s, as its new heart. Initially, their inspiration was Soviet, with an emphasis on heavy industry and a series of poor-quality high-rise housing programmes. Most of the traditional courtyard houses, which were seen to encourage individualism, were destroyed. In their place anonymous concrete buildings were thrown up, often with inadequate sanitation and little running water. Much of the new social planning was misguided; after the destruction of all the capital's dogs – for reasons of hygiene – in 1950, it was the turn of sparrows in 1956. This was a measure designed to preserve grain, but it only resulted in an increase in the insect population. To combat this, all the grass was pulled up, which in turn led to dust storms in the windy winter months.

In the zeal to be free of the past and create a modern, "people's capital", much of Beijing was destroyed or co-opted: the Temple of Cultivated Wisdom became a wire factory and the Temple of the God of Fire produced electric lightbulbs. In the 1940s, there were eight thousand temples and monuments in the city; by the 1960s, there were only around 150. Even the city walls and gates, relics mostly of the Ming era, were pulled down, their place taken by ring roads and avenues.

More destruction was to follow during the **Great Proletarian Cultural Revolution** – to give it its full title – that began in 1966. Under Mao's guidance, Beijing's students organized themselves into a political militia – the **Red Guards**, who were sent out to destroy the Four Olds: old ideas, old culture, old customs and old habits. The students attacked anything redolent of capitalism, the West or the Soviet Union; few of the capital's remaining ancient buildings escaped destruction.

Capitalism with Chinese characteristics

Mao's hold on power finally slipped in the 1970s, when his health began to decline. A new attitude of pragmatic reform prevailed, deriving from the moderate wing of the Communist Party, headed by Premier **Zhou Enlai** and his protégé, **Deng Xiaoping**.

In July 1976, a catastrophic earthquake in the northeast of the country killed half a million people. The Chinese hold that natural disasters always foreshadow great events, and no one was too surprised when Mao himself died on September 9. Deprived of their figurehead, and with memories of the Cultural Revolution clear in everyone's mind, Mao's supporters in the Party quickly lost ground to the right, and Deng was left running the country.

The subsequent move away from Mao's policies was rapid: in 1978, anti-Maoist dissidents were allowed to display wall posters in Beijing, some of which actually criticized Mao by name. Though such public airing of political grievances was later forbidden, by 1980 Deng and the moderates were secure enough to officially sanction a cautious questioning of Mao's actions. In the capital, his once-ubiquitous portraits and statues began to come down. However, criticism of Mao was one thing – criticism of the Party was viewed quite differently. When demonstrators assembled in **Tian'anmen Square** in 1989, protesting at corruption and demanding more freedom, the regime dealt with them brutally, sending tanks and soldiers to fire on them (see p.49).

Deng's "open door" policies of economic liberalization and welcoming foreign influences brought about new social – rather than political – freedoms, massive Westernization, and the creation of a consumer culture. Western fast food, clothes and music, and Japanese motorbikes became (and remain) all the rage.

The present day

Deng stepped down in the early 1990s. His successors – **Hu Jintao** and **Wen Jiabao** are now at the helm – have been pragmatic technocrats. In the last two decades, growth has been stellar – around ten percent a year – and the urban Chinese are much better off: in the 1970s, the "three big buys" – consumer goods that families could realistically aspire to – were a bicycle, a watch and a radio; in the 1980s, they were a washing machine, a TV and a refrigerator; now, like their counterparts in South Korea and Japan, the middle classes own cars and computers. But the **embrace of capitalism** has brought with it new problems: short-term gain has become the overriding factor in planning, with the result that the future is mortgaged for present wealth – Beijing's cultural heritage has vanished as *hutongs* are pulled down to clear space for badly made skyscrapers. As success is largely dependent on *guanxi* (personal connections), the potential for corruption is enormous; witness the men who stand outside Beijing subway stations, selling receipts so that cadres on junkets can pad their expense accounts. Not everyone has benefited from the bonanza, and China's income disparities have become grotesque – eighty percent of the nation earns little more than a subsistence living, which is hard to imagine as you wander the shiny new malls. Peasants, attracted by the big city's prospects, now flood to Beijing en masse – you'll see plenty outside Beijing Zhan, many of them finding the capital as novel as any foreigner does. The lucky ones end up working on building sites, though even they, far from home and un-unionized, are often exploited. Though the majority are family men who send the little money that they earn home, they are treated with suspicion by most city-dwellers – indicative of China's new class divisions, or the resurfacing of old resentments.

The glitz and pomp of the **2008 Olympic games**, in which China topped the medals table, served to mark the city's arrival on the world stage. Before the games, Beijing benefited from massive investment in infrastructure, including new subway lines and freeways. Historic sites were opened, renovated, or, it sometimes appears, invented. And this restless **reinvention** continues today. A ramshackle charm has been lost in the wholescale redevelopment, but on the whole the city has improved. It will never perhaps be memorable for attractiveness, but it's undeniably dynamic, new and exciting.

Books

You won't find much variety in **English-language reading** materials when book shopping in Beijing; your best bet are the many cheap editions of the **Chinese classics**, published in English translation by two Beijing-based firms, Foreign Languages Press (FLP) and Panda Books (some of these titles are published outside China, too).

In the reviews below, books that are especially recommended are marked ★; the publisher is listed only if it's based in China or elsewhere in Asia, and o/p signifies that a book is out of print.

History

Peter Fleming *The Siege at Peking*. A lively account of the events that led up to June 20, 1900, when the foreign legations in Beijing were attacked by the Boxers and Chinese imperial troops.

Harrison Salisbury *The New Emperors* (o/p). Highly readable account of the lives of China's twentieth-century "emperors", Mao Zedong and Deng Xiaoping, which tries to demonstrate that communist rule is no more than an extension of the old imperial Mandate of Heaven.

Arthur Waldron *The Great Wall of China* (o/p). More for the academic than the casual reader, this book traces the origins and history of the wall.

Justin Wintle *The Rough Guide History of China* (o/p). Pocket-sized but detailed chronicle of China's history, with the key events and people put into context in a chronological year-by-year format.

Jan Wong *Red China Blues*. Jan Wong, a Canadian of Chinese descent, went to China as an idealistic Maoist in 1972 at the height of the Cultural Revolution, and was one of only two Westerners permitted to enrol at Beijing University. She describes the six years she spent in China and her growing disillusionment, which led eventually to her repatriation. A touching, sometimes bizarre, inside account of the bad old days.

Culture and society

★ **Jasper Becker** *The Chinese*; *City of Heavenly Tranquility*; *Beijing in the history of China*. *The Chinese* is a classic, weighty, erudite but very comprehensible introduction to Chinese society and culture; lighter and breezier, *City of Heavenly Tranquility* is a great collection of stories about Beijing's history, including a hard-hitting condemnation of how most physical remains of that history have recently been destroyed.

Ian Buruma *Bad Elements: Chinese rebels from LA to Beijing*. Interviews with Chinese dissidents, both at home and in exile, make for a compelling, if inevitably rather jaundiced, view of the country.

Gordon G. Chang *The Coming Collapse of China*. This book theorizes that China's recent success is only skin deep, and that the country is about to fall apart, thanks largely to incompetent leadership. (It's worth noting that people have been saying this for years – and it hasn't happened yet.)

Roger Garside *Coming Alive: China after Mao*. Garside was a diplomat at the British Embassy in Beijing in 1968–70 and 1976–79. Here he describes the aftermath of the Cultural Revolution.

Martin Jacques *When China Rules the World*. Comprehensive overview, both troubling and enlightening, of the ascendancy of the Chinese state and the impact that will have on the rest of the world.

James Kynge *China Shakes the World*. Another critical but acute overview of Chinese society and government and the challenges ahead.

Michael Meyer *The Last Days of Old Beijing*. Combines a history of Beijing's *hutongs* with a memoir of what it was like to live in them, immersed in the local community.

Marco Polo *The Travels*. Said to have inspired Columbus, *The Travels* is a fantastic read, full of amazing insights picked up during Marco Polo's 26 years of wandering in Asia between Venice and the Peking court of Kublai Khan. It's not, however, a coherent history, having been ghost-written by a romantic novelist from Marco Polo's notes.

Guides and reference books

Giles Beguin and Dominique Morel *The Forbidden City*. A good introduction to the complex, and to the history of the emperors who lived there, though the best thing about this pocket book (as with most books about the Forbidden City) is the illustrations.

Lin Xiang Zhu and Lin Cuifeng *Chinese Gastronomy* (o/p). A classic work, relatively short on recipes but strong on cooking methods and the underlying philosophy. It wavers in and out of print, sometimes under different titles – look for "Lin" as the author name. Essential reading for anyone serious about learning the finer details of Chinese cooking.

Jessica Rawson *Ancient China: Art and archaeology*. By the then deputy keeper of Oriental antiquities at the British Museum, this scholarly introduction to Chinese art puts the subject in its historical context. Beginning its account in Neolithic times, the book explores the technology and social organization that shaped the development of Chinese culture up to the Han dynasty.

Mary Tregear *Chinese Art*. Authoritative summary of the main strands in Chinese art from Neolithic times, through the Bronze Age and up to the twentieth century. Clearly written and well illustrated.

Religion and philosophy

Asiapac Comics Series (Asiapac, Singapore). Available at Beijing's Foreign Language Bookstore, this entertaining series of books presents ancient Chinese philosophy in cartoon format, making the subject accessible without losing too much complexity. They're all well written and well drawn; particularly good is the Sayings of Confucius.

Confucius *The Analects*. Good, modern translation of this classic text, a collection of Confucius's teachings focusing on morality and the state. *I Ching*, also known as *The Book of Changes* is another classic volume from Confucius that teaches a form of divination. It includes coverage of some of the fundamental concepts of Chinese thought, such as the duality of *yin* and *yang*.

Lao Zi *Tao Te Ching*. This, the *Daodejing* in pinyin, is a collection of mystical thoughts and philosophical speculation that form the basis of Taoist philosophy.

Arthur Waley (trans) *Three Ways of Thought in Ancient China*. Translated extracts from the writings of three of the early philosophers – Zhuang Zi, Mencius and Han Feizi. A useful introduction.

Biography and autobiography

Pallavi Aiyar *Smoke and Mirrors*. There are plenty of memoirs about the expat experience in Beijing; this one stands out as it was written from an Indian perspective. Amusing, anecdotal and full of acute observations.

E. Backhouse and J.O. Bland *China Under the Empress Dowager* (o/p). Classic work on imperial life in late nineteenth-century China. It's based around the diary of a court eunuch, which is now generally accepted to have been forged (Backhouse was the prime suspect; see the review of *Hermit of Peking* by Hugh Trevor-Roper).

Jung Chang *Wild Swans* and *Mao: The Untold Story*. Enormously popular in the West, *Wild Swans* is a family saga covering three generations that chronicles the horrors of life in turbulent twentieth-century China. It serves as an excellent introduction to modern Chinese history, as well as being a good read. *Mao: The Untold Story* is a massive and well-researched character assassination; indeed, it's hard not to suspect that axes are being ground.

Rachel Dewoskin *Foreign Babes in Beijing*. Breezy account of an American girl's adventures among the city's artsy set in the 1990s. The most interesting parts concern the author's experiences working as an actress on a Chinese soap opera.

Pu Yi *From Emperor to Citizen* (FLP, Beijing). The autobiography of the last Qing emperor, Pu Yi, who lost his throne as a boy and was later briefly installed as a puppet emperor during the Japanese occupation. He ended his life employed as a gardener.

Rius *Mao for Beginners*. Lighthearted, entertaining comic book about Mao Zedong and Maoism.

Jonathan Spence *Emperor of China: Self portrait of Kang Xi*. A magnificent portrait of the longest-reigning and greatest emperor of modern China.

Hugh Trevor-Roper *Hermit of Peking: The Hidden Life of Sir Edmund Backhouse*. Sparked by its subject's thoroughly obscene memoirs, *Hermit of Peking* uses external sources in an attempt to uncover the facts behind the extraordinary and convoluted life of Edmund Backhouse – Chinese scholar, eccentric recluse and phenomenal liar – who lived in Beijing from the late nineteenth century until his death in 1944.

Marina Warner *The Dragon Empress*. Exploration of the life of the Empress Dowager Cixi, one of only two female rulers of China. Warner lays bare the complex personality of a ruthless woman whose reign, marked by vanity and greed, culminated in the collapse of the imperial ruling house and the founding of the republic.

Chinese literature

Cyril Birch (ed) *Anthology of Chinese Literature from Earliest Times to the Fourteenth Century*. This survey spans three thousand years of Chinese literature, embracing poetry, philosophy, drama, biography and prose fiction. Interestingly, different translations of some extracts are included.

Cao Xueqing *Dream of Red Mansions* (available in a Penguin edition and from FLP, Beijing). Sometimes published under the English title *Dream of the Red Chamber*, this intricate eighteenth-century comedy of manners follows the fortunes of the Jia clan through the emotionally charged adolescent lives of Jia Baoyu and his two girl cousins, Lin Daiyu and Xue Baochai. The version published in the West by Penguin fills five paperbacks; the FLP edition, available in Beijing, is much simplified and abridged.

Chen Sue *Beijing Doll*. This rambling confessional details the teenage writer's adventures in the indie music scene. With plenty of sex and drugs, it caused quite a stir when it came out and was, predictably, banned.

Lao She *Rickshaw Boy* (FLP, Beijing). One of China's great modern writers, Lao She was driven to suicide during the Cultural Revolution. This story is a haunting account of a young rickshaw puller in pre-1949 Beijing.

Lu Xun *The True Story of Ah Q* (FLP, Beijing). Widely read in China today, Lu Xun is regarded as the father of modern Chinese writing. *Ah Q* is one of his best tales: short, allegorical and cynical, about a simpleton who is swept up in the 1911 revolution. (You can pick up a copy at Beijing's Lu Xun Museum.)

Luo Guanzhong *Romance of the Three Kingdoms* (various editions published in the West; also published by FLP, Beijing). One of the world's greatest historical novels. Though written 1200 years after the events it depicts, this vibrant tale vividly evokes the battles, political schemings and myths surrounding China's turbulent Three Kingdoms period.

Ma Jian *Red Dust*; *The Noodle Maker*; *Beijing Coma*. Satirist Ma Jian is one of China's most insightful living writers, though most of his work is banned in China. *Red Dust* is a travelogue about an epic, beatnik-style jaunt around China in the 1980s, documenting a set of chaotic lives, not least the narrator's own; *The Noodle Maker* is a dark novel concerning the friendship between a writer of propaganda and a professional blood donor, and *Beijing Coma*, his weightiest tome, concerns the events of 1989.

Steven Owen *Anthology of Chinese Literature*. Unimaginably compendious, this colossal book contains delightfully translated excerpts and analyses from every era of Chinese literature up to 1911.

Wang Shuo *Playing For Thrills*; *Please Don't Call Me Human*. The bad boy of contemporary Chinese literature, Wang Shuo writes in colourful Beijing dialect about the city's seamy underbelly. These are his only novels translated into English: the first is a mystery story whose boorish narrator spends most of his time drinking, gambling and chasing girls; the second, banned in China, a bitter satire portraying modern China as a place where pride is nothing and greed is everything, as a dignified martial artist is emasculated in order to win an Olympic gold medal.

Wu Cheng'en *Journey to the West* (FLP, Beijing). Absurd, lively rendering of the Buddhist monk Xuanzang's pilgrimage to India to collect sacred scriptures, aided by – according to popular myth – Sandy, Pigsy, and the irrepressible Sun Wu Kong, the monkey king. Arthur Waley's version, published in the West under the title *Monkey*, retains the tale's spirit while shortening the hundred-chapter opus to paperback length.

Language

Language

Chinese

As the most widely spoken language on earth, Chinese is hard to overlook. **Mandarin Chinese**, derived from the language of Han officialdom in the Beijing area, has been systematically promoted over the past hundred years to be the official, unifying language of the Chinese people, much as modern French, for example, is based on the original Parisian dialect. It is known in mainland China as *putonghua*, "common language". All Beijingers will speak and understand it; but note that working-class Beijingers have a distinctive accent, adding a croaky "r" sound to the end of many words.

Chinese **grammar** is delightfully simple. There is no need to conjugate verbs, decline nouns or make adjectives agree – Chinese characters are immutable, so Chinese words simply cannot have different "endings". Instead, context and fairly rigid rules about word order are relied on to make those distinctions of time, number and gender that Indo-European languages are so concerned with. Instead of cumbersome tenses, the Chinese make use of words such as "yesterday" or "tomorrow" to indicate when things happen; instead of plural endings they simply state how many things there are. For English speakers, Chinese word order is very familiar, and you'll find that by simply stringing words together you'll be producing perfectly grammatical Chinese. Basic sentences follow the subject-verb-object format; adjectives, as well as all qualifying and describing phrases, precede nouns.

From the point of view of foreigners, the main thing that distinguishes Mandarin from familiar languages is that it's a tonal language. In order to pronounce a word correctly, it is necessary to know not only the sounds of its consonants and vowels but also its correct tone – though with the help of context, intelligent listeners should be able to work out what you are trying to say even if you don't get the tones quite right.

Pinyin

Back in the 1950s it was hoped eventually to replace Chinese characters with an alphabet of Roman letters, and to this end the **pinyin system**, a precise and exact means of representing all the sounds of Mandarin Chinese, was devised. It comprises all the Roman letters of the English alphabet (except "v"), with the four tones represented by diacritical marks, or accents, which appear above each syllable. The old aim of replacing Chinese characters with *pinyin* was abandoned long ago, but in the meantime *pinyin* has one very important function, that of helping foreigners pronounce Chinese words. However, there is the added complication that in *pinyin* the letters don't all have the sounds you would expect, and you'll need to spend an hour or two learning the correct sounds.

You'll often see *pinyin* in Beijing, on street signs and shop displays, but only well-educated locals know the system very well. The Chinese names in this book have been given both in characters and in *pinyin*; the pronunciation guide below is your first step to making yourself comprehensible. For more information, see the *Rough Guide Mandarin Chinese Phrasebook*, or *Pocket Interpreter* (FLP, Beijing; it's available at Beijing's Foreign Language Bookstore).

Pronunciation

There are four possible **tones** in Mandarin Chinese, and every syllable of every word is characterized by one of them, except for a few syllables, which are considered toneless. In English, to change the tone is to change the mood or the emphasis; in Chinese, to change the tone is to change the word itself. The tones are:

First or "high" *ā ē ī ō ū*. In English this level tone is used when mimicking robotic or very boring, flat voices.

Second or "rising" *á é í ó ú*. Used in English when asking a question showing surprise, for example "eh?"

Third or "falling-rising" *ǎ ě ǐ ǒ ǔ*. Used in English when echoing someone's words with a measure of incredulity. For example, "John's dead." "De-ad?!"

Fourth or "falling" à è ì ò ù. Often used in English when counting in a brusque manner – "One! Two! Three! Four!".

Toneless A few syllables do not have a tone accent. These are pronounced without emphasis, such as in the English **u**pon.

Note that when two words with the third tone occur consecutively, the first word is pronounced as though it carries the second tone. Thus *ně* (meaning "you") and *hǎo* ("well, good"), when combined, are pronounced *ní hǎo*, meaning "how are you?"

Consonants

Most consonants, as written in *pinyin*, are pronounced in a similar way to their English equivalents, with the following exceptions:

c as in ha**ts**

g is hard as in **g**od (except when preceded by "n", when it sounds like sa**ng**)

q as in **ch**eese

x has no direct equivalent in English, but you can make the sound by sliding from an "s" to an "sh" sound and stopping midway between the two

z as in su**ds**

zh as in fu**dg**e

Vowels and diphthongs

As in most languages, the vowel sounds are rather harder to quantify than the consonants. The examples below give a rough description of the sound of each vowel as written in *pinyin*.

a usually somewhere between f**a**r and m**a**n

ai as in **eye**

ao as in c**ow**

e usually as in f**ur**

ei as in g**ay**

en as in hyph**en**

eng as in s**ung**

er as in b**ar** with a pronounced "r"

i usually as in b**ee**, except in zi, ci, si, ri, zhi, chi and shi, when i is a short, clipped sound, like the American military "s**i**r".

ia as in **ya**k

ian as in **yen**

ie as in **yeah**

o as in s**aw**

ou as in sh**ow**

ü as in the German **ü** (make an "ee" sound and glide slowly into an "oo"; at the mid-point between the two sounds you should hit the ü-sound.

u usually as in **fool**, though whenever u follows j, q, x or y, it is always pronounced **ü**

ua as in s**ua**ve

uai as in **why**

ue as though contracting "you" and "air" together, **you'air**

ui as in **way**

uo as in **wo**re

Useful words and phrases

When writing or saying the name of a Chinese person, the surname is given first; thus Mao Zedong's family name is Mao.

Basics

I	我	*wǒ*
You (singular)	你	*nǐ*
He	他	*tā*
She	她	*tā*
We	我们	*wǒmen*
You (plural)	你们	*nǐmen*
They	他们	*tāmen*
I want...	我要	*wǒ yào...*
No, I don't want...	我不要	*wǒ bú yào...*
Is it possible...?	可不可以	*kě bù kěyǐ...?*
It is (not) possible	(不)可以...	*(bù)kěyǐ*
Is there any/Have you got any...?	你有没有	*nǐ yǒu méiyǒu...?*
There is/I have	有...	*yǒu...*
There isn't/I haven't	没有...	*méiyǒu*
Please help me	请帮我忙..	*qǐng bāng wǒ máng*
Mr...	...先生	*xiānshēng*
Mrs...	...太太	*tàitai*
Miss...	...小姐	*xiǎojiě*

Communicating

I don't speak Chinese	我不会说中文	*wǒ búhuì shuō zhōngwén*
Can you speak English?	你会说英语吗	*nǐ huì shuō yīngyǔ ma?*
Can you get someone who speaks English?	请给我找一个会说英文的人	*qǐng gěiwǒ zhǎo yīgè huìshuō yīngwén de rén?*
Please speak slowly	请说得慢一点	*qǐng shuōde màn yīdiǎn*
Please say that again	请再说一遍	*qǐng zài shuō yī biàn*
I understand	我听得懂	*wǒ tīngdedǒng*

I don't understand	我听不懂	*wǒ tīngbùdǒng*
I can't read Chinese characters	我看不懂汉字	*wǒ kànbùdǒng hànzì*
What does this mean?	这是什么意思	*zhèshì shénme yìsi?*
How do you pronounce this character?	这个字怎么念	*zhègè zì zěnme niàn?*

Greetings and basic courtesies

Hello/How do you do/ How are you?	你好	*nǐhǎo*
I'm fine	我很好	*wǒ hěnhǎo*
Thank you	谢谢	*xièxie*
Don't mention it/ You're welcome	不客气	*búkèqi*
Sorry to bother you...	麻烦你	*máfán nǐ*
Sorry/I apologize	对不起	*duìbùqǐ*
It's not important/No problem	没关系	*méiguānxì*
Goodbye	再见	*zàijiàn*
Excuse me	不好意思	*bùhǎoyìsi*

Chit-chat

What country are you from?	你是哪个国家的	*nǐ shì nǎgè guójiā de?*
Britain	英国	*yīngguó*
England	英国/英格兰	*yīngguó/yīnggélán*
Scotland	苏格兰	*sūgélán*
Wales	威尔士	*wēi'ěrshì*
Ireland	爱尔兰	*ài'érlán*
America	美国	*měiguó*
Canada	加拿大	*jiānádà*
Australia	澳大利亚	*àodàlìyà*
New Zealand	新西兰	*xīnxīlán*
South Africa	南非	*nánfēi*
China	中国	*zhōngguó*
Outside China	外国	*wàiguó*
What's your name?	你叫什么名字	*nǐ jiào shénme míngzi?*
My name is...	我叫....	*wǒ jiào...*
Are you married?	你结婚了	*nǐ jiéhūn le ma?*
I am (not) married	我(没有)结婚(了)	*wǒ (méiyǒu) jiéhūn (le)*
Have you got (children)?	你有没有孩子	*nǐ yǒu méiyǒu háizi?*
Do you like...?	你喜不喜欢.....	*nǐ xǐ bù xǐhuān....?*
I (don't) like...	我不喜欢....	*wǒ (bù) xǐhuān...*
What's your job?	你干什么工作	*nǐ gàn shénme gōngzuò?*
I'm a foreign student	我是留学生	*wǒ shì liúxuéshēng*
I'm a teacher	我是老师	*wǒ shì lǎoshī*
I work in a company	我在一个公司工作	*wǒ zài yígè gōngsī gōngzuò*
I don't work	我不工作	*wǒ bù gōngzuò*
I'm retired	我退休了	*wǒ tuìxīu le*

Clean/dirty	干净/脏	*gānjìng/zāng*
Hot/cold	热/冷	*rè/lěng*
Fast/slow	快/慢	*kuài/màn*
Good/bad	好/坏	*hǎo/huài*
Big/small	大/小	*dà/xiǎo*
Pretty	漂亮	*piàoliang*
Interesting	有意思	*yǒuyìsi*

Numbers

Zero	零	*líng*
One	一	*yī*
Two	二/两	*èr/liǎng**
Three	三	*sān*
Four	四	*sì*
Five	五	*wǔ*
Six	六	*liù*
Seven	七	*qī*
Eight	八	*bā*
Nine	九	*jiǔ*
Ten	十	*shí*
Eleven	十一	*shíyī*
Twelve	十二	*shíèr*
Twenty	二十	*èrshí*
Twenty-one	二十一	*èrshíyi*
One hundred	一百	*yībǎi*
Two hundred	二百	*èrbǎi*
One thousand	一千	*yīqiān*
Ten thousand	一万	*yīwàn*
One hundred thousand	十万	*shíwàn*
One million	一百万	*yībǎiwàn*
One hundred million	一亿	*yīyì*
One billion	十亿	*shíyì*

* 两/*liǎng* is used when enumerating, for example "two people" is *liǎng gè rén.* 二/*èr* is used when counting.

Time

Now	现在	*xiànzài*
Today	今天	*jīntiān*
(In the) morning	早上	*zǎoshàng*
(In the) afternoon	下午	*xiàwǔ*
(In the) evening	晚上	*wǎnshàng*
Tomorrow	明天	*míngtiān*
The day after tomorrow	后天	*hòutiān*
Yesterday	昨天	*zuótiān*
Week/month/year	星期/月/年	*xīngqī/yuè/nián*

Next/last week/month/year	下/上 星期/月/年	*xià/shàng xīngqī/yuè/nián*
Monday	星期一	*xīngqī yī*
Tuesday	星期二	*xīngqī èr*
Wednesday	星期三	*xīngqī sān*
Thursday	星期四	*xīngqī sì*
Friday	星期五	*xīngqī wǔ*
Saturday	星期六	*xīngqī liù*
Sunday	星期天	*xīngqī tiān*
What's the time?	几点了	*jǐdiǎn le?*
Morning	早上	*zǎoshàng*
Afternoon	中午	*zhōngwǔ*
10 o'clock	十点钟	*shídiǎn zhōng*
10.20	十点二十	*shídiǎn èrshí*
10.30	十点半	*shídiǎn bàn*

Travelling and getting around town

North	北	*běi*
South	南	*nán*
East	东	*dōng*
West	西	*xī*
Airport	机场	*jīchǎng*
Ferry dock	船码头	*chuánmǎtóu*
Left-luggage office	寄存处	*jìcún chù*
Ticket office	售票处	*shòupiào chù*
Ticket	票	*piào*
Can you sell me a ticket to…?	可不可以卖给我到…的票	*kěbùkěyǐ màigěi wǒ dào…de piào?*
I want to go to…	我想到…去	*wǒ xiǎng dàoqù*
I want to leave at (8 o'clock)	我想(八点钟)离开	*wǒ xiǎng (bādiǎnzhōng) líkāi*
When does it leave?	什么时候出发	*shénme shíhòu chūfā?*
When does it arrive?	什么时候到	*shénme shíhòu dào?*
How long does it take?	路上得多长时间	*lùshàng děi duōcháng shíjiān?*
CITS	中国国际旅行社	*zhōngguó guójì lǚxíngshè*
Train	火车	*huǒchē*
(Main) train station	主要火车站	*(zhǔyào) huǒchēzhàn*
Bus	公共汽车	*gōnggòng qìchēzhàn*
Bus station	汽车站	*qìchēzhàn*
Long-distance bus station	长途汽车站	*chángtú qìchēzhàn*
Express train/bus	特快车	*tèkuài chē*
Fast train/bus	快车	*kuài chē*
Ordinary train/bus	普通车	*pǔtōng chē*
Timetable	时间表	*shíjiān biǎo*
Map	地图	*dìtú*
Where is…?	…在 哪里	*…zài nǎlǐ?*

Go straight on	往前走	*wǎng qián zǒu*
Turn right	往右走	*wǎng yòu zǒu*
Turn left	往左拐	*wǎng zuǒ guǎi*
Taxi	出租车	*chūzū chē*
Please use the meter	请打开记价器	*qǐng dǎkāi jìjiàqì*
Underground/subway station	地铁站	*dìtiě zhàn*
Bicycle	自行车	*zìxíng chē*
Can I borrow your bicycle?	能不能借你的自行车	*néngbùnéng jiè nǐdē zìxíngchē?*
Bus	公共汽车	*gōnggòng qìchē*
Which bus goes to…?	几路车到…去	*jǐlùchē dào … qù?*
Number (10) bus	(十)路车	*(shí) lù chē*
Does this bus go to…?	这车到…去吗	*zhè chē dào … qù ma?*
When is the next bus?	下一班车几点开	*xiàyìbānchē jǐdiǎn kāi?*
The first bus	头班车	*tóubān chē*
The last bus	末班车	*mòbān chē*
Please tell me where to get off	请告诉我在哪里下车	*qǐng gàosù wǒ zài nǎlǐ xiàchē?*
Museum	博物馆	*bówùguǎn*
Temple	寺庙	*sìmiào*
Church	教堂	*jiàotáng*

Accommodation

Accommodation	住宿	*zhùsù*
Hotel (upmarket)	宾馆	*bīnguǎn*
Hotel (cheap)	招待所，旅馆	*zhāodàisuǒ, lǚguǎn*
Hostel	旅舍	*lǚshè*
Do you have a room available?	你们有房间吗	*nǐmen yǒu fángjiān ma?*
Can I have a look at the room?	能不能看一下方向	*néngbùnéng kàn yíxià fángjiān?*
I want the cheapest bed you've got	我要你这里最便宜的床位	*wǒ yào nǐ zhèlǐ zuìpiányi de chuángwèi*
Single room	单人房	*dānrén fáng*
Twin room	双人房	*shuāngrén fáng*
Double room with a big bed	双人房间带大床	*shuāngrénfángjiān dài dàchuáng*
Three-bed room	三人房	*sānrén fáng*
Dormitory	多人房	*duōrén fáng*
Suite	套房	*tàofáng*
(Large) bed	(大)床	*(dà) chuáng*
Passport	护照	*hùzhào*
Deposit	押金	*yājīn*
Key	钥匙	*yàoshi*
I want to change my room	我想换房	*wǒ xiǎng huànfáng*

Shopping, money and the police

How much is it?	这是多少钱	*zhèshì duōshǎo qián?*
That's too expensive	太贵了	*tài guì le*
I haven't got any cash	我没有现金	*wǒ méiyǒu xiànjīn*
Have you got anything cheaper?	有没有便宜一点的	*yǒu méiyǒu piányì yìdiǎn de?*
Do you accept credit cards?	可不可以用信用卡	*kě bù kěyǐ yòng xìnyòngkǎ?*
Department store	百货商店	*bǎihuò shāngdiàn*
Market	市场	*shìchǎng*
¥1 (RMB)	一块（人民币）	*yí kuài (rénmínbì)*
US$1	一块美金	*yí kuài měijīn*
£1	一个英镑	*yí gè yīngbàng*
Change money	换钱	*huàn qián*
Bank	银行	*yínháng*
Travellers' cheques	旅行支票	*lǚxíngzhīpiào*
ATM	提款机	*tíkuǎnjī*
PSB	公安局	*gōng'ānjú*

Communications

Post office	邮电局	*yóudiànjú*
Envelope	信封	*xìnfēng*
Stamp	邮票	*yóupiào*
Airmail	航空信	*hángkōngxìn*
Surface mail	平信	*píngxìn*
Telephone	电话	*diànhuà*
Mobile phone	手机	*shǒujī*
SMS message	短信	*duǎnxìn*
International telephone call	国际电话	*guójì diànhuà*
Reverse charges/collect call	对方付钱电话	*duìfāngfùqián diànhuà*
Fax	传真	*chuánzhēn*
Telephone card	电话卡	*diànhuàkǎ*
I want to make a telephone call to (Britain)	我想给（英国）打电话	*wǒ xiǎng gěi (yīngguó) dǎ diànhuà*
I want to send an email to the US	我想发一个邮件到美国	*wǒ xiǎng fā yīgè yóujiàn dào měiguó*
Internet	网路	*wǎngluò*
Internet café/bar	网吧	*wǎngbā*
Email	电子邮件	*diànzǐyóujiàn*

Health

Hospital	医院	*yīyuàn*
Pharmacy	药店	*yàodiàn*
Medicine	药	*yào*
Chinese medicine	中药	*zhōngyào*
Diarrhoea	腹泻	*fùxiè*
Vomit	呕吐	*ǒutù*

Fever	发烧	*fāshāo*
I'm ill	我生病了	*wǒ shēngbìng le*
I've got flu	我感冒了	*wǒ gǎnmào le*
I'm (not) allergic to…	我对…(不)过敏	*wǒ duì … (bù) guòmǐn*
Antibiotics	抗生素	*kàngshēngsù*
Condom	避孕套	*bìyùntào*
Tampons	卫生棉条	*wèishēng miántiáo*

A menu reader

General

Restaurant	餐厅	*cāntīng*
House speciality	招牌菜	*zhāopái cài*
How much is that?	多少钱	*duōshǎo qián?*
I don't eat (meat)	我不吃(肉)	*wǒ bùchī (ròu)*
I would like...	我想要…	*wǒ xiǎng yào...*
Local dishes	地方菜	*dìfāng cài*
Snacks	小吃	*xiǎochī*
Menu/set menu/English menu	菜单/套菜/英文菜单	*càidān/tàocài/yīngwéncàidān*
Small portion	少量	*shǎoliàng*
Chopsticks	筷子	*kuàizi*
Knife and fork	刀叉	*dāochā*
Spoon	勺子	*sháozi*
Waiter/waitress	服务员	*fúwùyuán*
Bill/cheque	买单	*mǎidān*
Cook these ingredients together	原料混合一块儿做	*yuánliào hùnhé yíkuàir zuò*
Not spicy/no chilli please	请不要辣椒	*qǐng búyào làjiāo*
Only a little spice/chilli	一点辣椒	*yìdiǎn làjiāo*
50 grams	两	*liǎng*
250 grams	半斤	*bànjīn*
500 grams	斤	*jīn*
1 kilo	1公斤	*yī gōngjīn*

Drinks

Beer	啤酒	*píjiǔ*
Coffee	咖啡	*kāfēi*
Milk	牛奶	*niúnǎi*
(Mineral) water	(矿泉)水	*(kuàngquán) shuǐ*
Wine	葡萄酒	*pútáojiǔ*
Yoghurt	酸奶	*suānnǎi*
Tea	茶	*chá*
Black tea	红茶	*hóng chá*
Green tea	绿茶	*lǜ chá*
Jasmine tea	茉莉花茶	*mòlìhuā chá*

Staple foods

Aubergine	茄子	*qiézi*
Bamboo shoots	笋尖	*sǔnjiān*
Bean sprouts	豆芽	*dòuyá*
Beans	豆子	*dòuzi*
Beef	牛肉	*niúròu*
Bitter gourd	苦瓜	*kǔguā*
Black bean sauce	黑豆豉	*hēidòuchǐ*
Bread	面包	*miànbāo*
Buns (filled)	包子	*bāozi*
Buns (plain)	馒头	*mántou*
Carrot	胡萝卜	*húluóbo*
Cashew nuts	腰果	*yāoguǒ*
Cauliflower	菜花	*càihuā*
Chicken	鸡	*jī*
Chilli	辣椒	*làjiāo*
Chocolate	巧克力	*qiǎokèlì*
Coriander (leaves)	香菜	*xiāngcài*
Crab	蟹	*xiè*
Cucumber	黄瓜	*huángguā*
Duck	鸭	*yā*
Eel	鳝鱼	*shànyú*
Eggs (fried)	煎鸡蛋	*jiānjīdàn*
Fish	鱼	*yú*
Fried dough stick	油条	*yóutiáo*
Garlic	大蒜	*dàsuàn*
Ginger	姜	*jiāng*
Green pepper (capsicum)	青椒	*qīngjiāo*
Green vegetables	绿叶蔬菜	*lǜyè shūcài*
Jiaozi (ravioli, steamed or boiled)	饺子	*jiǎozi*
Lamb	羊肉	*yángròu*
Lotus root	莲藕	*liánǒu*
MSG	味精	*wèijīng*
Mushrooms	磨菇	*mógū*
Noodles	面条	*miàntiáo*
Omelette	摊鸡蛋	*tānjīdàn*
Onions	洋葱	*yángcōng*
Oyster sauce	蚝油	*háoyóu*
Pancake	摊饼	*tānbǐng*
Peanut	花生	*huāshēng*
Pork	猪肉	*zhūròu*
Potato (stir-fried)	(炒)土豆	*(chǎo) tǔdòu*
Prawns	虾	*xiā*
Preserved egg	皮蛋	*pídàn*
Rice noodles	河粉	*héfěn*
Rice porridge (aka "congee")	粥	*zhōu*

Rice, boiled	白饭	*báifàn*
Rice, fried	炒饭	*chǎofàn*
Salt	盐	*yán*
Sesame oil	芝麻油	*zhīma yóu*
Shuijiao (ravioli in soup)	水饺	*shuǐjiǎo*
Sichuan pepper	四川辣椒	*sìchuān làjiāo*
Snake	蛇肉	*shéròu*
Soup	汤	*tāng*
Soy sauce	酱油	*jiàngyóu*
Squid	鱿鱼	*yóuyú*
Straw mushrooms	草菇	*cǎogū*
Sugar	糖	*táng*
Tofu	豆腐	*dòufu*
Tomato	蕃茄	*fānqié*
Vinegar	醋	*cù*
Water chestnuts	马蹄	*mǎtí*
White radish	白萝卜	*báiluóbo*
Wood ear fungus	木耳	*mùěr*
Yam	红薯	*hóngshǔ*

Cooking methods

Boiled	煮	*zhǔ*
Casseroled (see also "Claypot")	焙	*bèi*
Deep-fried	油煎	*yóujiān*
Fried	炒	*chǎo*
Poached	白煮	*báizhǔ*
Red-cooked (stewed in soy sauce)	红烧	*hóngshāo*
Roast	烤	*kǎo*
Steamed	蒸	*zhēng*
Stir-fried	清炒	*qīngchǎo*

Everyday dishes

Braised duck with vegetables	蔬菜炖鸭	*shūcài dùn yā*
Cabbage rolls (stuffed with meat or vegetables)	菜卷	*càijuǎn*
Chicken and sweetcorn soup	玉米鸡丝汤	*yùmǐ jīsī tāng*
Chicken with bamboo shoots and baby corn	笋尖嫩玉米炒鸡片	*sǔnjiān nènyùmǐ chǎojīpiàn*
Chicken with cashew nuts	腰果鸡片	*yāoguǒ jīpiàn*
Claypot/sandpot (casserole)	砂锅	*shāguō*
Crispy aromatic duck	香酥鸭	*xiāngsū yā*
Egg flower soup with tomato	蕃茄蛋汤	*fānqié dàntāng*
Egg fried rice	蛋炒饭	*dànchǎofàn*
Fish ball soup with white radish	白萝卜鱼蛋汤	*báiluóbo yúdàn tāng*
Fish casserole	砂锅鱼	*shāguōyú*
Fried shredded pork with garlic and chilli	大蒜辣椒炒肉片	*dàsuàn làjiāo chǎo ròupiàn*

Hotpot	火锅	*huǒguō*
Kebab	串肉	*chuànròu*
Noodle soup	汤面	*tāngmiàn*
Pork and mustard greens	芥菜叶炒猪肉	*jiè càiyè chǎo zhūròu*
Pork and water chestnut	马蹄猪肉	*mǎtízhūròu*
Prawn with garlic sauce	蒜汁虾	*suànzhīxiā*
"Pulled" noodles	拉面	*lā miàn*
Roast duck	烤鸭	*kǎoyā*
Scrambled egg with pork on rice	滑蛋猪肉饭	*huádàn zhūròufàn*
Sliced pork with yellow bean sauce	黄豆肉片	*huángdòu ròupiàn*
Squid with green pepper and black beans	豆豉青椒炒鱿鱼	*dòuchǐ qīngjiāo chǎo yóuyú*
Steamed eel with black beans	豆豉蒸鳝	*dòuchǐ zhēng shàn*
Steamed rice packets wrapped in lotus leaves	荷叶蒸饭	*héyè zhēngfàn*
Stewed pork belly with vegetables	回锅肉	*huíguōròu*
Stir-fried chicken and bamboo shoots	笋尖炒鸡片	*sǔnjiān chǎo jīpiàn*
Stuffed bean-curd soup	豆腐汤	*dòufu tāng*
Sweet and sour spare ribs	糖醋排骨	*tángcù páigǔ*
Sweet bean paste pancakes	赤豆摊饼	*chìdòu tānbǐng*
White radish soup	白萝卜汤	*báiluóbo tāng*
Wonton soup	馄饨汤	*húntun tāng*

Vegetables and eggs

Aubergine with chilli and garlic sauce	大蒜辣椒炒茄子	*dàsuàn làjiāo chǎo qiézi*
Aubergine with sesame sauce	芝麻酱拌茄子	*zhīmájiàng bàn qiézi*
Bean curd and spinach soup	菠菜豆腐汤	*bōcài dòufu tāng*
Bean-curd slivers	豆腐花	*dòufuhuā*
Bean curd with chestnuts	栗子豆腐	*lìzi dòufu*
Pressed bean curd cabbage	白菜豆腐	*báicài dòufu*
Egg fried with tomatoes	蕃茄炒蛋	*fānqié chǎo dàn*
Fried bean curd with vegetables	豆腐炒蔬菜	*dòufu chǎo shūcài*
Fried bean sprouts	炒豆芽	*chǎodòuyá*
Spicy braised aubergine	炖香辣茄子条	*dùn xiānglà qiézitiáo*
Stir-fried bamboo shoots	炒冬笋	*chǎodōngsǔn*
Stir-fried mushrooms	炒鲜菇	*chǎo xiāngū*
Vegetable soup	蔬菜汤	*shūcài tāng*

Regional dishes

Northern

Aromatic fried lamb	炒羊肉	*chǎoyángròu*
Fish with ham and vegetables	火腿蔬菜鱼片	*huǒtuǐ shūcài yúpiàn*
Fried prawn balls	炒虾球	*chǎoxiāqiú*
Mongolian hotpot	蒙古火锅	*ménggǔ huǒguō*

Beijing (Peking) duck	北京烤鸭	*běijīng kǎoyā*
Red-cooked lamb	红烧羊肉	*hóngshāo yángròu*
Lion's head (pork rissoles casseroled with greens)	狮子头	*shīzitóu*

Sichuan and western China

Boiled beef slices (spicy)	水煮牛肉	*shuǐzhǔ niúròu*
Crackling-rice with pork	爆米肉片	*bàomǐ ròupiàn*
Crossing-the-bridge noodles	过桥米线	*guòqiáo mǐxiàn*
Carry-pole noodles (with a chilli-vinegar-sesame sauce)	担担面	*dàndànmiàn*
Deep-fried green beans with garlic	大蒜煸四季豆	*dàsuàn biǎn sìjìdòu*
Dong'an chicken (poached in spicy sauce)	东安鸡子	*dōng'ān jīzi*
Doubled-cooked pork	回锅肉	*huíguōròu*
Dry-fried pork shreds	油炸肉丝	*yóuzhà ròusi*
Fish-flavoured aubergine	鱼香茄子	*yúxiāng qiézi*
Gongbao chicken (with chillies and peanuts)	公保鸡丁	*gōngbǎo jīdīng*
Green pepper with spring onion and black bean sauce	豆豉洋葱炒青椒	*dòuchǐ yángcōng chǎo qīngjiāo*
Hot and sour soup (flavoured with vinegar and white pepper)	酸辣汤	*suānlà tāng*
Hot-spiced bean curd	麻婆豆腐	*mápódòufu*
Rice-flour balls, stuffed with sweet paste	汤圆	*tāngyuán*
Smoked duck	熏鸭	*xūnyā*
Strange flavoured chicken (with sesame-garlic-chilli)	怪味鸡	*guàiwèijī*
Stuffed aubergine slices	馅茄子	*xiànqiézi*
Tangerine chicken	桔子鸡	*júzijī*
"Tiger-skin" peppers (pan-fried with salt)	虎皮炒椒	*hǔpí qīngjiāo*
Wind-cured ham	扎肉	*zhāròu*

Southern Chinese/Cantonese

Baked crab with chilli and black beans	辣椒豆豉焙蟹	*làjiāo dòuchǐ bèi xiè*
Barbecued pork ("char siew")	叉烧	*chāshāo*
Casseroled bean curd stuffed with pork mince	豆腐碎肉煲	*dòfu suìròu bǎo*
Claypot rice with sweet sausage	香肠饭	*xiāngchángfàn*
Crisp-skinned pork on rice	脆皮肉饭	*cuìpíròufàn*
Fish-head casserole	焙鱼头	*bèiyútóu*
Fish steamed with ginger and spring onion	清蒸鱼	*qīngzhēngyú*
Fried chicken with yam	芋头炒鸡片	*yùtóu chǎo jīpiàn*
Honey-roast pork	叉烧	*chāshāo*

Lemon chicken	柠檬鸡	*níngméngjī*
Litchi (lychee) pork	荔枝肉片	*lìzhiròupiàn*
Salt-baked chicken	盐鸡	*yánshuǐjī*

Dim sum

Dim sum	点心	*diǎnxīn*
Barbecued pork bun	叉烧包	*chāshāobāo*
Crab and prawn dumpling	蟹肉虾饺	*xièròu xiā jiǎo*
Custard tart	蛋挞	*dàntà*
Doughnut	油炸圈饼	*yóuzhà quānbǐng*
Pork and prawn dumpling	烧麦	*shāomài*
Fried taro and mince dumpling	蕃薯糊饺	*fānshǔ hújiǎo*
Lotus paste bun	莲蓉糕	*liánrónggāo*
Moon cake (sweet bean paste in flaky pastry)	月饼	*yuèbǐng*
Paper-wrapped prawns	纸包虾	*zhǐbāoxiā*
Prawn crackers	虾片	*xiā piàn*
Prawn dumpling	虾饺	*xiā jiǎo*
Spring roll	春卷	*chūnjuǎn*
Steamed spare ribs and chilli	辣椒蒸排骨	*làjiāo zhēng páigǔ*
Stuffed rice-flour roll	肠粉	*chángfěn*
Stuffed green peppers with black bean sauce	豆豉馅青椒	*dòuchǐ xiàn qīngjiāo*
Sweet sesame balls	芝麻球	*zhīmá qiú*

Fruit

Fruit	水果	*shuǐguǒ*
Apple	苹果	*píngguǒ*
Banana	香蕉	*xiāngjiāo*
Grape	葡萄	*pútáo*
Honeydew melon	哈密瓜	*hāmìguā*
Longan	龙眼	*lóngyǎn*
Lychee	荔枝	*lìzhī*
Mandarin orange	橘子	*júzi*
Mango	芒果	*mángguǒ*
Orange	橙子	*chéngzi*
Peach	桃子	*táozi*
Pear	梨	*lí*
Persimmon	柿子	*shìzi*
Plum	李子	*lǐzi*
Pomegranate	石榴	*shíliú*
Pomelo	柚子	*yòuzi*
Watermelon	西瓜	*xīguā*

Glossary

Arhat Buddhist saint.

Bei North.

Binguan Hotel; generally a large one, for tourists.

Bodhisattva A follower of Buddhism who has attained enlightenment, but has chosen to stay on earth to teach rather than enter nirvana; Buddhist god or goddess.

Boxers The name given to an anti-foreign organization that originated in Shandong in 1898. Encouraged by the Qing Empress Dowager Cixi, they roamed China attacking westernized Chinese and foreigners in what became known as the Boxer movement.

Canting Restaurant

Cheongsam Long, narrow dress slit up the thigh.

CITS China International Travel Service. Tourist organization primarily interested in selling tours, though they can help with obtaining train tickets.

CTS China Travel Service. Tourist organization similar to CITS.

Cultural Revolution Ten-year period beginning in 1966 and characterized by destruction, persecution and fanatical devotion to Mao.

Dagoba Another name for a *stupa*.

Dong East.

Fandian Restaurant or hotel.

Fen Smallest denomination of Chinese currency – there are one hundred fen to the yuan.

Feng Peak.

Feng shui A system of geomancy used to determine the positioning of buildings.

Gong Palace.

Guanxi Literally "connections": the reciprocal favours inherent in the process of official appointments and transactions.

Guanyin The ubiquitous Buddhist Goddess of Mercy, who postponed her entry into paradise in order to help ease human misery. Derived from the Indian deity Avalokiteshvara, she is often depicted with up to a thousand arms.

Gulou Drum tower; traditionally marking the centre of a town, this was where a drum was beaten at nightfall and in times of need.

Guomindang (GMD) The Nationalist Peoples' Party. Under Chiang Kaishek, the GMD fought Communist forces for 25 years before being defeated and moving to Taiwan in 1949, where it remains a major political party.

Han Chinese The main body of the Chinese people, as distinct from other ethnic groups such as Uigur, Miao, Hui or Tibetan.

Hui Muslims; officially a minority, China's Hui are, in fact, ethnically indistinguishable from Han Chinese.

Hutong A narrow alleyway.

Immortal Taoist saint.

Jiao (or mao) Ten fen.

Jie Street.

Jiuba Bar or pub.

Lamaism The esoteric Tibetan and Mongolian branch of Buddhism, influenced by local shamanist and animist beliefs.

Laowai A slang term for foreigner.

Ling Tomb.

Little Red Book A selection of "Quotations from Chairman Mao Zedong", produced in 1966 as a philosophical treatise for Red Guards during the Cultural Revolution.

Lu Street.

Luohan Buddhist disciple.

Maitreya Buddha The Buddha of the future, at present awaiting rebirth.

Mandala Mystic diagram which forms an important part of Buddhist iconography, especially in Tibet; *mandalas* usually depict deities and are stared at as an aid to meditation.

Men Gate/door.

Miao Temple.

Middle Kingdom A literal translation of the Chinese words for China.

Nan South.

Palanquin A covered sedan chair, used by the emperor.

Peking The old English term for Beijing.

PLA The People's Liberation Army, the official name of the Communist military forces since 1949.

PSB Public Security Bureau, the branch of China's police force which deals directly with foreigners.

Pagoda Tower with distinctively tapering structure.

Pinyin The official system of transliterating Chinese script into Roman characters.

Putonghua Mandarin Chinese; literally "Common Language".

Qiao Bridge.

Qiapo Another word for a *cheongsam* (see opposite).

RMB Renminbi. Another name for Chinese currency literally meaning "the people's money".

Red Guards The unruly factional forces unleashed by Mao during the Cultural Revolution to find and destroy brutally any "reactionaries" among the populace.

Renmin The people.

Renminbi The official term for the Chinese currency, literally, "people's money".

Si Temple, usually Buddhist.

Siheyuan Traditional courtyard house.

Spirit wall Wall behind the main gateway to a house, designed to thwart evil spirits, which, it was believed, could move only in straight lines.

Spirit Way The straight road leading to a tomb, lined with guardian figures.

Stele Freestanding stone tablet carved with text.

Stupa Multi-tiered tower associated with Buddhist temples that usually contains sacred objects.

Ta Tower or pagoda.

Tai ji A discipline of physical exercise, characterized by slow, deliberate, balletic movements.

Tian Heaven or the sky.

Uigur Substantial minority of Turkic people, living mainly in Xinjiang.

Waiguoren Foreigner.

Xi West.

Yuan China's unit of currency. Also a courtyard or garden (and the name of the Mongol dynasty).

Zhan Station.

Zhong Middle; China is referred to as *zhongguo*, the Middle Kingdom.

Zhongnanhai The compound, next to the Forbidden City, that serves as Communist Party Headquarters.

Zhonglou Bell tower, usually twinned with a *gulou*. The bell it contained was rung at dawn and in emergencies.

Zhuang Villa or manor.

Travel store

Small print and

Index

A Rough Guide to Rough Guides

Published in 1982, the first Rough Guide – to Greece – was a student scheme that became a publishing phenomenon. Mark Ellingham, a recent graduate in English from Bristol University, had been travelling in Greece the previous summer and couldn't find the right guidebook. With a small group of friends he wrote his own guide, combining a highly contemporary, journalistic style with a thoroughly practical approach to travellers' needs.

The immediate success of the book spawned a series that rapidly covered dozens of destinations. And, in addition to impecunious backpackers, Rough Guides soon acquired a much broader and older readership that relished the guides' wit and inquisitiveness as much as their enthusiastic, critical approach and value-for-money ethos.

These days, Rough Guides include recommendations from shoestring to luxury and cover more than 200 destinations around the globe, including almost every country in the Americas and Europe, more than half of Africa and most of Asia and Australasia. Our ever-growing team of authors and photographers is spread all over the world, particularly in Europe, the US and Australia.

In the early 1990s, Rough Guides branched out of travel, with the publication of Rough Guides to World Music, Classical Music and the Internet. All three have become benchmark titles in their fields, spearheading the publication of a wide range of books under the Rough Guide name.

Including the travel series, Rough Guides now number more than 350 titles, covering: phrasebooks, waterproof maps, music guides from Opera to Heavy Metal, reference works as diverse as Conspiracy Theories and Shakespeare, and popular culture books from iPods to Poker. Rough Guides also produce a series of more than 120 World Music CDs in partnership with World Music Network.

Visit www.roughguides.com to see our latest publications.

Rough Guide credits

Text editor: Samantha Cook
Layout: Jessica Subramanian
Cartography: Deshpal Dabas
Picture editor: Emily Taylor
Production: Rebecca Short
Proofreader: Serena Stephenson
Cover design: Nicole Newman, Dan May
Photographer: Tim Draper
Editorial: **London** Andy Turner, Keith Drew, Edward Aves, Alice Park, Lucy White, Jo Kirby, James Smart, Natasha Foges, James Rice, Emma Beatson, Emma Gibbs, Kathryn Lane, Monica Woods, Mani Ramaswamy, Harry Wilson, Lucy Cowie, Alison Roberts, Lara Kavanagh, Eleanor Aldridge, Ian Blenkinsop, Charlotte Melville, Joe Staines, Matthew Milton, Tracy Hopkins; **Delhi** Madhavi Singh, Jalpreen Kaur Chhatwal, Jubbi Francis
Design & Pictures: **London** Scott Stickland, Dan May, Diana Jarvis, Mark Thomas, Nicole Newman, Sarah Cummins; **Delhi** Umesh Aggarwal, Ajay Verma, Ankur Guha, Pradeep Thapliyal, Sachin Tanwar, Anita Singh, Nikhil Agarwal, Sachin Gupta
Production: Liz Cherry, Louise Minihane, Erika Pepe
Cartography: **London** Ed Wright, Katie Lloyd-Jones; **Delhi** Rajesh Chhibber, Ashutosh Bharti, Rajesh Mishra, Animesh Pathak, Jasbir Sandhu, Swati Handoo, Lokamata Sahu
Marketing, Publicity & roughguides.com: Liz Statham
Digital Travel Publisher: Peter Buckley
Reference Director: Andrew Lockett
Operations Coordinator: Becky Doyle
Operations Assistant: Johanna Wurm
Publishing Director (Travel): Clare Currie
Commercial Manager: Gino Magnotta
Managing Director: John Duhigg

Publishing information

This fourth edition published June 2011 by
Rough Guides Ltd,
80 Strand, London WC2R 0RL
11, Community Centre, Panchsheel Park, New Delhi 110017, India

Distributed by the Penguin Group

Penguin Books Ltd,
80 Strand, London WC2R 0RL

Penguin Group (USA)
375 Hudson Street, NY 10014, USA

Penguin Group (Australia)
250 Camberwell Road, Camberwell, Victoria 3124, Australia

Penguin Group (NZ)
67 Apollo Drive, Mairangi Bay, Auckland 1310, New Zealand

Rough Guides is represented in Canada by Tourmaline Editions Inc. 662 King Street West, Suite 304, Toronto, Ontario M5V 1M7

Cover concept by Peter Dyer.

Typeset in Bembo and Helvetica to an original design by Henry Iles.

Printed in Singapore

216pp includes index
A catalogue record for this book is available from the British Library
ISBN: 978-1-84836-656-5

1 3 5 7 9 8 6 4 2

Help us update

We've gone to a lot of effort to ensure that the fourth edition of **The Rough Guide to Beijing** is accurate and up-to-date. However, things change – places get "discovered", opening hours are notoriously fickle, restaurants and rooms raise prices or lower standards. If you feel we've got it wrong or left something out, we'd like to know, and if you can remember the address, the price, the hours, the phone number, so much the better.

Please send your comments with the subject line "**Rough Guide Beijing Update**" to ⓔmail@uk.roughguides.com. We'll credit all contributions and send a copy of the next edition (or any other Rough Guide if you prefer) for the very best emails.

Find more travel information, connect with fellow travellers and book your trip on ⓦwww.roughguides.com

Acknowledgements

Simon: Many thanks to Noe, Du, Yang Yen, Summer, Craig and Shen Ye.

Photo credits

All photos © Rough Guides except the following:

Introduction

Night view of Beijing's "Bird's Nest" stadium © Liu Liqun/Corbis
Red carp ornament, Dongyue Temple, Spring Festival © Tao/Robert Harding

Things not to miss

04 Houhai Lake at night © Lou Linwei /Alamy
10 Monk at Yonghe Gong © Commercial Megapress Collection/Alamy

Capital cuisine colour section

Making noodles in a market © Christopher Tozer/Alamy
Beijing duck © PhotoLibrary
Fangshan Imperial Kitchen © Dennis Cox/Alamy
Eating noodles at a food stall © Impact Photos/Alamy
Beijing open air market © Ron Watts/Corbis
Mapo dofu © Bon Appetit/Alamy

Temple life colour section

Lanterns with wishes hanging on tree branch, Temple Of Great Mercy, Badachu © Tao/Robert Harding
The 17m-high sandalwood statue of Maitreya Buddha, Yonghe Gong © Christian Kober/Robert Harding
Dongyue Temple © Atlantide Phototravel/Corbis
Drummers performing during Spring Festival © Bruce Connolly/Corbis
People worshipping gods in White Cloud Taoist temple © Tao/Alamy
A monk enters Yonghe lamasery © Brad Mitchell/Alamy

Index

Map entries are in colour.

N

O

P

Q

R

S

T

U

V

W

X

Y

Z

Map symbols

maps are listed in the full index using coloured text

Chapter division boundary
Province boundary
Road
Railway
Path
River
Wall
Gate
Bridge
Hill
Airport
Subway station
Bus stop/station
Point of interest
Internet access
Tourist office
Telephone office
Post office
Hospital
Embassy/consulate
Observatory
Museum
Temple
Dagoba
Mosque
Market
Building
Church
Stadium
Park

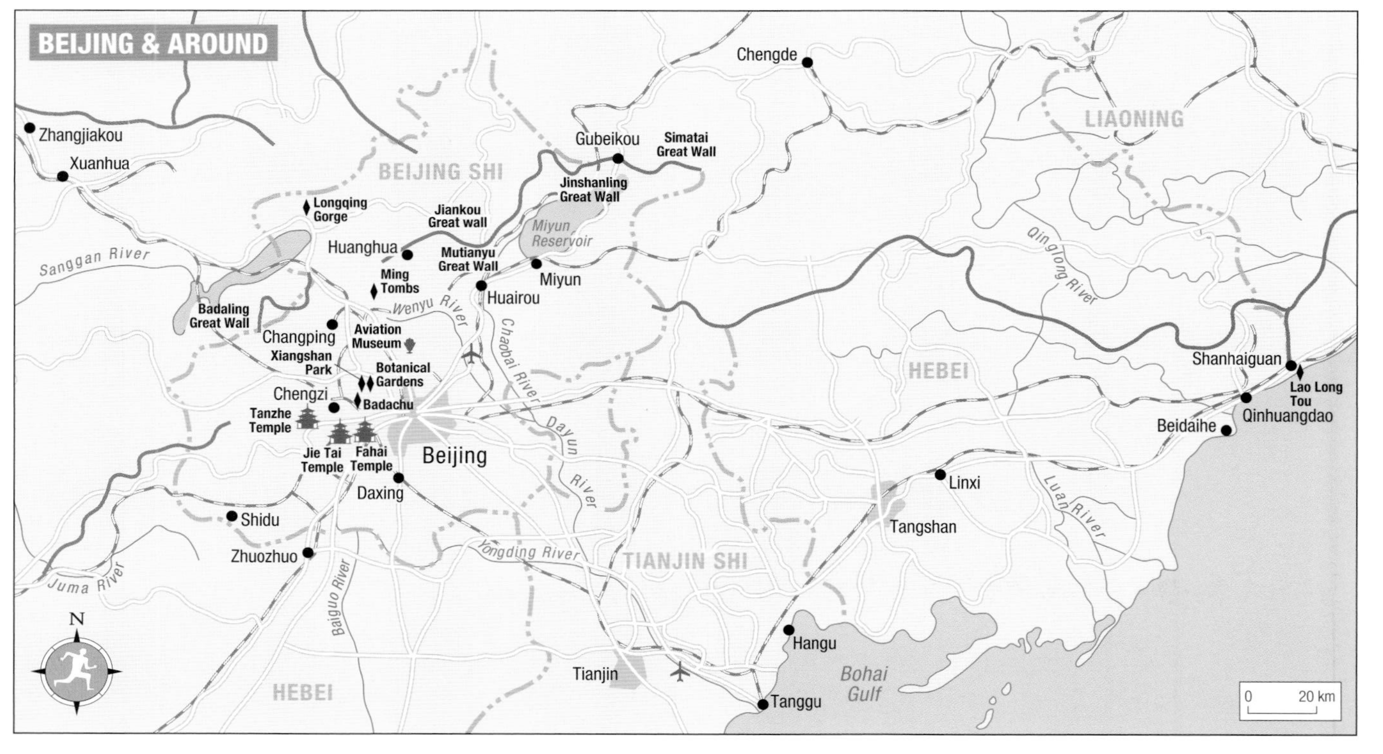
BEIJING & AROUND
Chengde
LIAONING
Zhangjiakou
Xuanhua
BEIJING SHI
Gubeikou
Simatai Great Wall
Jinshanling Great Wall
Longqing Gorge
Jiankou Great wall
Miyun Reservoir
Qinglong River
Sanggan River
Huanghua
Mutianyu Great Wall
Miyun
Ming Tombs
Huairou
Wenyu River
Badaling Great Wall
Changping
Aviation Museum
Chaobai River
Xiangshan Park
Botanical Gardens
HEBEI
Shanhaiguan
Lao Long Tou
Chengzi
Badachu
Qinhuangdao
Tanzhe Temple
Beidaihe
Dayun River
Jie Tai Temple
Fahai Temple
Beijing
Daxing
Linxi
Luan River
Shidu
Tangshan
Zhuozhuo
Yongding River
TIANJIN SHI
Juma River
Baiguo River
Hangu
N
Bohai Gulf
Tianjin
HEBEI
Tanggu
0 20 km

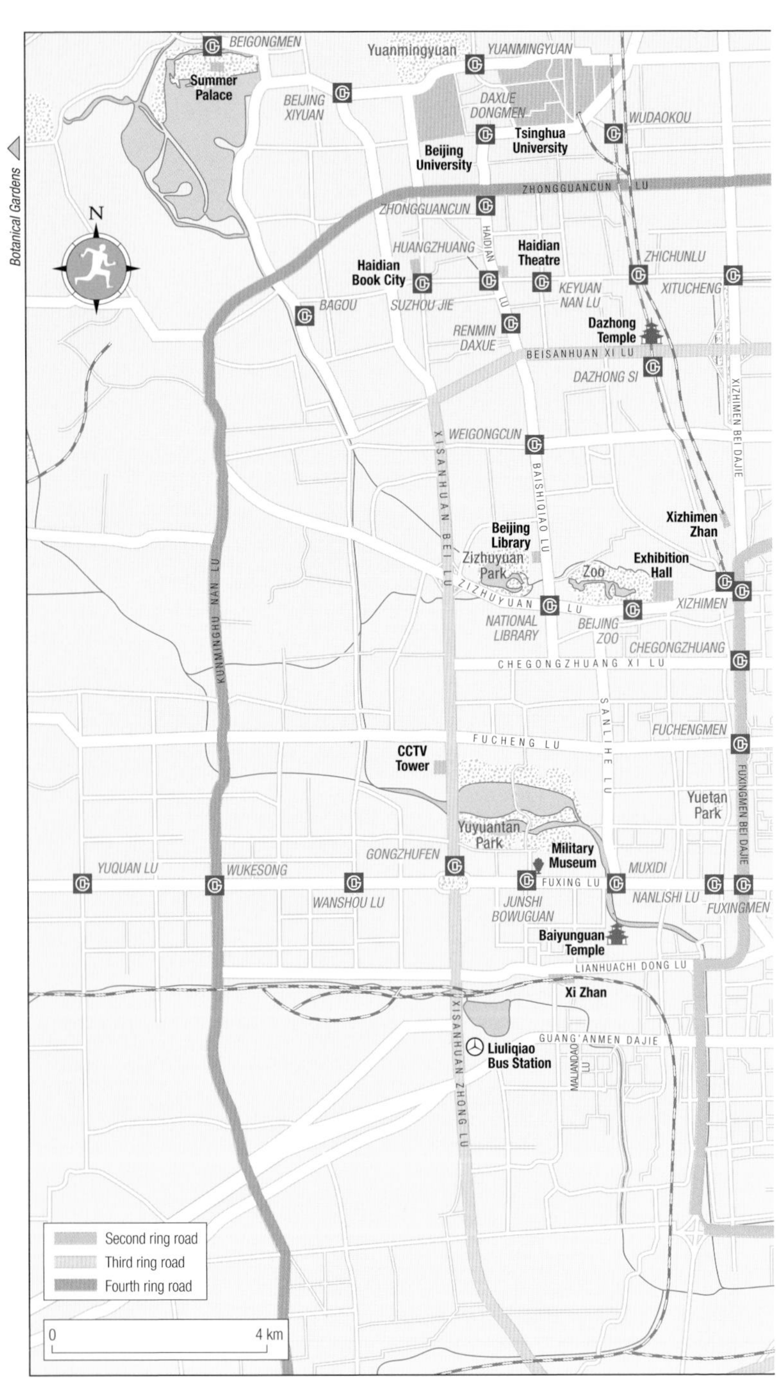
BEIGONGMEN
Summer Palace
Yuanmingyuan
YUANMINGYUAN
BEIJING XIYUAN
DAXUE DONGMEN
WUDAOKOU
Tsinghua University
Beijing University
Botanical Gardens
N
ZHONGGUANCUN LU
ZHONGGUANCUN
HAIDIAN LU
HUANGZHUANG
Haidian Theatre
Haidian Book City
ZHICHUNLU
XITUCHENG
KEYUAN NAN LU
BAGOU
SUZHOU JIE
RENMIN DAXUE
Dazhong Temple
BEISANHUAN XI LU
DAZHONG SI
XIZHIMEN BEI DAJIE
WEIGONGCUN
XISANHUAN BEI LU
BAISHIQIAO LU
Xizhimen Zhan
Beijing Library
Zizhuyuan Park
Zoo
Exhibition Hall
ZIZHUYUAN LU
XIZHIMEN
NATIONAL LIBRARY
BEIJING ZOO
CHEGONGZHUANG
KUNMINGHU NAN LU
CHEGONGZHUANG XI LU
SANLIHE LU
FUCHENGMEN
FUCHENG LU
CCTV Tower
Yuetan Park
FUXINGMEN BEI DAJIE
Yuyuantan Park
Military Museum
GONGZHUFEN
YUQUAN LU
WUKESONG
MUXIDI
FUXING LU
WANSHOU LU
JUNSHI BOWUGUAN
NANLISHI LU
FUXINGMEN
Baiyunguan Temple
LIANHUACHI DONG LU
Xi Zhan
GUANG'ANMEN DAJIE
Liuliqiao Bus Station
MALIANDAO LU
XISANHUAN ZHONG LU
Second ring road
Third ring road
Fourth ring road
0
4 km

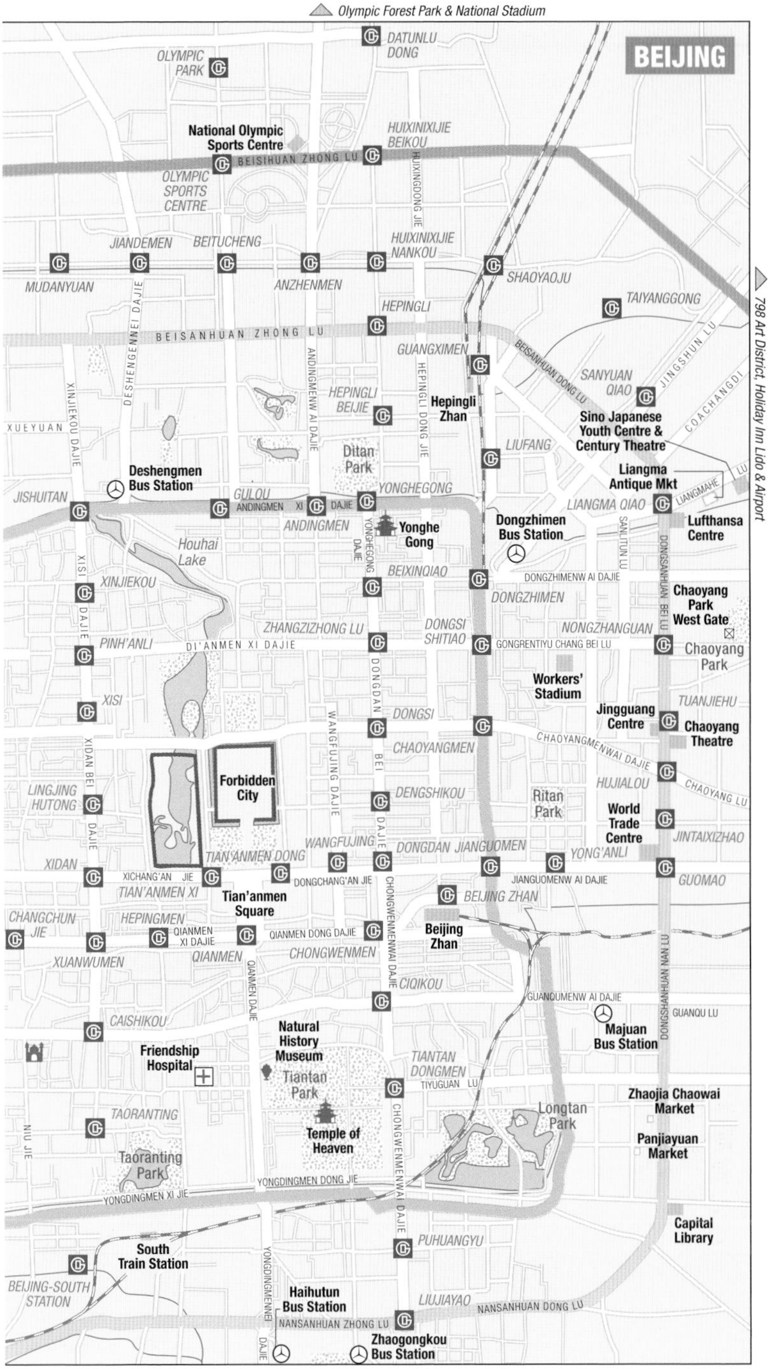

BEIJING

Olympic Forest Park & National Stadium

798 Art District, Holiday Inn Lido & Airport

DATUNLU DONG
OLYMPIC PARK
National Olympic Sports Centre
HUIXINIXIJIE BEIKOU
BEISIHUAN ZHONG LU
OLYMPIC SPORTS CENTRE
HUIXINGDONG JIE
JIANDEMEN
BEITUCHENG
HUIXINIXIJIE NANKOU
SHAOYAOJU
MUDANYUAN
ANZHENMEN
TAIYANGGONG
HEPINGLI
DESHENGENNEI DAJIE
BEISANHUAN ZHONG LU
GUANGXIMEN
BEISANHUAN DONG LU
JINGSHUN LU
ANDINGMENW AI DAJIE
HEPINGLI DONG JIE
SANYUAN QIAO
COACHANGDI
XINJIEKOU DAJIE
HEPINGLI BEIJIE
Hepingli Zhan
XUEYUAN
Sino Japanese Youth Centre & Century Theatre
LIUFANG
Ditan Park
Deshengmen Bus Station
Liangma Antique Mkt
LIANGMAHE LU
JISHUITAN
GULOU
YONGHEGONG
ANDINGMEN XI DAJIE
LIANGMA QIAO
ANDINGMEN
Yonghe Gong
Dongzhimen Bus Station
SANLITUN LU
Lufthansa Centre
Houhai Lake
YONGHEGONG DAJIE
XISI DAJIE
XINJIEKOU
BEIXINQIAO
DONGZHIMENW AI DAJIE
DONGSANHUAN BEI LU
DONGZHIMEN
Chaoyang Park West Gate
ZHANGZIZHONG LU
DONGSI SHITIAO
NONGZHANGUAN
PINH'ANLI
DI'ANMEN XI DAJIE
GONGRENTIYU CHANG BEI LU
Chaoyang Park
Workers' Stadium
XISI
DONGDAN
WANGFUJING DAJIE
TUANJIEHU
DONGSI
Jingguang Centre
Chaoyang Theatre
CHAOYANGMENWAI DAJIE
CHAOYANGMEN
Forbidden City
BEI
XIDAN BEI DAJIE
HUJIALOU
LINGJING HUTONG
DENGSHIKOU
Ritan Park
CHAOYANG LU
World Trade Centre
WANGFUJING
DONGDAN
JIANGUOMEN
JINTAIXIZHAO
XIDAN
TIAN'ANMEN DONG
YONG'ANLI
XICHANG'AN JIE
DONGCHANG'AN JIE
JIANGUOMENW AI DAJIE
GUOMAO
TIAN'ANMEN XI
Tian'anmen Square
BEIJING ZHAN
CHONGWENMENNEI DAJIE
CHANGCHUN JIE
HEPINGMEN
Beijing Zhan
QIANMEN XI DAJIE
QIANMEN DONG DAJIE
XUANWUMEN
QIANMEN
CHONGWENMEN
CHONGWENMENWAI DAJIE
CIQIKOU
QIANMEN DAJIE
GUANQUMENW AI DAJIE
DONGSHANHUAN NAN LU
GUANQU LU
CAISHIKOU
Majuan Bus Station
Natural History Museum
Friendship Hospital
Tiantan Park
TIANTAN DONGMEN
TIYUGUAN LU
Zhaojia Chaowai Market
Temple of Heaven
Longtan Park
TAORANTING
NIU JIE
Panjiayuan Market
Taoranting Park
YONGDINGMEN DONG JIE
YONGDINGMEN XI JIE
CHONGWENMENWAI DAJIE
Capital Library
PUHUANGYU
South Train Station
YONGDINGMENNEI DAJIE
BEIJING-SOUTH STATION
Haihutun Bus Station
LIUJIAYAO
NANSANHUAN DONG LU
NANSANHUAN ZHONG LU
Zhaogongkou Bus Station

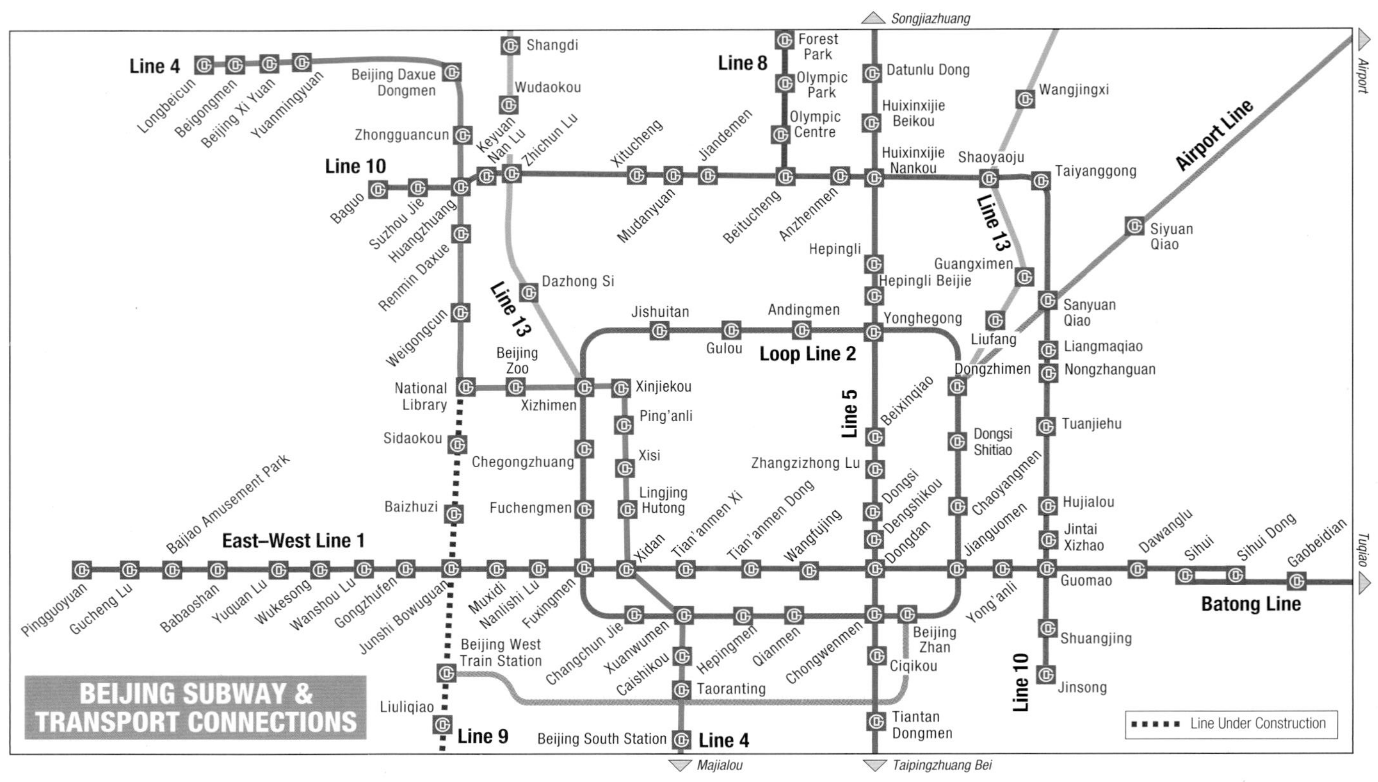
BEIJING SUBWAY & TRANSPORT CONNECTIONS
Line Under Construction
Songjiazhuang
Airport
Tuqiao
Majialou
Taipingzhuang Bei
Line 4
Longbeicun
Beigongmen
Beijing Xi Yuan
Yuanmingyuan
Beijing Daxue Dongmen
Zhongguancun
Line 10
Baguo
Suzhou Jie
Huangzhuang
Renmin Daxue
Weigongcun
National Library
Shangdi
Wudaokou
Keyuan Nan Lu
Zhichun Lu
Xitucheng
Mudanyuan
Jiandemen
Beitucheng
Anzhenmen
Line 8
Forest Park
Olympic Park
Olympic Centre
Datunlu Dong
Huixinxijie Beikou
Huixinxijie Nankou
Shaoyaoju
Wangjingxi
Taiyanggong
Airport Line
Siyuan Qiao
Line 13
Guangximen
Liufang
Hepingli
Hepingli Beijie
Yonghegong
Sanyuan Qiao
Liangmaqiao
Nongzhanguan
Dazhong Si
Jishuitan
Andingmen
Gulou
Loop Line 2
Beijing Zoo
Xizhimen
Xinjiekou
Ping'anli
Xisi
Lingjing Hutong
Dongzhimen
Line 5
Beixinqiao
Dongsi Shitiao
Tuanjiehu
Sidaokou
Chegongzhuang
Zhangzizhong Lu
Dongsi
Dengshikou
Chaoyangmen
Hujialou
Jintai Xizhao
Bajiao Amusement Park
Baizhuzi
Fuchengmen
Tian'anmen Xi
Tian'anmen Dong
Wangfujing
Dongdan
Jianguomen
Dawanglu
Sihui
Sihui Dong
Gaobeidian
East–West Line 1
Pingguoyuan
Gucheng Lu
Babaoshan
Yuquan Lu
Wukesong
Wanshou Lu
Gongzhufen
Junshi Bowuguan
Muxidi
Nanlishi Lu
Fuxingmen
Xidan
Guomao
Yong'anli
Batong Line
Changchun Jie
Xuanwumen
Caishikou
Hepingmen
Qianmen
Chongwenmen
Beijing Zhan
Ciqikou
Shuangjing
Jinsong
Line 10
Beijing West Train Station
Taoranting
Tiantan Dongmen
Liuliqiao
Line 9
Beijing South Station
Line 4